CONTEMPORARY JEWISH PHILOSOPHY

Contemporary Jewish Philosophy introduces the most important Jewish philosophers of recent times from the point of view of their original approach to both Judaism and philosophy, and includes Hermann Cohen, Franz Rosenzweig, Martin Buber, Leo Strauss and Emmanuel Lévinas.

It shows how for them the dialogue between Judaism and philosophy is necessary in order to avoid on one side, an attachment to Jewish tradition which is only nationalistic or non-rational; on the other, an idea of philosophy which first of all focuses on the problems of nature, human existence in the world, or God as the origin of being. For all these thinkers the main result of the encounter between the civilization coming from Jerusalem, and that coming from Athens, is ethics. Therefore they defend the concept of humanity as a species whose characteristic is not so much theoretic reason as the capacity for moral feelings such as respect for the law, friendship, love, empathy for the suffering of others.

In reconstructing the intellectual evolution of each of these twentieth-century philosophers with a view to their meaning today, this book is unique and goes beyond the standard historical account provided by other books. *Contemporary Jewish Philosophy* is essential reading for researchers and students of philosophy, Judaism and the history of religions.

Irene Kajon is Professor of Moral Philosophy at the University of Rome "La Sapienza." A leading interpreter of Jewish philosophy, she is the author of *Ebraismo e sistema di filosofia in Hermann Cohen* (Padova, 1989) and *Fede ebraica e ateismo dopo Auschwitz* (Perugia, 1993).

ROUTLEDGE JEWISH STUDIES SERIES
Series editor: Oliver Leaman
University of Kentucky

Studies, which are interpreted to cover the disciplines of history, sociology, anthropology, culture, politics, philosophy, theology, religion, as they relate to Jewish affairs. The remit includes texts which have as their primary focus issues, ideas, personalities and events of relevance to Jews, Jewish life and the concepts which have characterised Jewish culture both in the past and today. The series is interested in receiving appropriate scripts or proposals.

MEDIEVAL JEWISH
PHILOSOPHY
An introduction
Dan Cohn-Sherbok

FACING THE OTHER
The ethics of Emmanuel Lévinas
Edited by Seán Hand

MOSES MAIMONIDES
Oliver Leaman

A USER'S GUIDE TO FRANZ
ROSENZWEIG'S STAR OF
REDEMPTION
Norbert M. Samuelson

ON LIBERTY
Jewish philosophical perspectives
Edited by Daniel H. Frank

REFERRING TO GOD
Jewish and Christian philosophical
and theological perspectives
Edited by Paul Helm

JUDAISM, PHILOSOPHY,
CULTURE
Selected studies by E. I. J. Rosenthal
Erwin Rosenthal

PHILOSOPHY OF THE
TALMUD
Hyam Maccoby

FROM SYNAGOGUE
TO CHURCH:
THE TRADITIONAL DESIGN
Its beginning, its definition,
its end
John Wilkinson

HIDDEN PHILOSOPHY OF
HANNAH ARENDT
Margaret Betz Hull

DECONSTRUCTING
THE BIBLE
Abraham ibn Ezra's introduction
to the Torah
Irene Lancaster

CONTEMPORARY JEWISH PHILOSOPHY

An introduction

Irene Kajon

Routledge
Taylor & Francis Group

LONDON AND NEW YORK

First published 2006
by Routledge
2 Park Square, Milton Park, Abingdon, Oxon OX14 4RN

Simultaneously published in the USA and Canada
by Routledge
270 Madison Ave, New York, NY 10016

Routledge is an imprint of the Taylor & Francis Group

© 2006 Irene Kajon

Typeset in Garamond by
Newgen Imaging Systems (P) Ltd, Chennai, India
Printed and bound in Great Britain by
Biddles Ltd, King's Lynn, Norfolk

British Library Cataloguing in Publication Data
A catalogue record for this book is available from the British Library

Library of Congress Cataloging in Publication Data
A catalog record for this book has been requested

ISBN10: 0–415–34163–9
ISBN13: 9–78–0–415–34163–9

CONTENTS

PREFACE TO THE ENGLISH EDITION

The present book is the English version of my *Il pensiero ebraico del Novecento. Una introduzione*, Roma: Donzelli, 2002. It is not exactly a translation: the English has been sometimes modified with regard to the Italian text. Moreover, in the notes and the bibliographical note, the English translations of the writings of the Jewish philosophers considered, and English critical literature on them are indicated instead of Italian translations and Italian critical literature. I hope, in this way, to make the book more useful to English speaking readers.

Dr Francesca Gleason translated chapters I–III from the Italian; I translated the rest; Mark Joseph revised the entire book in English. I am very indebted to both for their careful and patient work, their competence and kindness. Professor Oliver Leaman gave me support, suggestions, and the benefit of his knowledge in the preparation of this book from the first steps until its conclusion: I give him my warmest thanks for his kind help.

I would like also to thank both the Italian and the English publishers, for their sympathetic understanding of my research and their interest in making Jewish philosophy more known and therefore more loved.

I. K.

Rome, November 2004 – Cheshvan 5765

PREFACE TO THE ITALIAN EDITION

There are two objectives inspiring the writing of this book. The first is to draw attention to a group of twentieth century Jewish thinkers who, though following different paths, aim for the same theoretical goal. They want to point out the possibility of human beings establishing their relation to the Other (either the Other as man or the Other as Transcendence) in a different manner from that which has so far been allowed by theoretical or practical reason, imagination or empirical feelings. Rather they point out strong, non-pathological affections, like compassion, love, fidelity. The second objective is to explain how these thinkers connect that main thesis to a philosophy that returns to Jewish sources, either as a starting point for philosophical analysis or as a way of expressing it.

The book offers a synthetic view of the path each author follows as he goes from a view marked by the Greek philosophical tradition to a thought directed towards the Other, and tries to set out the historical knowledge needed to evaluate what they say. It presents itself both as a defence of philosophy as metaphysics (a metaphysics reflecting first on what we do in society, coinciding therefore with ethics and politics), and as a defence of Judaism – one that tries to unify Jewish religious tradition and Jewish secularism.

It seems to me that it is just these notions of philosophy and Judaism that now need our attention. Today they are often suppressed, in the case of philosophy by a view of it as a science for specialists, or as a science that cannot give man any sense of Being, or values for him to live by. And, in the case of Judaism, by a view that has as its centre either the revealed law or the people unified through history alone. Yet philosophy was born as a reflection on Being and the meaning of human life, and Judaism as the willingness to hear divine commandments that can also be heard by all peoples, through the use of reason.

We hope this book will bring readers to nourish the idea of the necessary relationship between living and thinking; it is the most important demand of both Judaism and philosophy.

I. K.
Rome, September 2002 – Elul 5763

1

PREMISES

1.1   The *parabola* of Western humanism

The Latin term *parabola* has two meanings. It means a *parable* or story, a teaching illustrated by plot or character. And as *parabola* it means a line that departs from a fixed point, extending itself to a climax and coming back to another point, distant but on the same plane.

Three books from the twentieth century on the history of philosophy each illustrate a *parabola* in both senses of the word. They contain *parables* that exemplify the general meaning of a culture, tales that tell of specific individuals and cultural currents, and *parabolas* or trajectories that are traced by the phenomena being studied. These books are aiming for much more than historical and philosophical review. By analyzing philosophical texts they describe a broader cultural reality; and they explain how events unfold, with a focus on their final ending. In addition, if these three works are considered in sequence, and in historical context, they represent a *parabola*, as will be seen. They appear as metaphors for the civilization of an entire age, and at the same time as different points of a descending line.

The first of these works was published by Bernhard Groethuysen in 1931 as *Philosophical Anthropology*.[1] Groethuysen uses the antithesis between "spirit" and "life" as a *leitmotiv* to interpret the history of Western philosophy from Plato to the dawn of modern times. According to the author the antithesis was already present in Plato's doctrine. From there it develops in different ways, here turned more towards "life," and here more towards "spirit." Finally the antithesis shows itself in a more radical form. The mechanistic vision of nature that was brought about by the scientific studies of the fifteenth and sixteenth centuries contrasts with the vision of man as soul or inner self that was brought about by modern introspection. Following this underlying theme, Groethuysen emphasizes man's inability to give a straightforward answer to the problem represented by his own being, since as a living human or individual he is a unique existence, and as a rational being he is pure conscience or human essence. Thus a deep laceration splits not only reflection on man, but Western culture too. It is a culture divided between on the one hand religion, literature, and "philosophy of life," and on the other, natural science and philosophy as theory.

So Groethuysen writes in his *Philosophical Anthropology*:

> Know thyself, such is the theme of every philosophical anthropology.
> Philosophical anthropology is reflection on oneself, an effort to understand
> himself carried out by man and always renewed. But the reflection on
> oneself can mean two things, depending on whether man refers to what
> happened to him in life and wishes to represent himself, or if he and life
> become a problem of knowledge; thus on whether he asks the question in
> point of life or in point of knowledge.[2]

In answering the question on man, "philosophy of life" begins from life and returns
to an individual existence, never elevating itself to universal or eternal truth.
Philosophy as theory abandons life completely in answering the question, turning its
focus on the general characteristics of human nature.

Groethuysen thinks that although these two views, underlying the history of
Western thought, may at times coexist in one person, they never interweave or find
a point of conjunction. So, whereas in his dialogues Plato contrasts the common man
and the philosopher, the Aristotelian view is characterized by the idea of the difference between man belonging to nature, and man endowed with intellectual faculties.
Later, in Graeco-Roman philosophy of life this contrast emerges as the battle between
submission to one's fate and the exercise of one's individual will and power. In
Renaissance philosophy, the split comes about between two tendencies, that is between
human empirical reality in its natural form, or in the plurality of its forms
(Machiavelli or Montaigne), and the pure intelligible or supersensible (Ficino or
Nikolaus von Cusa). Then, the emphasis placed on the "I" as a single entity by the
main religious personalities of the Reformation opposes the emphasis on knowledge
required by Descartes and the Cartesians.

So Groethuysen reconstructs the histories of the "philosophies of life" and of the
"philosophies of spirit," and finds in the point reached by Western culture at the
beginning of modernity a most dramatic antithesis, that is between man's isolation
within himself as an individual and his attainment of tranquility as a universal being
within the sphere of contemplation. But in both cases man loses the universal sense
of his being in the world, divided as he is between his existence and this sense.

The second book among contemporary works on the history of philosophy tracing
parabolas is Karl Löwith's *From Hegel to Nietzsche*, first published in 1941.[3] Löwith
looks at the thought of the period from the mid-1800s to the first decades of the
1900s. He distinguishes Christianity and philosophy, the path of the former aimed
at asserting the individual, Transcendence and faith, the latter at affirming universality, nature, society and reason. Löwith says that in the Hegelian system
Christianity and philosophy finally establish a close relationship, having failed until
then to reach unity, their dialogue notwithstanding. In fact, in the Hegelian system
Christian revelation and philosophical reason or *Logos* mutually found one another.
Revelation is proven by philosophical thought and is also its premise. After Hegel,
however, the Hegelian schools are divided between a right wing, advocating

Christian revelation, and the left, supporter of philosophy. The division exemplifies the crisis in a culture whose highest point was Hegelian doctrine. Löwith qualifies as "Christian bourgeois" the culture that witnessed the practical conciliation of Christianity and philosophy, the former transmitting values of respect for the individual's inner life, defence of personal rights, and freedom of conscience, and the latter transmitting values such as scientific learning, State tolerance of all religions, and citizen participation in politics as free and equal citizens, that is, as human beings. It was a conciliation achieved through the Hegelian centre. After Hegel, this culture was replaced by a world in which the individual and society, reference to God and existence in time, belief and knowledge oppose each other. Although Kierkegaard and Marx each stand for one side of the conflict, the first expressing as an individual a faith that is known to be in incurable contrast with the world, the second sustaining as philosopher a science solely directed towards social and political relationships, Nietzsche with his deep lacerations nearly represents the embodiment of both sides.

Typical of Hegelian thought was the *discors concordia* between eternity and history, *Bildung* and work. In its place a state of permanent and violent conflict comes about between the desire to escape the world and the desire to be immersed in it. So Löwith writes in his book:

> In place of the Hegelian mediation the will formed as a decision to separate what Hegel had unified: the ancients and Christianity, God and the world, the inner and outer self, essence and existence.[4]

Thus, although Hegel had hoped to overcome the dualism between Christian revelation and philosophical knowledge, in the period of the Hegelian crisis and the following decades it returns, and in a harder and harsher way. The final result of this turn of events is "nihilism," which the author relates to German philosophy because in it he finds the focal point for all the rays of Western philosophy, and the many different tendencies of Western culture as well. Löwith says that nihilism assumes two forms. The first form is the "nihilism of weakness," denying existence and the variety and newness of experience. This is for the sake of finding a refuge from existence itself in the immobility of Being. The second is the "nihilism of power," rejecting any presence of reason or spirit in existence in order to celebrate everything that exists and lives, including man's selfish instincts. Nietzsche, who was divided between the thesis of the "eternal return" and the thesis of the "Will to power," between the "One" and the "Dispersion of Being," shows these two sides of nihilism. The crisis of Hegelianism, in Löwith's interpretation, leads to Nietzsche.

The third book outlining the history of Western thought under the guise of a *parable/parabola* is Michel Foucault's work *The Words and the Things*, published in 1966.[5] In order to shed light on the concepts used in the human sciences of the twentieth century, to reconstruct their genesis, and to derive from them a perspective about our times, Foucault analyzes the ways in which experience is organized in three different ages: first, the Cartesian age, then, the period between the end of the 1700s and the first decades of the 1800s, and finally the phase between the mid-1800s and the end of that century. Now, if one reconstructs this history – from Descartes until the crisis of positivism – one will notice, according to Foucault, how the idea of man at the centre, the subject organizing reality, belongs only to the second age. It is an idea upheld by the thinkers of the Enlightenment, Kant and the representatives of German idealism; is the base of economics, politics, all the other human and social sciences, a base forming their methods and concepts at this time. Now, in the Cartesian era, representations that reflect objective order, that is to say something existing outside man, are the criteria used to systematize data. The period running from the mid-1800s to the end of the century can be defined as the age when human consciousness disintegrates. It seems that the a priori of consciousness is not good enough to deal with the abundance of empirical situations and experiences. And so the concept of the non-centrality of man, maintained in an earlier period, before the humanism of the Enlighteners and idealists, returns in the era following the Enlightenment and idealism, if in a different guise. The anti-humanism of the age that had no more trust in reason has visible consequences in the twentieth century. Although interest in history was no longer supported by the notion of a universal human subject after the middle of the century, it still guided research in the human and social sciences at the end of the 1800s. Now it was replaced by an interest in certain norms, rules and systems sustaining human life, of which man himself seems unaware. So writes Foucault, considering the emergent situation in linguistics, economics, ethnology, and psychoanalysis from the first decades of the twentieth century onward.

> On the horizon of any human science the plan exists to bring man's consciousness back to its own true conditions, to return human consciousness to the contents and forms that gave it birth, and that elude consciousness.[6]

The idea that man is not master on this earth is shared by the human and social sciences in the twentieth century with the supporters of the rationality of a Cartesian or classical type. Certainly, these sciences have not merely returned to that rationality; they in no way go back to the notion of an external reality ordered according to hierarchies or structures having God as their beginning and final end. Once the human and social sciences reach awareness of their own status, they show Western culture as having an inherent direction, one that has not emerged until now. But this is only because, although it is weakened, the humanistic vision and inspiration of the previous period is still present. As Foucault says in the final pages of *The Words and the Things*:

> If such tendencies should disappear as they have appeared, if they – as a consequence of some event which we can at the most forecast, of which however we do not know for now either the form or the promise – should precipitate as happened at the turn of the eighteenth century for the basis of classical thought, we can certainly venture that man would be cancelled, as on the edge of the sea a face made of sand.[7]

Thus Foucault, in an investigation directed to a specific field and to the analysis of a path that, moving away from its beginning, returns to exactly the same point, though on a different plane, reflects on the destiny of Western thought.

Now if these three books on different ages in the history of philosophy, all using the idea of the *parable/parabola*, are put together, then they themselves seem to form a *parabola* in both its meanings.

First of all, in fact, the *parabola* consists in the line that these works describe: from the split between living and philosophizing, making it impossible to find a univocal answer to the question of man, according to Groethuysen, one arrives at the cancellation of man sketched by Foucault, while having the rise and development of nihilism as represented by Löwith as an intermediate point.

In the second place, the *parabola* consists in the fact that these books which indeed dwell upon partial aspects, nevertheless relate the comprehensive history of Western civilization; they show how this civilization is hardly able to defend man and even seems to give up on the attempt. Groethuysen, Löwith and Foucault are three renowned representatives of that historiographic current that, in our times, acknowledges and analyzes a crisis in the course followed by humanistic ideas and dispositions. It is a crisis with deep roots in Europe and the West's intellectual history.[8] But why has not Western culture the strength – notwithstanding the richness and multiformity of its prevailing directions – to give an answer today to the question of man in a clearer and more convincing way than it did in past centuries? Perhaps the conceptual tools, used for the most part in Western philosophical and religious tradition until now, are not good enough to understand how in ancient times the idea of humanity entered ordinary life? After seeing the disquieting results of the history of Western thought, it could be instructive to examine carefully once again those human experiences which are the sources of this idea, before philosophy and the different religious doctrines establish their influence on human life.

1.2 The witness in Primo Levi's *If This is a Man*

Primo Levi's book *If This is a Man* – an autobiography – comes as a warning to remember that man is more than something to be used or the object of some arbitrary and violent will. The title and the poem preceding the tale make it clear. "Consider if this is a man/ Who works in the mud/ Who doesn't know peace." The title first given to the poem was then given to the book itself.[9] Levi himself was captured as a "partigiano" by the Fascists, handed over by the Fascists to the German SS, and deported by them to Auschwitz, where he was detained between February 1944 and January 18, 1945. This was the date when the Germans abandoned the camp because of the imminent arrival of the Russian army.

In this tale there are many pages where Primo Levi weighs the idea of humanity against what man had become at Auschwitz. He opposes the sphere of common language, lacking words to describe the "demolition of a human being," and the "reduction of man to suffering and needs."[10] The human world in which a question is posed and an answer expected, however limited the means of expression available to the partners in dialogue, is contrasted with the brutal denial of the possibility of even asking questions;[11] reasonable and meaningful norms with being confined to regulations and prohibitions without any reason;[12] a variety of experiences, encounters and activities with the horribly dull repetitiveness of working, eating, sleeping, getting sick and recovering, or dying;[13] feeling confidence and trust with being afraid and hostile, undermining even the rapport between man and nature;[14] and freedom of thought and will with the transformation of man into an automaton.[15]

The book is addressed to men so that they will nevermore allow themselves to be deprived by other men of their own humanity. The obligation to be a witness of what happened at Auschwitz arises from this deep perception that a violation of humanity occurred there. A terrifying dream was lined in Auschwitz – of telling others what was happening and not being believed.[16] In this case, witnessing is rendered by telling others faithfully of events that point to an extremely serious danger. Those who have experienced this danger wish to warn others of it. In this case, it is not so much the desire for justice that moves the witness but seeing himself as the representative of a human community that he seeks to protect from a tragic threat.[17]

How, then, does Levi present the idea of humanity? It is, after all, the source inspiring his book, grounding the duty to be a witness.

If This is a Man contains many reflections on human nature. Although the author highlights human weakness, fragility and much wickedness, the denotation "humanity" itself remains unchallenged by these qualities, because they only belong to a corruptible and perishable world. This denotation in *If This is a Man* emerges neither from knowledge nor from faith contained in a religious teaching. The idea of humanity is described as an immediate truth seeming to reach man from a mysterious beyond, truth that is not proven with reason, but through words and behavior. Now the term "witness" fits here as well. A witness is not only someone who gives a report, or documents events he or she participated in, to inform and advise. A witness is also a human being immediately certain of a truth that seems to keep him in touch with a beyond – a beyond human finiteness.

Dante wrote "Think of your breed; for brutish ignorance/ Your mettle was not made; you were made men/ To follow after knowledge and excellence." Levi writes, in the chapter entitled "The Canto of Ulysses," that when he recited these verses to his companion Jean, called Pikolo, he was overwhelmed by their meaning and simply forgot himself. "As if I also was hearing it for the first time: like the blast of a trumpet, like the voice of God."[18] Pikolo immediately grasped the verses' meaning, and his friend's desire that they be understood exactly. "Pikolo begs me to repeat it" – the author continues – "How good Pikolo is, he feels that he is doing me good."[19]

Later on Levi relates how before the cry of the man who was last among those who dared to rebel, there was not one of the prisoners forced to be present at his execution who wasn't deeply shaken, in spite of their heavy resignation. "Everybody heard the cry of the doomed man, it pierced the ancient and thick barriers of inertia and submissiveness, it struck the living core of man in each of us. – Kamaraden, ich bin der Letzte!"[20] Later, as Levi remembers, a secret feeling of shame oppressed him and the friend he used to share the food with, preventing them, after they had satisfied "the daily ragings of hunger," from "looking each other in the face."

The author also recounts that he told the "Hungarian boy Kraus" about a fictional dream where both were happy in his Italian home, in the warmth of a family circle. And he did this because all of a sudden he saw that he was before a human being. "I look at him and I see his eyes behind the drops of rain on his glasses, and they are the eyes of the man Kraus."[21] Even if only for a "brief moment" what took place there was "an important event," whose memory it is good to keep. "It is worth recounting it now, perhaps for the same reason that it happened then."[22]

In bringing these episodes to light, Levi shows that witnessing is given by those who feel that there is a pure kingdom, uncontaminated and good, beyond an infernal world, and this in spite of everything. The author sees those men who are good and wise, mild and strong as living proofs of this kingdom. Levi gratefully remembers his companion Alberto and the Italian civilian, a working man, Lorenzo, who fed him day by day giving him part of his meager rations. Those human beings are the witnesses. For sure, senselessness isn't cancelled by the pure world, just contrasted. Exactly the idea of this kingdom, however, permits the world of civilization, language, reciprocal assistance, and justice in everyday life.

Such is the way the thought of humanity comes to mind and influences human beings – in hearing a writer describing a limit-situation, a place and time where all established laws and consolidated rules collapsed, producing a return to the first and most elementary strata of experience.[23]

Now, should not the form and aspects of the idea of humanity at Auschwitz, according to Primo Levi, impact on today's philosophical defences of Western humanism? And in this case, shouldn't the term witness, standing for someone who has an immediate perception of an ethical beyond, and who tries to act on this perception, be used as a philosophical concept? If philosophers would, as philosophers, think about this kind of witnessing, it would perhaps provide a strong justification for a witness's behavior even in the first sense of the term, one who reports on what happened with the purpose of avoiding further offences to humanity.

1.3 Philosophical tradition, Judaism, new thought

Now, there is a group of Jewish thinkers of the twentieth century whose intellectual evolution brought them to criticize Western thought. The premise and main subject of their work became a specific idea about humanity – as I shall try to show – the same one found in Primo Levi's *If This is a Man*. They are Hermann Cohen, Franz Rosenzweig, Martin Buber, Leo Strauss and Emmanuel Levinas.[24]

This book is an introduction to these authors' philosophies: in their dialogue with Western humanism and in the context of its crisis, one wishes to emphasize the type of humanism they have come to uphold, while outlining the content of their writings. It seems to me that what they mean by the word "humanity" could be both that which allows us to consider them together, and the means to evidence their originality within the scope of twentieth-century philosophy.

In certain phases of the development of their thinking their originality becomes evident, first in that they connect the ethical and political spheres (for them, the "I" is neither a mere single human being, nor a mere part of a public organization), and second, in relating the ethical–political field to Transcendence. They give a Jewish interpretation here: Transcendence doesn't need to be mediated to enter human reality, cannot become incarnate, isn't reducible to an image, is defined by ethical attributes and is the model for human actions that stay forever imperfect. Humanity is therefore defined simultaneously by morality and existence in time.

I would like to underline here only those features of their biographies and teachings that show the affinity between them. Later in this book we will see both their biographies and writings in detail, and we will study their different languages and styles.

All of them begin their philosophical life as scholars or followers of specific philosophers – Kant, Hegel, Spinoza, Husserl – or of a particular philosophical current – idealism, "philosophy of life" or phenomenology. Then, they look at Judaism as philosophers, convinced as they are that they can find in Jewish sources orientations, methods, concepts, and means of expression not known to the Western philosophical tradition, and indispensable to the building of a "new thought" (the term is introduced by Rosenzweig, but the concept it indicates is true also for the others). In fact, they think that the Western philosophical tradition developed especially through the contributions of the Greeks and Christianity.

When these thinkers discover in the Jewish sources a different concept of reason or "spirit" than that maintained by Western philosophical tradition, or when they interpret experience in relation to the experience of God, man and the world from which the Hebrew Bible came, all of them criticize Parmenides, or Parmenides' identification of thinking and being. Parmenides and his followers exclusively place the *Logos* at the foundation of philosophical reflection and do not consider the connection of the *Logos* with language, eros, sensibility, and common moral rules. While the traditional type of philosophical thinking is founded on reason, and either considers faith, passions and feelings opposed to it, or doesn't give them the importance they deserve, the root of the new way of thinking is affectivity, or what we could call a moral sensitivity. The affects of love, pity, justice, fidelity, loyalty, responsibility are the very bases of the *Logos* that man turns towards the Being, or the various spheres of being in his or her knowledge.

Finally, Cohen, Rosenzweig, Buber, Strauss and Levinas say that thought that is open to Judaism keeps both the notion of one's individual existence and the ethical concept of God. For them, God is first of all the remote and hidden origin of the Law, and then He is the creator and the redeemer. God is included and also not included within human horizons. A man can be in touch with the supersensible and conceive it; but the supersensible cannot in any way simply be the object of our minds.

Such are the fundamental characteristics of this Jewish philosophical current, optimistic about human nature and therefore defending an authentic theodicy.

2

HERMANN COHEN (1842–1918)

2.1 The contrast between mechanism and freedom in the early writings

Cohen left the rabbinical seminary of Breslau in 1863.[1] He started his dissertation on Plato and Aristotle in Berlin, and presented it at Halle in 1865 as the crowning work of his university studies in philosophy. After this, between 1866 and 1869, Cohen published three articles in the journal directed by Moritz Lazarus and Haim Steinthal, at the time the most important representatives of the current called *Völkerpsychologie*.[2] The object of these three articles was the way in which the mechanism of consciousness, either through cultural environment or certain physical states, can produce particular doctrines or representations.

In the first of these essays, Cohen proved how Plato had elaborated his theory of ideas in a specific cultural context. Since in Greek art there is a perfect correspondence between the spiritual and the material, for Plato the idea is first of all "vision" (*Gesicht*), or an ideal element perceived by the mind as a specific form or image. So "mythical fantasy," which besides art also produces Greek tragedy and poetry, is at the base of Platonic philosophy. That is the context where this philosophy is integrated and its firm ground. A scholar of social or individual psychology who did not focus on this context, would be missing the historical meaning of Plato's philosophy. In the second essay Cohen distinguishes psychological analysis from metaphysics, regarding the identification of the "a priori" inherent in our spirit and its relation to Being. He also distinguishes psychological analysis from deductive criticism, relating to the theoretical function of concepts. Then he went on to ponder the mythological notions of God and the soul. He showed the origins of these notions in perceptive states, and connected these states to movements of the nervous system. Thus, even notions regarding the supersensible had their genesis in sensibility and in the human body. So Cohen writes:

> Psychology – as it is totally separated from the metaphysical question, and as there is no innate concept for it – must divide any representation given in science, or in the naive spirit, into its elements. Its task, faced with even the most respectable concept, is to ask: through what has this concept come about, from where, and how? – in case this quality of respectability can be connected with the concept.[3]

In his third essay Cohen first explained how "poetic fantasy" had its source in "mythical fantasy" in terms of both form and content; then, he linked poetry and language, poetry and music, and poetry and ethics. Thus, through a psychological analysis, which has the hypothesis of the "unity of consciousness" as its fundamental principle, it is possible to prove how a particular spiritual process sets other processes in motion. Naturally, each process moves away from the one which first brought it about, and a great distance separates, for example, the mythical concepts of ethics from the ethical concepts successively established in art and literature. However, the investigation which retraces the very beginning of spiritual processes, makes it possible to understand how spirit itself operates and the meaning it bears, even when it has moved far away from its original roots.

So in his early writings Cohen advocates a psychology that denies creative mental activity preferring to study those states which connect spirit with man's natural being or man's history. In the third of these writings, nevertheless, there is a comment indicating that Cohen is inspired to go in another direction from that of the *Völkerpsycholog*. Here, there is a reference to the clear difference between Greek art, linked with myth, and the Jewish idea of God which forbids His portrayal in perceptible forms. "How small must the Zeus of Phaedias have appeared to a rigorous monotheist!"[4] – Cohen exclaims, when he examines the difference between Greek and Jewish culture which also had its literary, poetic and musical productions. These, however, were centered not on the forms given to nature or man by the artist, but on the idea of God as beyond any image or representation.

Thus Cohen, reflecting on Jewish culture, was led to an important question: whether the Jewish idea of God, implying complete detachment from sensibility, could have originated from it, as explained by the psychological analysis of consciousness developed in the *Völkerpsychologie*, or whether this idea had another source. Wouldn't this idea perhaps encourage a different view of spirit from that which describes it as closely bound to the senses or to a specific environment? This might still be so even when the philosopher, the artist or the poet is able to elaborate the influences deriving from those sources (a possibility which Cohen certainly did not exclude). Isn't Jewish monotheism perhaps the strongest evidence of the mind's ability to separate from the plane of the natural world to see what is definitely supersensible through an act of freedom?

Now, it is this second line of research, regarding the productions of mind and culture, that Cohen follows in two essays on Jewish themes, written during the same years in which he wrote the pieces we have been looking at. So, besides psychological analysis which sees the human being as influenced by causal connections, a consideration of man appears in Cohen characterizing him by a creative intelligence: in an active manner, breaking his ties with nature, man orders the phenomena of both the natural world and the human world through pure concepts. The author focused particularly on the first aspect of human intelligence, knowledge production, in his text *Heinrich Heine and Judaism*;[5] and dealt particularly with the second aspect of human intelligence, producing action in society and history, in his text *The Sabbath in its Historical–Cultural Meaning*.[6]

In the first of these articles Cohen demonstrates how besides many other influences in Heine, there is a Jewish inspiration when he exalts the autonomy of man as both a theoretical and a practical subject. Spinoza is the figure Heine is referring to, according to Cohen, when he defends this position: Heine supports not so much Spinoza's philosophical system, as the main reasons inspiring this system. Because of the influence Spinoza had on him, Heine places no opposition between Jewish monotheism and pantheism. Unlike Goethe's pantheism that confuses spirit with nature, Heine's peculiar version separates rational activity, ordering perceptions and inclinations, from the variability of natural events. As Spinoza had done before, Heine interprets the Jewish idea of God, transcending the natural and human world, in the sense of the excellence of the human spirit which soars above the world existing in space and time: so the human spirit knows the world according to the ideal measures found in natural science and, alternatively, transforms the world according to moral rules. Even Heine's fondness for Greek culture, which brings him to disdain asceticism and to exalt a life in nature and history, should be evaluated, in Cohen's view, in the light of his "pantheistic–monotheistic" attitude.[7] Whereas in Goethe art represents the climax of human activity, Heine considers knowledge and ethics directed towards humanity's progress the main purpose. Heine considers that the human spirit itself is divine because it is able to reach pure ideas and to act without any selfish interest. In Cohen's view, Spinoza and Heine are great figures of modern Judaism, that is to say of a Judaism which transfigures its rigorous monotheism into a humanism founded on the idea of the absolute freedom of the human spirit. It is precisely the Jewish idea of God that proves – as Cohen states in *Heinrich Heine and Judaism* – how not all human representations can be traced back to a psychological mechanism. In fact, this idea is based on a complete split with the world of impulses, passions, and representations in which man as a natural being lives: "It was born in the darkness of consciousness, and thus it is obscure, as is everything which is sublime."[8] And from exactly this sublime idea modern science and morality have originated: a humanity which has freed itself from ties with those traditions still influenced by myth, has produced modernity. The "glorification" (*Verherrlichung*) of man is expressed by a pantheism which is not pagan, and is seen instead as the development and the renewal of the Jewish notion of God.

In his article *The Sabbath in its Historical–Cultural Meaning* Cohen emphasizes first of all how the ethical ideas of the modern era – freedom, equality, and fraternity – have origins in Judaism: on the day of rest from work, the Sabbath, all human beings are recognized as equal in their dignity and divine in their origin. He goes on to explain how the concept of the Sabbath, claimed by the Jews since the most ancient times, cannot be related either to natural impulses and selfish feelings, or to the influence on the people of Israel of other peoples with whom they were in contact: only the human mind, free from any tie with the earthly and sensible, could create such a notion, later adopted by all the civilized peoples of the world. The Sabbath was for ancient Israel a day dedicated to God in abstaining from any activity directed towards one's physical sustenance or the transformation of nature: "Not fasts, not wild dancing, not debauchery of one's senses characterize its celebration, but rest from work."[9] The Sabbath originates in one idea only: this idea is part of an understanding of the world characterized by Cohen as "perfect idealism" (*geschlossene Idealismus*). The idealism received in the modern age no longer upholds a transcendent God with regard to man, but exalts man himself who – in the imitation of Prometheus – develops in history, on an ascending path towards the ideal.

Therefore, two directions of thought coexist in Cohen's writings between 1866 and 1869, one of a naturalistic or materialistic tendency – according to the teachings of the *Völkerpsychologie* – and the other idealistic. The idealism which Cohen maintains in these years could be defined as immanent because its main notion is the action of the human spirit in constructing culture.[10] Cohen takes this second direction in interpreting Judaism and its role in modernity.[11] This immanent idealism was to prevail over naturalism or materialism in 1871 when Cohen participated in the lively discussion on Kant in German culture at that time, upholding his own particular and original position.

2.2 Interpreting the Kantian doctrine of the "a priori" in the works on Kant

After his participation in the dispute between Kuno Fischer and Adolf Trendelenburg concerning the evaluation of the Kantian "a priori" – where he had criticized both interpretations of it, the first for being addressed only towards subjectivism, the second for its primary emphasis on objectivism[12] – Cohen published a book entitled *The Kantian Theory of Experience*.[13] He presented his reading of Kant as a philosopher of human knowledge of the natural world. Some welcomed the book as a contribution of great significance opening a new epoch in Kantian studies, while others, were perplexed by this work which not only analyzed the *Critique of Pure Reason* and the *Prolegomena to any Future Metaphysics which will present Itself as Science*, but also developed a theory of knowledge, based on them, completely centered on the activity of the spirit. Spirit was considered in this work as a set of functions constructing the objectivity of nature: in this way the author set a limit to the meaning and importance of the doctrine of sensibility, characterized by receptivity, and to the doctrine of the thing in itself as the cause of sensations; both doctrines were considered secondary for the core of Kant's theory of knowledge.[14]

Right from the preface of *The Kantian Theory of Experience*, Cohen explains to the reader his guiding intentions in interpreting the Kantian books on knowledge. He certainly intends, in presenting Kant's thought, to respect philology and history; however, his purpose is systematic, of "founding again the Kantian 'a priori' doctrine."[15] It is not so much a question of clarifying Kant's position within the history of philosophy, as of recognizing in Kant the philosopher who effectively showed how man can have objective knowledge of things. Cohen intends to prove in his work how Kant, "this hero of the German spirit,"[16] opened a way, in this field, that can lead to further valuable results. Cohen himself wishes to continue on this way, and build a theory of the human spirit on foundations Kant ensured.

Cohen dedicates the first five chapters of his book to Kant's evaluation of space and time. He points out how it is just such an evaluation, which differs both from

Leibniz's, who considers space and time as concepts, and from Hume's, who holds that space and time are concepts derived from impressions, that leads Kant to set up a new notion of the "a priori," and therefore of experience. The "a priori" pertains neither to those concepts of reason dogmatically identified with the being of things, nor to what is innate from a psychological point of view, but to what allows our knowledge to be real. "Kant" – Cohen writes – "calls 'a priori' that knowledge (*Bekenntnis*) which is universally valid and rigorously necessary."[17] Mathematics is closely linked to the "a priori" in the Kantian sense: time and space are the "a priori" principles of sense experience as they enable the validity of geometric and arithmetic knowledge. Mathematics does not reflect reality in itself, but has its own subsistence and consistency. Kant's "Copernican revolution" consists not in attending to consciousness, in the subjective or psychological meaning of this term, but in seeing the determination of objectivity accomplished through the "a priori." Thus, mathematics itself takes on the form of "experience." Hence – so Cohen holds – the real meaning of "transcendental" in Kantian thought: "Kant calls transcendental that knowledge which does not deal so much with objects, as with our 'a priori' concepts of objects."[18] Thus, the philosophical problem which Kant presents is not at all that of the relationship between consciousness and objects, but that of what allows our knowledge to be valid. Therefore, in a way of knowing that has the "a priori" character, oppositions disappear between concept–object, idea–thing, subjective–objective, and form–content: Kantian doctrine only considers the objective knowledge we have of the world, and emphasizes that which renders it so. The subject, in the Kantian sense – according to Cohen – is only the subjective side of objective experience. While idealistic subjectivism and realism inevitably lead to scepticism with regard to the possibility of experiencing the world, critical Kantian idealism gives reasons for the certainty of such experience and for the reality of the common world of mathematics and natural science: "Objective is only that which subjectivity 'a priori' 'produces', 'constructs'."[19] Through this notion of "a priori" which forms the "foundation of the entire system,"[20] the difference between forms of sensibility and forms of intellect does not seem radical – the "a priori" and the phenomena are simply correlated terms. The fact that experience is constituted by the complex of phenomena – the objective side of knowledge – makes it impossible or senseless to ask the question: "Is there ever a being?"[21] Phenomena are objective exactly because they are based on the "a priori" of that consciousness which identifies itself with the structure of experience. The fact that this meaning of the "a priori" has not been clarified by Kantian critique, explains, in Cohen's opinion, the mistaken paths and the sterile disputes that have arisen in the name of Kant: as if his teaching consisted in a new metaphysical or psychological doctrine rather than one concerning the conditions that make objective experience possible, given in human culture.

In chapters 6–13 of *The Kantian Theory of Experience* the author discusses the problems of the "transcendental deduction of categories" and the "self" in the *Critique of Pure Reason*. He also enquires how "a priori" forms of sensibility come together with intellectual activity, and thus asks about the difference between simple "perception judgements" (*Wahrnehmungsurtheilen*), having only subjective value, and "experiential

13

judgements" (*Erfahrungsurtheilen*), which also have objective value. With regard to the first problem, Cohen maintains that such a "deduction" is addressed to solving the question of the universality and necessity of knowledge – which is completely different from the question of the genesis of knowledge in a metaphysical or empirical sense – and that the two different versions of this "deduction," one found in the 1781 and the other in the 1787 edition of the *Critique*, do not oppose each other. In both, in fact, Kant underlines the active role of the intellect in constructing experience, entrusting to the intellectual functions that "recognition of the representations" (*Recognition der Vorstellungen*) which allows us to reach stability and organic unity in "learning" and "reproducing" phenomena. Only in the later version, however, are the psychological aspects of the "deduction" clearly separated from those analyzed by transcendental logic. Concerning the second problem, Cohen insists on the fact that the "self" should not be seen as an intelligible or empirical reality, but only as the "condition" upon which, in the end, Kant makes the objectivity of knowledge depend. In the *Critique* the "self" indicates not a "substance," but an "action" or a "process," as it is identified with consciousness' synthetic activity related to experience. "The objective unity of self-consciousness" – Cohen writes – "consists in the synthetic unity of the representations under the category."[22] One must thus distinguish in a radical manner the "self" of "transcendental apperception" from the "self" as it is given either by "internal sense" – and in this case it can only be an internal "phenomenon" – or the self given by "intellectual intuition" – when it becomes that "soul" which experience cannot consider as one of its objects because of the conditions of its validity. In chapters 6–13 Cohen also reflects on the Kantian doctrines of "schematism" and "synthetic 'a priori' principles." He remarks that Kant's analysis of the processes of "schematization" carried out by the imagination should be considered subordinate to that analysis dedicated to determining the "transcendental principles": as functions of the intellect these "principles" allow us to bring unity and coherence to our knowledge of nature; they are those forms in which given or possible experience is finally necessarily and universally structured through the action of consciousness, identified with the "I think" of mathematics and science.

The final two chapters of *The Kantian Theory of Experience* introduce Kant's transcendental idealism as "empirical realism," that is as an enquiry into our actual experience of nature, and they outline the scope of this "empirical realism" through an interpretation of the "thing in itself" as "limit-concept" (*Grenzbegriff*). In fact, if the intellect breaks away from the deceptive view of objects as real entities beyond itself or as supersensible, then the "thing in itself" cannot but indicate what is produced by the "intellectual intuition" once it assumes the role of producing knowledge: the "thing in itself" is, in this case, only an "illusion" (*Schein*) produced by the intellect which abandons its reference to objectivity in trying to know objects other than those proposed by mathematics and science. At the same time, however, exactly because of the interpretation of Kantian thought as "empirical realism" and of the "thing in itself" as a negative concept within the theory of experience, a possibility opens to extend "critical idealism" to other spheres of culture bearing the character of objectivity. Since there are no longer for Kant "things in themselves" presupposed by knowledge, but only facts having a rational structure, as with mathematics and the scientific knowledge of nature, then it becomes possible to extend the transcendental method to other ideal facts. The doctrine of the "antinomies," developed in the "transcendental dialectic" (the second part of the "transcendental logic" in the *Critique* after the "transcendental analytic"), already makes evident – according to Cohen – how Kant transformed the opposition between different points of view on Being, expressed up to then by philosophical thinking – origin or eternity of the world, reduction to simple elements or infinite divisibility, causality or finality, necessity or freedom – into a harmonious set of the different principles produced by consciousness. In this way one may say that Kant truly represents a turning point in the history of philosophy. So Cohen writes in the conclusion of his first book: "To resolve the difference between things in the diversity of ideas – this is the secret of idealism. The history of human thought discovers this secret and, with this secret, discovers itself as the history of idealism."[23] Thus, Kant constitutes the fixed point of a philosophical reflection that intends both to retrace the steps of its journey, and to study in further depth and extend its field.

In *The Kantian Theory of Experience* – as has been seen – Cohen gave a precise determination to the idea of freedom as a faculty of the spirit able to produce culture, which he had alluded to in his first writings dedicated to Judaism. In the Kantian "a priori" doctrine he found the methodological tools for proving that the activity of spirit and the results of human culture are correlated. In this book, while analyzing Kantian writings on knowledge, Cohen highlighted the constructive functions of sensibility, imagination, and intellect, placing greater emphasis on the latter. In his following two books dedicated to Kant, he underlines the productive role of ideas, expressed by reason, and teleological principles, expressed by the faculty of judgment. While the first have as their correlative part the ethical world, the latter have as their correlation the world of art and experience of nature's finality. So Cohen was – on the German scene of his time – the interpreter of Kant as *Kulturphilosoph* who in the most radical and rigorous form defended the thesis that central to Kant is the idea of spirit's autonomy, beyond natural or historical conditions that might affect it. Humanity's scientific, artistic and moral culture has universal value because it is independent of the specific conditions in which it comes about. Conditions are connected with particular places and times while culture (in the true sense of this term) has rationality or spirituality: if the spirit remained, as it were, tied to nature or history, then its productions would not be important, meaningful and necessary to all human beings. For Cohen, Kant was the German philosopher who had first been able to grasp the deep meaning of culture, and to render it, with full self-consciousness, the object of a philosophical analysis. Against any provincialism and human closure into limited horizons, Kant had exalted a free humanity that produces a meaningful ideal world.[24] In his previous work on Kant, Cohen had laid out both the question of knowledge and philosophy's passage from knowledge to other spheres. In human culture these spheres seem to have objectivity. Cohen's book *The Kantian Foundation of Ethics*[25] follows a path depending on the method established there.

The first part of this book is dedicated to explaining the transition between reflection on experience and ethics. Whereas the first consists in an enquiry into experience as based on mathematics and the science of nature – experience which is "being" (*Sein*) – the second consists in an investigation of ethical concepts and judgments which can be collected under the heading of "having to be" (*Sollen*). As the first differs both from metaphysics and psychology, the second likewise differs both from religion or theology and anthropology. But, since only in the case of the theory of experience may one refer to ideal facts considered valid by everyone, like those of pure and applied mathematics, while the moral world still appears fragmented and uncertain, then the first constitutes the necessary premise for the second. Thus Cohen in the first part of *The Kantian Foundation of Ethics* shows how the "thing in itself," in the reflection on knowledge, indicates only the negative *pendant* of objectivity, while in moral philosophy it becomes the positive idea of *noumenon*: the *noumenon* is conceived no more by theoretical reason which first discovers it, but by a practical reason which invites action according to ethical principles. Amongst the ideas defined by theoretical reason that become ideas for practical use (because the *noumenon* transforms from an object of thinking to a rule for actions), the idea of freedom in particular appears as what upholds the sphere of morality: freedom in Kantian thought is – according to Cohen – not the possibility of choosing, but the "regulative principle" of the unity of actions directed to a goal, that is, the antithetical term to that of the determination, according to causal laws, of events in the natural world. "Ethics" – Cohen writes – "is founded, according to its possibility, on the regulative use of one of the cosmological ideas. Ethics therefore may be defined as the exposition (*Darstellung*) of the regulative use of the cosmological idea of freedom."[26] Freedom is, in such a case, not self-determination, but orientation of the practical reason or pure will moved by its own end or by itself. The idea of freedom is at the base of ethical knowledge as "synthetic a priori knowledge" – like theoretical knowledge, but also unlike it because founded on other concepts and principles: in place of causal necessity and natural principles, teleology and principles of morality. So, the reality (*Realität*) of the idea of freedom – which is not to be confused with empirical existence (*Wirklichkeit*) because it means ideal consistency and firmness – is assured by the objective validity of knowledge of nature. In fact, only starting out from reflection on experience is it possible to reach ethics as a philosophical discipline, addressed as it is to a field of culture bearing certainty and worth: the validity of morality is proved by the validity of scientific knowledge.

The second part of *The Kantian Foundation of Ethics* highlights how beginning with the idea of freedom understood in a cosmological sense, many other important arguments in Kant's ethics may be drawn. For example, the connection between the *Sein* of the *Sollen*, that is, between the ideal being of the "having to be," and empirical or historical reality (*Wirklichkeit*) can be clarified through this idea of freedom: the ideal gives to the actual the direction to be pursued because the ideal already expresses the law of praxis and has a finalistic meaning. The *Autonomie*, on which Kant grounds moral law, becomes through the notion of freedom as an idea with regulative value, *Autotelie*, that is, the concept of humanity as "end in itself" (individuals are "ends in themselves" only because they have a pure will). The formalism of the moral law, through the cosmological idea of freedom, acquires a precise content: it means the respect for rationality itself in man, as the end to keep in mind, in every specific ethical action. The notion of the "primacy of practical reason" – through the central position held by the idea of freedom as depending on the theory of knowledge – does not mean an opposition to theoretical reason and a reference to a metaphysical or empirical subject; rather, it means that theoretical reason recognizes the value of the moral field, once it has reached, through the expansion of its own concepts, just this field. Finally, the idea of God, through the relation between the idea of freedom and the idea of the world, takes on the meaning of a final unity between the spheres which these ideas control, the sphere of morality and the sphere of nature.

In the third and last part of the *Kantian Foundation of Ethics*, built on the ground of his philosophical analysis of being, first related to mathematics and mathematical natural science, Cohen describes how the individual moral life is subordinated to morality's being. Here he examines the terms of "duty" (*Pflicht*), and "respect" (*Achtung*) for the moral law as typical concepts of Kantian ethics: "duty" and "respect" are the effects of practical reason on human sensibility. The theory of postulates and the doctrine of the *summum bonum*, present in the *Critique of Practical Reason*, are excluded from this area of the "application" of the moral law to human nature: in fact, Cohen thinks that these doctrines are not exclusively oriented by ethical concepts, but by the need to prove the compatibility of the moral and the natural being of man as moved by desire for happiness – respect for the moral law should be considered, according to Cohen, as the only and exclusive motive of the empirical will in moral actions.

In 1889 Cohen – after the publication of other writings on mathematics and natural science, in which he emphasized the constructive function of the idea in the process of knowledge, and deprived sensibility of cognitive value,[27] and the publication of the second edition, revised and expanded, of the *Kantian Theory of Experience*[28] – concluded his exegesis and systematic meditation on Kant with *The Kantian Foundation of Aesthetics*.[29] If in the first two books on Kant he had examined the concepts and principles of theoretical knowledge, and the ideas and law of practical knowledge, in this third book he dealt with the determination of the subject which is at the base not only of works of art, but also of culture in its totality. Even in the world of art, as in that of science and morality, Cohen searched out and highlighted forms and rules. These seemed to him, however, in the case of art, not "a priori," already outlined, impersonal elements, as in the other two areas, but – coming from the *Critique of Judgement* – productions of artistic genius and therefore again and again determined by the artist. At the end of the book the author extended just such a close connection between the subjective and the objective, which is evident in aesthetics, to the whole of *Kulturphilosophie*. Thus, for Cohen, in *The Kantian Foundation of Aesthetics*, Kant was the author of a philosophical system centered on a subjectivity which expresses and finds itself in the objectivity of *Kultur*. "The system means for Kant not a closed totality of concepts" – thus Cohen summarized his comprehensive interpretation of Kant – "but the totality of the productive modes of consciousness

17

(*Bewusstsein*): each mode, singularly (*für sich*) analyzed, gives a distinctive content."[30] The subject which produces culture is humanity itself, the *homo noumenon*, that is, the intelligible or ideal humanity, which sees itself in its spiritual creations as in a mirror.

In this way Cohen, who in his early Jewish writings on Spinoza and Heine had exalted the modern idea of the freedom of mind, and defended an immanent idealism, critical of the transcendence of God, then came in his Kantian books to a critical idealism directed by art as the highest human activity, model of all the other activities. In art there is no radical differentiation between form and content, the material and the ideal: the image is the point in which creative subjectivity and created objectivity come together.

2.3   The idea of humanity as producer of culture in the *Philosophical System*

Cohen's plan of a *Philosophical System* arises from his interpretation of Kantian thought as a philosophy of culture founded on the autonomy of spirit: spirit has mathematics and natural science, moral judgments and artistic works as its objective terms. The point of composing such a *System* was on the one hand to continue on the path taken by Kant, who had transformed metaphysics from a science of being into a philosophy of culture, and on the other to develop what he had not fully accomplished: for example, the determination of reason as the fundamental instrument of knowledge, because of its unifying activity (which implied a denial of sensibility as a specific source); the connection between ethics and the human sciences (which was the result of an analogy between the theory of experience and ethics); and the definition of the last concept of subjectivity as a ground for all the cultural *Fakta* (which allowed one to understand the comprehensive meaning of the *System*).

After the publication in 1896 of his *Introduction* to the *History of Materialism* by Friedrich Albert Lange, where he offers the idea of philosophy as the self-consciousness of culture, referring to the history of philosophy and to social and political problems of his times,[31] Cohen publishes between 1902 and 1912 a *Philosophical System*, made up of three parts entitled *Logic of Pure Knowledge*, *Ethics of Pure Will*, and *Aesthetics of Pure Feeling*.[32] The author entrusts a great task to this trilogy: the *System* must show readers how through spirit, humanity becomes one, and how humanity should carry on so that, even in the historical and political realm, unification and harmony become possible. The individual must find in this trilogy an articulated illustration of his belonging to a plane in which he – as a member of humanity – lives no longer only in time, and look at this supersensible plane in order to give a meaning to his existence.

In the *Preface* to the first edition of his *Logic of Pure Knowledge* Cohen eloquently explains his intent: the logic that he presents not only teaches "the laws and rules of the universal use of reason," and therefore refers to mathematics and – among all the natural sciences – mathematical science; it is also "the foundation of a philosophical system" whose aim is the celebration of reason, idealism and cosmopolitanism. This logic, which does not depend on the actual temporal context, which is extremely favorable to irrational or romantic tendencies, and is mostly inspired by Greek science and philosophy, shows how reason operates in the world; it is a logic that considers as its defenders and supporters those philosophers who are guided by the sciences and culture. Cohen finds the spirit of Kantian enlightenment, the climax of German thought, still alive in the academic institutions and universities of Germany, and is confident that they will be able to welcome his message, and thus consider philosophy – as humanity's self-consciousness in culture – the core of their activity.

The logic which Cohen presents in this book – through references to Parmenides, Plato, Leibniz, and Kant (whose dualism between sensibility and thought is often criticized) – upholds pure thought not as the instrument of reasoning, beyond the contents, as occurs in formal logic, but as the producer of its objects. The notion of "origin," built out of a reflection on infinitesimal calculus, is the starting point of this logic: categories and judgments which appear in all the sciences, as in every human experience, have their source here; this notion allows one to conceive thinking as a continuous, but productive movement, as a unifying and, at the same time, dividing energy. Data remain, in this thinking process, within pure thought: thus, the results of pure thought are knowledge having the character of universal validity. Pure thought expresses four classes of judgments (Cohen dedicates a part of his book to each of these classes): judgments of the laws of thinking, which require, before judgments of identity and contradiction, judgment of origin; judgments of mathematics, which consist in judgments of reality (*Realität*), plurality (*Mehrheit*), and totality (*Allheit*); judgments of the mathematical natural sciences, which are those of substance (*Substanz*), law (*Gesetz*), and concept (*Begriff*); and finally judgments of method (*Methodik*), which refer to possibility, reality (*Wirklichkeit*) and necessity. In *Logic of Pure Knowledge* Cohen especially fights against what he calls "the illusion of perception"[33]: space and time, depending on pure thought, are also categories or intellectual concepts; certainly, perception is connected to individual conscience (*Bewusstheit*), existence (*Dasein*), the individual (*Einzelne*), and reality (*Wirklichkeit*), whose notions belong to the sciences; and yet, even these elements, under scrutiny, seem nothing more than "self-productions of pure thought," themes introduced by pure thought itself. So the author, making Being identical with thinking, sides with Parmenides and the Eleatics against all those who subordinate logic to other human faculties: "What is then the full sense of logic? We think that the old man of Elea characterized this sense for all eternity."[34]

Idealism, as "true realism," represents – according to Cohen – the basis of a new psychology. He outlines the plan of this psychology in the final pages of *Logic of Pure Knowledge*: in lieu of a psychology which considers consciousness (*Bewusstsein*) only as an element inserted within natural or historic reality, a psychology as the science of humanity's cultural consciousness must be established. Philosophy analyzes the many directions of culture, and reduces them to a unity so that this psychology can then expound the subject of humanity as a reality truly living only in spirit: "Psychology may tend to idealize the ideal man of culture only through and in reference to this very unity of the consciousness of culture."[35]

In *Ethics of Pure Will*, Cohen develops the position he set up in the first part of his *System*: just as logic ponders the methods and concepts of mathematics and mathematical science of nature, so as to focus on the action of pure thought, so ethics examines the concepts upheld in human sciences, particularly "juridical science" (*Rechtswissenschaft*), in order to clarify the action of pure will; as logic does not pay attention to the individual's theoretical situation because it considers this situation only in the light of pure knowledge, so ethics does not deal with the moral situation of the individual because it evaluates this situation only in the light of the pure will. Just as pure thinking is characterized by movement, pure will – which is nothing more than the deepening and transformation of thought – has traits of activity and tension (in fact, the will is connected to other parts of consciousness, purified of any relation to the receptive faculty of sensibility, like "affect" and "feelings," and this increases its auto-activity). However, there is a fundamental difference between logic and ethics with regard to their common reference to the sciences as points of anchorage: while logic is addressed to the *Fakta* of mathematics and mathematical natural sciences, which are universally recognized as objective, ethics is oriented by a jurisprudence which does not yet have the universally recognized *status* of objective science. Therefore, moral concepts which do not refer to the field of nature, but to actions (*Sollen*), have the quality of "having to be" (*Sollen Sollens*), while they cannot help having as a basis for their discovery an ideal *Faktum* (*Sein Sollens*).[36] Thus, the concepts of "personality," "action," "self-conscience," "self," "law," "freedom" – in the different meanings of "autonomy" (*Selbstgesetzgebung*), "self-determination" (*Selbstbestimmung*), "self-responsibility" (*Selbstverantwortung*), "self-conservation" (*Selbsterhaltung*) – and "guilt" and "punishment," which appear in the first seven chapters of *Ethics of Pure Will*, all have at the same time a moral meaning and a meaning oriented by juridical science. In this context, Cohen considers the State as both a fact to be brought back to the conditions which make it possible, and as a reality to be created according to ideal principles. If on one side coercion by the existing political power is justified as such, on the other the coercion is transformed into a rational instrument needed to achieve the ideal political constitution. Finally, Cohen inserts the State itself in the project of a federation of States: this project is inspired by ideas expressed by juridical science, considered both as a cultural *Faktum* and as a science to be set up.[37] The 8 and 9 chapters, which deal respectively with *The Ideal* and *The Idea of God*, can be read as consequences of Cohen's identification of the ethical field with the field of pure will (this is not, however – as will be seen in the following paragraph – the only possible reading of these chapters). As real being for logic is not received through perceptions, but founded on pure thinking, so real being for ethics is the ideal as moral perfection. The ideal is what ensures the reality (*Wirklichkeit*) of morality in history, and the continuous, infinite progress of morality in history. As the *Sein* formed by pure thought refers to space – producing the notion of a world which, as the totality of phenomena, always is to be determined – likewise the *Sein* formed by pure will refers to time – producing the notion of the never ending perfecting of the imperfect towards perfection. The *Sein* of pure thought and the *Sein* of pure will come together in the idea of God, as the "crowning of the system": God is "the truth" rather than "a person" and, as the final point of logic and ethics, is beyond them, and in this sense "transcendent."

In the final chapters of *Ethics of Pure Will*, on the concept of virtue and the determination of virtues, Cohen defines virtues as "indications of the path" (*Wegweiser*) towards morality. He subordinates to the virtues guided by the notion of "totality" (the State or humanity are *Allheit* or "totality"), by the feeling of honor or respect (*Ehre*), and by thought more than by will, such as truthfulness (*Wahrhaftigkeit*), courage, and justice – those guided by the notion of "community" (family, nationality or religious association are "communities" or *Gemeinschaften*), by the feeling of love (*Liebe*), and by the will more than by thought, such as modesty, faithfulness and humanity. This last virtue, however, holds a special position: *Humanität* is not only "equity," allowing the person who is judging to evaluate the particular case and to compare it to other cases; *Humanität* – and this is how Cohen concludes the book – is also that attitude which allows us to understand how all the works created by humanity as an ideal subject in history form a harmonious whole, even in their difference or discordance. Humanity, in this second sense, is the virtue which expresses awareness of the subjective side of universal history, of the multiformity of human spirit in culture. Cohen discusses the virtue of humanity in the last chapter of *Ethics of Pure Will*. Transformed in the feeling of humanity, it becomes what is at the base of artistic productions in *Aesthetics of Pure Feeling*. Since the feeling, which unifies respect and love for humanity, has in itself both pure thought and pure will, it follows that the specific analysis of this feeling means analyzing the entire consciousness of culture: this analysis pays attention to the subjective side of culture no less than its objective side.

So, in the third part of his *System of Philosophy*, Cohen reflects upon the results he had reached in the two previous works, through a phenomenology of the various stages and directions of consciousness; and he also reflects upon the various modes and instruments of aesthetic consciousness. If logic is the base of the philosophical system of culture, aesthetics is the climax of this system. Mathematical and scientific reason, which transforms itself into practical reason, gains depth as a creative activity in art: this activity always finds appropriate rules and laws anew, depending on individual subjectivity. As mathematics and natural science, carried out methodically, first came to light in Greece, so Greek art gave models and inspiration to the poets and artists of German and European classicism. In this book, Cohen puts emphasis on the ability to "communicate" (*Mitteilen*), as art's distinctive quality with respect to the natural sciences or ethics. To art he entrusts, following Kant and Schiller, the education of mankind to *Humanität* and, through *Humanität*, to the awareness of the functions and tasks of human consciousness. Art, through "beauty" – which Cohen specifies in the two forms of the "sublime" and "humour" – teaches man to comprehend man, not so much as a single individual, but as a type of humankind (as Shakespeare and Rembrandt demonstrate), that is, the variety of figures or forms which human essence can take on. Epic, lyric, drama, novel, music, architecture, sculpture, painting, unified by the author in "poetry" as the "linguistic form" (*Sprachform*) of the arts, are the ways in which humanity is described.

In his *Aesthetics of Pure Feeling*, Cohen's analysis of aesthetic consciousness had shown the subjective aspect of *Kultur* as an ensemble of *Fakta*. The psychology that

Cohen then mentioned, in the end, was defined as an "encyclopedia of the philosophical system." Describing this project, Cohen finished the construction of his philosophical system. Thus, from intellectualism – which had at the beginning inspired him, and remained at the root of his philosophy of culture – he reached aestheticism – in the sense of a position which claims not only the centrality of art in the whole of human experience, but also the character of free creative play for every spiritual activity.

2.4 The problems of the individual and the foundation of ethics in the Jewish writings

In the years in which Cohen interprets Kant and writes his systematic books, he also publishes a number of writings on Judaism.[38] Two themes, which are important both in the interpretation of Kant and in the *Philosophical System*, are discussed in these writings: the first concerns the individual and the second the foundation of ethics. However, they are presented in a different manner than that found in the writings not pertaining directly to Judaism. In these, as we have seen, the problem of the individual is solved either by reducing the living man to one who turns towards the moral law out of respect for it, shutting out happiness as philosophically irrelevant, or to a juridical person: in fact, only the idea allows a true foundation for reality, given only apparently by perception.[39] As regards the problem of ethics, it is solved in the sense that ethics presupposes logic, either through the connection between theory and practice provided by the ideas of reason, or through moral philosophy referring first to natural science and then to the human sciences, especially to juridical science.[40] But in some of the Jewish writings, as will be seen, the individual appears as a human being who has his own internal moral life and, after going wrong, aspires to his conciliation with God, others and himself; and also, the founding of ethics is closely connected to the idea of God as unique, and not representable except through moral attributes. In this way Cohen not only defends his faith as a member of the Jewish community – that having a subjective value; he also upholds the philosophical meaning of Jewish monotheism – implying a universal or objective value to be placed besides pure philosophic knowledge. Certainly, Cohen in these Jewish texts does not deny the position which he holds as a philosopher inspired by the idealistic tradition, from Parmenides to Kant; but he introduces within this tradition – and in inevitable contrast to it – concepts which he draws directly from the Jewish sources and from Jewish religious existence. However, he does not try to find a connection in these writings of his between the two fundamental tendencies of his life and education – the idealistic scientific one and the Jewish one.

The indissoluble tie between the idea of God as it is proclaimed by Judaism – a God beyond man's thinking, who eludes humanization and is also beyond nature and history – and the possibility of ethics in human culture, is maintained by Cohen in his response to the anti-Jewish articles of Heinrich von Treitschke,[41] in an essay on the idea of the Messiah[42] and in contributions on medieval Jewish thought.[43] In the first of these texts the idea of the humanization of the divine introduced by

Christianity, from which the modern idea of man's autonomy derives, is contrasted with the Jewish idea of the "incomparability" of God; only from this idea can the thought of what is beyond time and gives a direction to history arise. In the second text, the messianic idea is explicitly related to Jewish monotheism; therefore Cohen denies that ethics can be built by philosophy without the contribution of Judaism. In the writings on Jewish medieval philosophy, he exalts the deep philosophical perspective open by Saadia ha-Gaon, Bahya ibn Paquda, and particularly Maimonides: they pointed out how in moral actions man takes as a model divine moral qualities (first of all divine love for human beings as an example for human love); they claimed that reason alone forms the tie between man and God notwithstanding their distance, and they meant by reason the heart, the spirit, the soul, the human spiritual faculties as a whole.

Instead, Cohen concentrates on the necessity, in moral philosophy, of taking into account the individual's life, his conflicts and dramas, his longing for peace, in an essay on the Jewish notion of "conciliation,"[44] and in writing on the Jewish notion of freedom.[45] In the first, with regard to the way in which tradition considers *Yom Kippur* (the Day of Atonement), he shows the ethical importance of the notions of sin before God, personal responsibility, repentance, return of the guilty man to the unity of his soul, and of the idea of relationship between God, community, and the individual as well. In the second, he distinguishes between freedom as autonomy, maintained by philosophical ethics, and freedom as choice which, according to Judaism, is the consequence of the purity of the soul before God: he emphasizes how both concepts of freedom are essential to ethics as a doctrine of pure will.

After 1912 – the year in which he publishes the third part of his *Philosophical System* – Cohen faces the problem of the relationship between ethics, as determined by his philosophical research, and religion, as determined by his knowledge of the Jewish sources and his participation in the life of the Jewish community: this problem remains precisely because he has not yet given univocal answers to the question of how to ground ethics, and the question of the individual. How is it possible to uphold at the same time the foundation of ethics on logic, and the foundation of ethics on a concept of God that first of all excludes any mental reference to natural phenomena? How can one reconcile the point of view of ethics as impossible to found *per se*, and the point of view that does not make morality dependent on science, and exalts morality before science? The philosophical foundation would presuppose both the pure knowledge of being opened by mathematics and natural science, and the pure will showed by juridical science (a juridical science mostly composed of the contributions of Roman law, medieval German law, and the legal system of modern Europe). Are the ideas that the individual is to be inserted within a universal structure of concepts (since the immediacy of existence is a deceptive notion), and that the individual has a life of his own, hidden from the sight of other individuals, and visible only to a God who judges and forgives, really compatible with each other?

Even in the systematic books – or in some of those writings through which Cohen completes or defines his philosophical system – one discovers, if one reads with care certain details or allusions, this double perspective regarding both ethical meditation, and the reflection on the individual. For example, in *Logic of Pure Knowledge*, alongside the notion of the origin as a method of reducing the material to the ideal, the author introduces origin understood as a way of determining a "nothing" which is already a "something" (as if the material could not be completely reduced to an idea). He does not refer to mathematics in order to explain this second meaning of origin, but to the negation of privations held by Maimonides in his theory of divine attributes.[46] And in the chapters of *Ethics of Pure Will* entitled *The Ideal* and *The Idea of God* Cohen not only maintains that the Ideal refers to time, as ideas of mathematical science of nature refer to space, and that God represents the point of convergence of logic and ethics; he also writes that the time to which the Ideal refers, does not at all presuppose space, because space indicates the "totality" of the world and the Ideal, instead, the "infinite" of the ethical task, and that God, ensuring both the subsistence of nature and the realization of morality in history, transcends both nature and history, and therefore is the unique true being.[47] In *Aesthetics of Pure Feeling*, where he grounds art – as we have seen – on the feeling of honor and love of humanity, Cohen admits that Jewish art, which finds expression especially in lyrics and music, presupposes instead the dialogue between "self" as individual and God, and that Jewish art does not portray God or man in sculpture or painting because it devotes itself exclusively to the celebration of God and to the description of man in contact with Him.[48] Finally, in *Religion and Morality* and *Religious Postulates*, Cohen both identifies religion with philosophical ethics, whose last point is the idea of God, and grounds ethics on religion, whose central concept is that of the unique God: in this way he attempts not to renounce, as he himself puts it, either "knowledge" or "faith."[49]

Cohen had left the chair of philosophy at the University of Marburg in 1912, at the age of 70, and between 1913 and 1914 gave a series of lectures in Berlin at the "Lehranstalt für die Wissenschaft des Judentums." Religion upholds both the idea of God's uniqueness and the idea of the individual; and it is just this question of the relation of religion to philosophical ethics and, through this part of the system, its relation to the whole of philosophy, that Cohen tackles. So in these lectures – later published with the title *The Concept of Religion in the System of Philosophy*[50] – Cohen discusses exactly what is the most problematic theme in his doctrine. However, the lectures, rather than giving a solution to Cohen's difficulties, only emphasize – as will be seen – the tension in Cohen's thought between the Greek and European tradition, whose climax is, according to him, Kantian idealism, and the Jewish tradition. It turns out to be difficult for the philosopher to insert religion, as expressed by Judaism, into a system of philosophy which remains centered on the idea of logic as its beginning and fundamental premise.

Thus, in the chapter of *The Concept of Religion* about the relation between religion and logic, the author insists on the affinity between Eleaticism, which gives unity to Being through the notion of the *Logos*, and monotheism which gives unity to Being through the idea of God; and he also stresses the deep difference between the One thought by the Eleatics as an immanent impersonal principle of the cosmos, and the One thought by the Jews as a Person transcending the natural and human world.

But, can the Jewish concept of Transcendence – whose origin is the love between the soul and a God never completely changeable into a simple object – find a real place within a philosophical system that is based on the absolute autonomy of pure thought, and studies the different forms of objects the spirit produces? Even in the chapter about the relation between religion and ethics, as in the chapter on logic, Cohen's will to reconcile the concept of systematic ethics, grounded on freedom as self-legislation, and religion, grounded on the correlation between man and God through a love which, according to Biblical terminology, coincides with knowledge, emerges. In this chapter religion is described as a form that has both "similarity" (*Gleichartigkeit*), and "peculiarity" (*Eigenartigkeit*) with regard to ethics. Is it, however, really possible to interpret the idea of God, as the protector and comforter of those who suffer and are in distress, as a simple specification of the idea of God defended by a humanity active in history? Can one really understand the concept of the individual who longs for redemption, or suffers for another, or assists another when in need, as a simple specification of the concept of "totality," which implies the full transformation of the individual in the universal, that is, the negation of the individual's life and uniqueness? Further, religion entrusts to the affect of love the discovery of the "other" similar to the "self," since all human beings are loved by God in the same way. Can one see this affect of love as a simple specification of the feeling of love in Cohen's ethics, which with regard to the feeling of honor or respect, has only a secondary value (as we have seen)? Especially in the chapter about the relation between religion and aesthetics, Cohen stresses more the difference between philosophical aesthetics and religion than their connection: certainly, both the artist and the person who has a religious experience look at man; but the first considers in man the type, the figure, or the model, and his interest in man is mediated by his vision as well as his serene and contemplative love; the second, instead, sees in man the individual, and his way of referring to him implies both an immediate correlation in which God is involved, as it were, and a painful, compassionate, active, healing love. If the artist and the religious individual are so different, then the position of religion in a philosophical system where aesthetics is based on the ideas of *Humanität* and artistic genius, becomes precarious; or – another possibility – the insertion of religion into the system raises questions about the system itself.[51]

In the closing chapter of *The Concept of Religion*, dealing with the relation between religion and psychology, Cohen seems to know that he must revise his philosophical system. In this chapter, in fact, psychology – the doctrine of the unity of consciousness as producer of culture – no longer seems to have logic as its condition, but religion: Cohen now considers the preservation of human finiteness essential to psychology, and maintains that only the religious concept of the relationship between man and God allows an understanding of such a finiteness, and therefore of humanity in man. The analysis of religion – Cohen says in the last chapter of his book – leads one to highlight certain aspects of consciousness not yet considered in thinking about knowledge, morality or art, such as the aspiration of the soul to be close to God, or desire, compassion, love as directed to God, and thus to other human beings. Can these aspects, however, be simply introduced in a reflection on consciousness which keeps to earlier theoretical directions, or do they encourage one to revise psychology as the doctrine of the totality and unity of all spiritual directions? The texts of the Jewish religious tradition should not be read, the author points out, through the eyes of the scientist or historian, that is, from a point of view external to them, but rather as writings from which it is possible to draw true meaning only when inspired by "reverence" (*Pietät*) with regard to the past and tradition. From here then the possibility of retracing the specificity of religion: "The peculiarity of religion opens up for us an important perspective on the essence of man, without which the inner life and the unity of man would be vain appearance and illusion."[52] This human essence is presented to us by the religious concepts of suffering for love, carrying upon oneself the sufferings of the world, atoning for another's sin. Only in these ways, according to Cohen, does man's spirit or reason manifest itself, not because they lead to an absolute redemption or liberation from pain or evil, but because they prove ethical strength superior to such events. The concreteness, depth and individuality of consciousness have their premise in this pure love; in it culture finds its anchorage and its final meaning. Only religion then, with its human climax in the figure of the "suffering servant," is truly able to produce the unity of consciousness. The psychology that takes religion as its condition, draws from it anti-pantheism, that is to say the thesis of the difference between the individual and God, and not from logic, ethics and aesthetics, which dissolve the finite in the infinite. The philosophical system is grounded in an interpretation of the Jewish sources which is respectful of their specific meaning exactly because of its dependence on the peculiarity of religion as necessary to psychology, the last and conclusive part of the system: "Systematic philosophy" – Cohen writes clearly and decisively at the end of his reflection on religion within the system – "is the doctrine of the unity of man in producing culture. This unity of man, however, is conditioned by his correlation with God."[53] Without religion having in God its center of gravity, consciousness would be missing that point which indicates true humanity in human beings and therefore gives unification and meaning to the whole of culture.

And yet, even in the last chapter of *The Concept of Religion* which introduces new and important thoughts, the author does not give up pursuing a direction, for the most part taken in earlier works, according to which it is, on the contrary, systematic philosophy, based on scientific reason, which provides religion its norms and instances of control. Actually, he stresses this direction again in the final pages of his book because he continues to consider this as the only path allowed by the idealistic philosophical tradition.

In *The Concept of Religion* Cohen had brought to light a completely new area for meditation when he had allowed religious man to speak with words taken directly from Scripture in order to express his real experience, and had rendered this man the premise for the man of culture (*Kulturmensch*). Cohen dedicated himself to the exploration of this area in the last years of his life: in his subsequent writings, however, he never noticed that in doing so he had undertaken a journey leading him on a completely different and contradictory route with regard the path he had previously followed.

2.5   The identification of reason with religious love
in the *opus postumum*

Within a structure still determined by an orientation of thought having scientific reason as its center, Cohen in his *Religion of Reason out of the Sources of Judaism*, written between 1916 and 1918 and published after his death,[54] introduces the idea that the human essence is to be found first of all in religious love, that is, that love which originates in a God transcending nature and man, and is turned towards one's destitute and helpless brethren. In this love, he sees the basis of the other functions of consciousness, addressed to knowledge of the being of nature or to art. Religious love does not consist at all in an intellectual intuition of the divine, nor in a feeling that allows the coincidence of the divine and the human, but in an affection which is aware (to love, in Biblical Hebrew, also means to know, as Cohen remarks) of the way in which God enters in relation with human beings, that is through morality – therefore an affection that keeps the distance between finiteness and what is beyond it. Religious love does not oppose itself to reason understood as man's spiritual faculty; this love is, in fact, reason itself. In this case, however, reason is not only a spiritual force; rather, it identifies with a force emanating from the entire human being once touched by divine love. This love expresses the meaning of the totality of moral laws and norms, an act of identification made before this force splits itself into the various abilities addressed to different spheres of culture. Cohen allows the religious meaning of reason to subsist side by side with the other one which considers it first of all a theoretical faculty. And so, it happens that the term "reason" takes on in the *opus postumum* a double aspect: it means the reason of science, referred to in philosophy, in examining the productions of religion; and it means the reason which directly produces religion, and which philosophical analysis accepts as its own premise. The expression "religion of reason," which appears in the title of this Cohenian work, acquires therefore an equivocal sense: it indicates both a religion which is subjected to criticism by philosophical reason which considers logic as its foundation, and a religion which is the result of reason intended as that pure spiritual faculty which permits the relation of man with a transcendent God from whom laws and ethical prescriptions derive.

Actually, in the *Introduction* of *Religion of Reason*, the author presents both these meanings of the term "reason" expressing different, even opposite orientations, as if they could be inserted in a coherent and unified picture. On the one hand, he maintains here that the concept of reason, as philosophy defines it, that is, founded on mathematics and mathematical natural science, produces religion understood as part of universal human culture; on the other hand, that the Jewish sources, which are the representations and models of religion as pure or original, are themselves immediately produced by reason, and thus offer a philosophy even before they enter into relation, in the course of their history, with science or philosophy directed by science. Reason, thus, becomes "problematic." Certainly, it can be characterized, in both cases mentioned, as opposing animal sensibility, opposing affection and intellect connected to the organic life of man, the material forces of economics and politics, and the violence of selfishness. In the first case, however, reason is at the base of the knowledge of nature and being – and it was the Greeks who were masters in this field; in the second case, reason is the basis of religion – and it was the Jews who were guides in this field. Thus we find ourselves, according to Cohen, having to place not only the two meanings of "reason," but also the two meanings of "philosophy" as expression of reason, one besides the other: "One cannot avoid noticing" – he says – "the fact that the concept of philosophy is changed and rendered precarious if it is not developed as scientific philosophy. But the universal character of reason, even in the absence of science, nevertheless connects religion to philosophy."[55] It is true that in such a case the philosophical doctrine of man seems to be divided between the point of view held by an ethics based on scientific philosophy, and a point of view oriented by ethics expressed by religion. One could try to insert the second conception of man – addressed as it is to the analysis both of the concrete relations between different human beings, and of the phenomena of one's individual existence – into the first. Nevertheless, as Cohen acknowledges, it is hard for such an attempt to be successful since religion proposes a complete doctrine of man, the world, and God which appears different from that maintained by philosophical ethics. One can only, then, keep both points of view without, however, renouncing research on the possibility of unifying them.

Although the author reconnects his meditation on the human being, which was developed through an analysis of Jewish texts – especially the Bible, rabbinical literature, medieval commentaries on the Bible, medieval Jewish thought, and the liturgy – to the previous reflection carried out in his systematic philosophical writings, as he had done in *The Concept of Religion*, the thesis comes out strongly from *Religion of Reason* that what forms the human essence is reason understood as religious love. Cohen highlights the identity of these two concepts by means of a philosophical exegesis of that Jewish literature: although this literature had a historical development and received the most varied motifs from different cultural environments, it derives from a single original inspiration. The chapters in which such an idea of man is expressed are, in particular, those dedicated to revelation, the creation of human being in reason, the spirit of holiness, the attributes of action, the individual as "self," conciliation, the law, religious love, the other human being (*Mitmensch*).

One could synthesize the content of these chapters as follows. The determination of revelation, if accomplished keeping in mind the way in which the philosophical Jewish tradition has mostly interpreted this concept, leads one to see in the human being the one who through reason is in correlation with God: "The rational essence (*Vernunftwesen*) of man" – so Cohen writes – "emerges only because of revelation."[56] One must not, however, conceive of the relation between man and God as a cause and effect relation, where God gives man revelation and thus automatically allows the emergence of rationality to take place within him. Only spirit, to which man elevates himself when he agrees to observe in freedom that law entering his life as given in revelation, forms the element which immediately brings together the two terms of the relation, notwithstanding the distance between them. We find ourselves here in a sphere not of natural phenomena or our knowledge of them, but one of pure moral relations existing independently and before every other sphere of human experience. Before belonging to the natural world man lives in his correlation with God through a spirit which may be defined as the spirit of holiness, that is to say of morality; and morality can be summarized in the two qualities of pity or mercy and justice. In revelation, interpreted in this manner, man himself (neither Moses nor the people of Israel alone, as the author says quoting the rabbinical exegesis) receives teachings and commandments whose overall meaning is to follow the spirit of morality. These teachings and commandments stand as precise rules which guide human actions in society. And it is only in this manner, as an individual responsible for his fellow man, that every man discovers himself as an "individual" and a "self." The rabbis see in the episode in which God, passing before Moses who hides his face, leaves the tracks of his path, causing Moses then to praise and sing hymns, the way in which divine actions which can be qualified as good and just – even though the divine person, who is beyond the human, still remains in part hidden – represent examples and models of human actions. Revelation gives the spirit of morality together with the law, and not rules that are external to man's will. Thus the divine spirit, which is the spirit of holiness, is immediately granted to human beings, and it is identified with thinking, the language and the whole of their spiritual faculties. Revelation, when moved by this spirit – as some Jewish commentators of the Bible hold – is uttered by man's own lips, and it is drawn from his own soul and heart. Human sensibility is also involved in the moment in which God reveals himself to the human heart as the One that bestows the law, as long as it is not considered in the sense of animal sensibility or selfishness. The spirit of holiness, which is man's own reason itself, represents the eternal in him, even though he lives in time and history. Reason is created in human beings in the sense that it is not original or autonomous in them: reason is granted to human beings by divine love towards them in revelation: "Reason, which in an eminent way is ethical reason, is derived from God."[57] Ethical reason is spirit itself present in man: it takes on this ethical aspect before shaping itself as theoretical reason. In ethical reason, love and knowledge are not separable: they are directed first of all to God, and then, without losing their connection with Him, to other human beings. Love in the religious sense thus includes knowledge in a moral context. This love, coming from God, transforms itself in man's love for Him, and through this, in "compassion" (*Mitleid*) once it is directed to the other suffering man. The other human being, as one's equal or neighbor, the *Mitmensch*, is discovered therefore by man only through a love which is no more than the reflection of his love for God in response to the divine love towards him. Love in the religious sense is therefore pure affection, fundamental strength of the soul, practical reason inspired by the heart. This love is produced by an external action on the individual who in this way is moved to action: it is not an immediate empirical feeling present in human nature. Cohen relates, within the text of his posthumous work, the discussion between Akiva and Ben Asai, found in the Jerusalem Talmud, about the comprehensive meaning of the Torah:

> Akiva says: "You must love your neighbor [*rea*]; he is like you. This is a great synthesis of the Torah." Ben Asai says: "This is the book of the origins of man: this is a greater synthesis than that." One thinks of the

proposition: "In the day in which God created Man, he made him in the image and likeness of God." Which foundation has precedence? [...] Evidently, Ben Asai is right.[58]

The love which man directs to the *Mitmensch*, starting from the love that God has for him as the most unselfish, pure, free from any motive dictated by nature, forms that human essence which is not even destroyed when man violates the moral law. This love renders man consistent, and makes of him an "individual" unified with himself in conciliation: this event is every time sought and again every time reached through God's forgiveness, which also implies the possibility of establishing each time relations based on morality with one's fellow man once more. There are not mediators in the process which brings the soul once more close to God after error or guilt, as the soul is already aware of its correlation with Him through the spirit of holiness, which itself indicates purity of intention. God sanctifies the soul giving it His law in love, and the soul comes back to him, not after having totally drawn away from Him, but having only strayed. Desire and humility in prayer distinguish the soul that returns to its initial state of observing divine commandments "in the name of heaven" – as the rabbinical expression goes. The human being then goes back to feeling "compassion" or "pity" (*Frömmigkeit*) for his fellow and companion looking towards the world: "Love for man is produced. As a miracle, as an enigma, it origi-nates from the head, nay from the heart of man."[59] Cohen asks himself if this love may not simply be an illusion in human reality – but a love, like the religious one, which fills man's heart, and through which he discovers the disassociation between guilt and suffering, and thus the suffering of the just and the innocent, far from being an illusion, shows itself instead as that which is most real in human life and in history. It is in this love that one discovers what properly defines the humanity of human beings. From this love originate natural or rational law, social legislation, and principles of political constitution ruling the life of civilized states, which – precisely because of their tacit recognition of these principles – could all be defined as "theocracies." The "suffering servant of God" is the model human being. Culture is simply the result of the developments of religious love as reason.

In the remaining chapters of *Religion of Reason* Cohen expounds the notions of creation and redemption as they appear in Jewish religious literature. Both notions have their centre in the notion of revelation intended as the disclosure, through the commandments, of divine love to human beings who respond to such a love by changing themselves into rational beings. The author explains the concept of creation as he thinks it is presented in Maimonides' *Guide of the Perplexed*;[60] and he also out-lines, in analyzing the Pentateuch and the Prophets, the idea of individual redemp-tion or the immortality of the soul, and then the idea of social or messianic redemption.[61]

And thus Cohen, late in life, formulated a doctrine of the human being that had as its hero not the scientist of nature, nor the individual who is directed in his actions by philosophical ethics – with science as its foundation and main guide – nor the artist, or the philosopher who sees it as his duty to celebrate all of these figures, but the simple man who, for the love of God, that is to say for the love of the morality which He represents and reveals, takes upon himself the suffering of others and works towards justice. The philosopher subordinates himself before this man, limiting himself only to illustrating his deeds. Human reason is nothing more than that religious love, and all the other directions of consciousness have their beginning and source in it. Still, Cohen, until the last phase of his life, never ceased to reflect on the philosophical system as founded on scientific reason. He published the third edition of his *Kantian Theory of Experience* with a new preface, in which he clarified the sense of his interpretation of Kant as a philosopher of a culture which has the *Logos* for its center.[62] He publicly defended German culture – from Luther to Kant – as founded on the concept of the autonomy of a harmonious humanity in which each spiritual function finds accordance with all the others, attempting also to prove, through using the term "spirit," the correspondence between this culture and Judaism.[63] And still he worked on his systematic psychology as having scientific consciousness as its firm ground.[64] But, in his final years, his vehement critique of Spinoza, who was accused of pantheism, of betraying his community, of not having understood how ethics must assume the idea of a God not coinciding with the unity of nature, of intellectual unscrupulousness originating from a heart that was cold and lacking compassion, proves how the center of gravity of his existence and his thought was represented by that Judaism which preserves in history the pure idea of the uniqueness of God.[65] There is thus a great distance between the young Cohen, who – as has been seen – had exalted Judaism as a source, through Spinoza, of modernity and the old Cohen who emphasizes the anti-modernity of Judaism as the cause of Spinoza's excommunication and as an absolutely necessary element for modernity itself, if this modernity intends to establish on a sure footing ethics as the principle of culture and to acknowledge the rights of the individual.

Nevertheless, in the last lecture he had the opportunity of giving, Cohen went back to Spinoza's idea of a philosophy based on that reason which comprehends being as the last criterion and measure of the truth of the Jewish religion and all the other religions.[66]

3

FRANZ ROSENZWEIG (1886–1929)

3.1 Searching for the ideal man in the diaries and letters of 1905 to 1913

From his youth Rosenzsweig enjoyed keeping diaries on his relationship with the outside world and on his inner life, and communicating his thoughts and opinions through letters to family, friends and colleagues. In the diaries and letters written between 1905 and the autumn of 1913 he talks about many things, describing figures from his *entourage*, characterizing the various university circles he associated with, recalling readings, expressing his opinion on the culture and events of his time, and his own moods and feelings.[1]

There is, however, one subject which moves through all of these writings as a recurring theme which can best be defined as the quest for the ideal man. It is this search that gave him an answer as to how to give meaning to his own life, about which he pondered from the first years of his university studies. One could say that in a relatively short period he underwent a series of rapid passages, demonstrating his existential and intellectual restlessness and the courage of his choices. He begins by exalting creative subjectivity which expresses itself in universal work that is a heritage for all of humanity; then celebrates the scientist who is oblivious of his or her own self in their work and is led by objective and rigorous rules; afterwards, he portrays the historian as the main actor because the historian is one who brings together his subjectivity and the objectivity brought to light; finally he reaches a phase where the religious man who has a connection with a transcendent and creator God coexists with a tragic individuality which sees no purpose in the world. From here – one step more – Rosenzweig reaches the conclusion that the man who accepts revelation and who thus lives contemporaneously in contact with God and in the world, cannot but witness his situation in two opposite ways, either restricting his activity to praying in a community detached from history or concentrating on action in a community immersed in historic developments. Each type of humanity which Rosenzweig presents as an ideal form in these writings also becomes the model he follows in his own life. So he adopts a different attitude each time in the years being considered – first that of the artist, or romantic subjectivity, second that of the scientist, third that of the historian, then that of *homo religiosus* which coexists, but in conflict, with tragic subjectivity, and finally that of the Jew who is aware that revelation implies a man committed to both prayer and action, but keeps for himself only the moment of turning to God through study and liturgy and leaves to post-Constantinian Christianity (that is to say the Christianity which ties its destiny to political power) the antithetical moment of working in time while looking towards redemption. The diaries and letters written by Rozensweig between 1905 and autumn 1913 illustrate these swings and changes in attitude; based on these writings the author from then on develops his philosophical doctrine and gives a new turn to his own existence.

Goethe is the hero of the diaries and letters between 1905 and 1906. Rozensweig remarks in a letter dated April 3, 1905 addressed to his cousin Gertrud Frank, that the God of whom he proclaims himself a follower is the God of the Pantheists, an expression of the forces of nature, no longer the "King of the World" that was dear to him during the years of his childhood and adolescence.[2] He reaches the God of the Pantheists attracted by the ideal, which he finds proclaimed in Goethe (his favorite reading as witness the letters to his parents of July 30, 1905, and to Gertrud Frank of September 29, 1905), of a harmonious balance between the subjectivity which is present in the world and the world itself. This ideal, in opposition to the point of view represented by Nietzsche's subject, who is isolated and at odds with reality, is mentioned in some notes written in his diary in this period (February 5 and 19, 1906). Whereas the "method" of Goethe is "intuition" (*Auschauung*), unifying subjective and objective, sensitivity and reason, perception and thing, Nietzsche's "method" is "scepsis." One must not conceive the subject as abstracted from nature and history and in relation with a transcendent sphere, but consider it in its connection with the objectivity which surrounds it: God, being the expression of the infinite, lives within the objectivity of the world and of culture. Through Goethe, Rosenzweig read in these years Plato and Kant: these philosophers seem to him, as mentioned in his notes of January 28 and May 22, 1906, authors who have particularly focused on the theory of art, that is to say on that sphere of human activity in which the individual comes to be universal by expressing himself in a work which becomes part of the culture. Rosenzweig appreciates Wilhelm Windelband for having brought to light this aspect of Plato and Kant, as he states in a note of March 27, 1906.[3] Through the thought of harmony between the single creator and the environment into which he inserts his creations – a harmony which he finds expressed in Goethe – Rosenzweig also evaluates the Greek world, opposed in its "classicism" to the world of "romanticism"; he traces back the origin of romantic movements in European culture to the Jewish and Christian idea of a God to whom the soul aspires in its desire; and he declares himself certainly in favor of "classicism" versus "romanticism," as seen in the notes of April 27 and May 6, 1906. In this juvenile phase of his reflection the author perceives the "complete man" – defined in a note of September 2, 1906 – as the individual who having discovered his *daimon*, and letting himself be guided by it, works for the development of culture. The culture will be renewed, even allowing for inevitable continuity, by the action of those who, being creative personalities, will produce meaningful results for all humanity. What this objective means for the action of individuals – whose importance is upheld against particularism and nationalism in the notes of February 9, 10, and 28, 1906 – is a humanism which relinquishes an ethics based either on the saying "Be holy as am I" from the Pentateuch, or on the saying "What you did to these little ones, you have done to me" from the Gospels, and rather founds the norms of behavior on man's autonomy. From this base, on which he comments in a remark of September 29, 1906, Rosenzweig defends the concept of a productive subjectivity which is reflected in its fruits, as the artist does with regard to his objects: thus the artist finds a meaning to his being in time; and Rosenzweig wishes – as he confesses in notes dated February 10 and 12, 1906 – to be strong enough to be such a subjectivity.

However 1907 is the year in which Rosenzweig, having embarked on the reading of the *Critique of Pure Reason*, under the guidance of Jonas Cohn in Fribourg, finds a substitute for Goethe as his mentor in thought and life: Kant interpreted as the founder of a scientific objectivism which assumes the negation of any subjective element.[4] Rosenzweig, who informs his cousin Hans Ehrenberg in a letter of March 6, 1907 of his interest in the "Ich denke" doctrine, developed in the "Transcendental Dialectic," in which he discovers the core of the *Critique*, exalts in a letter written to his mother on November 18, 1907 the criticism of all metaphysics and the transformation of philosophy in the theory of the scientific knowledge of nature carried out by Kant. Scientists and medical doctors and not those who deal with the practical matters of life, seem to him the best suited to read Kant's works. Kant's positive idealism, which assumes that objects are not independent of our way of knowing them, and which therefore effectively contrasts with scepticism – as stated in a note dated March 20, 1907 – now seems to indicate a direction to Rosenzweig, that of the serious study of nature, which he considers the best suited to provide long lasting and beneficial results.

Soon, however, Rosenzweig claims to be unsatisfied with a point of view which, through a more careful consideration of reality's complexity, seems to be flawed by abstraction and pure formalism. The Kantian doctrine – he notes in his diary on May 20 and 29, 1908 – belongs to an age, like the eighteenth century, in which individualism does not allow one to have a deep and true relation with reality. The philosophical development from Kant to Fichte to Hegel, on which he reflects in a note dated May 29, 1908, seems to him thus to have an internal justification of its own. Rosenzweig now tends, as he himself says in a note of May 24, 1908, towards a position in which the "Self" directed particularly towards the world may reconcile itself to the world in its concreteness. Hegel, thus, now becomes the figure he considers as the source of inspiration for his own activity. The work that the historian carries out when he expresses his own subjectivity through the reconstruction of an objective past, seems in this period to Rosenzweig as that which best corresponds to his aspiration of bringing together feeling and science, view and thought, as he himself puts it in a letter to his mother on October 30, 1908. Until the beginning of 1910, he trusts that the Hegelian program of understanding in the best way possible one's own time, that is to say the true powers which act in it and which show its rationality in the light of the idea, expressed in the "Preface" to Hegel's *Outlines of the Philosophy of Law*, of the identity between the real and the rational – may be retrieved and carried out even in one's own era. Rosenzweig is certainly not unaware that history is not only made up of events which have an ideal meaning, but also of tragedies and horrors, which the historian must recognize, rather than dealing with his object as if it were a "Platonic dialogue," as he puts it in a letter to Hans Ehrenberg of October–November 1908. However, he judges favorably that Hegelian attitude, already considered positively by Friedrich Meinecke, his teacher of modern history in Fribourg beginning in the autumn of 1908, in the work *Cosmopolitanism and the National State*: this attitude encourages one to become conscious of the meaning of the historical reality in which one lives, in order to get a guide to one's individual behavior.[5]

The failure of the meeting in January 1910 in Baden-Baden of young philosophers and historians from South West Germany – which had been convened in the name of Hegel both with the purpose of offering valuable interpretations of the social and political reality of the time and practical suggestions for the future, and with the purpose of forming a community of intellectuals involved in the culture of their time and active in the pursuit of historical continuity, as can be surmised from the exchange of letters between Rosenzweig and Hans Ehrenberg, Walter Sohm and Franz Frank in December 1909 – convinced Rosenzweig of the impossibility of maintaining in the twentieth century a perspective of thought and life originating in the nineteenth century. After the Baden-Baden failure, Hegel represented for Rosenzweig, the nineteenth century, that is to say an era of the past in the history of civilization, during which culture had been identified with the divine and the individual had found the place for his becoming eternal precisely within culture, elevating his own individuality to a common spiritual sphere. The dissertation dedicated to Hegel as a central character in German history from the age of Restoration to the end of the nineteenth century, was begun in Fribourg under the guidance of Meinecke in the summer of 1909, at a time in which he still professed himself a follower of the Hegelian system. It was elaborated and written only in the following years and reflects this state of mind, already detached from the perspective which had been outlined in Hegel's thought and critical of the Hegelian system.[6] Rosenzweig's Hegelian period – from 1908 to 1910 – resulted in this conclusive work which would be evaluated by Hegelian criticism, after Rosenzweig's time, as one of the most important and significant monographs on Hegel.[7]

During his meditative period between winter 1910 and summer 1913, Rosenzweig gave his own life and his concept of existence a double direction: on the one hand, the author kept close to religion, understood in the sense he defines as characteristic of the twentieth century, that is to say religion as the connection between the individual and a God beyond history, although never ceasing to refer also to the God of the Jewish and Christian tradition (he refers to this particular reading of religion in a letter to Hans Ehrenberg of September 26, 1910). On the other hand, he thought about writing a book dedicated to the history of tragic individuality in Germany beginning with Lessing, to be entitled *The Hero*, of which he had already outlined some chapters, as he recounts in a letter addressed to Gertrud Oppenheim of September 28, 1911. Thus, on the threshold of the serious social and political crisis which would lead to the First

World War, Rosenzweig confessed to Hans Ehrenberg, in a letter written at the end of November 1912, to no longer having any fixed point of reference in a world which has become for him devoid of meaning, and thus to finding himself in the tragic situation of an individual receiving only "equivocal perceptions" from his contact with reality. However, although denying that God is present in history and culture and reserving contact with Him not for humanity, but only for the individual, he accepts the idea of a God who is in contact with the people of Israel and, through them, with humanity, as is stated in his note written on September 1, 1910.

On July 7, 1913, Rosenzweig had a dramatic discussion with Eugen Rosenstock, whom he had met in Baden-Baden and seen again in Leipzig – where he had moved to pursue his legal studies – and with his cousin Rudolf Ehrenberg, in which he was confronted with the inconsistency of his position, which on one side looks to a gnostic God placed beyond the absurdity of the world, and on the other to a God who reveals Himself, as held by Judaism and Christianity. So Rosenzweig was forced to recognize the lack of stability of his ideas and, with them, of his existence. The idea of God as creator which appears in the first verse of the Bible, if upheld with coherence and with all of its consequences, is enough to free one from the nihilism to which inevitably the historicistic point of view is subjected: actually, historicism renounces finding values which are independent of the development of events in time and abandons itself to such events; on the contrary, the Bible offers an Absolute beyond history. Thus Rosenzweig, after this discussion, adheres without reservation to the Biblical point of view, adding to his faith in the God who "at the beginning created heaven and earth" the faith in ideals which, being beyond time, give a meaning to historical events. Divine revelation in the world no longer only implies the connection between the individual and God, but also the connection between God and a humanity that moves on in its history and culture. This change in Rosenzweig from a faith limited to the inner life of the individual to a faith that does not relate only to inner conscience, but comes together with the vision of history and culture as meaningful, explains why he could think of connecting to Christianity immediately after July 7, 1913. The Christian religion – as he had learned from Hegel and as he acknowledges in the letters of November 2 and 6, 1909 addressed to his parents with regard to Hans Ehrenberg's conversion to Christianity – seems to him as the religion which had imbued German and European culture, even when this culture had subjected it to criticism. To profess revelation thus implies accepting Christian revelation as having two meanings, the meaning of upholding the connection between man and a God who, while still intervening in time, remains beyond time, and the meaning of asserting the connection between God and the history of the whole of humanity. But Hegel had also taught Rosenzweig that modern Christianity had finally accepted the Gospel of John proclaiming the end of the dualism between heaven and earth, and the divine becoming immanent. So, in contrast to a Christianity that carries on its evangelization of the world, and in modernity risks losing the idea of diversity between the eternal and the historical, Judaism re-achieves a role in history because of its rigorous belief in the transcendence of God with regard to the world. In October 1913, Rosenzweig decided to remain a Jew.

In the letters to Rudolf Ehrenberg of October 31 and November 1, 1913, the author recounts how, beginning with his renunciation of gnosticism and historicism, he felt he could fully participate in the Biblical orientation, seeing at first his point of reference in the Christian revelation, and then returning to Judaism.[8]

But Rosenzweig, while still having as his model the man who on one side remains in contact with the only God, beyond images, through words and silent gestures, and on the other goes towards the world in order to transform it in view of the final redemption of humanity, nevertheless keeps a dualistic perspective. In fact, how can the first attitude find a connection with the second one, if it seems to be the prerogative of a community which remains absolutely closed within itself in prayer, isolated from history and always the same, in spite of time? How can such a community communicate with the world if its life is carried on in an absolutely different sphere to that of daily activities? And how can the second attitude draw teachings from the first one, if it does not have within itself any need to concentrate on the final transcendent point to which it aspires, and loses itself instead in ordinary activities? The iconography, present in the portals of the medieval cathedrals of some regions of Germany, of the Synagogue and of the Church as two women placed one besides the other, the first blindfolded and with her sceptre shattered, the second with her eyes wide open, with the crown and the sceptre – to which Rosenzweig himself makes reference at the end of his letter to Rudolf Ehrenberg dated November 1, 1913, using an image to represent his thought – clearly demonstrates, in reality, the lack of a relationship between the two communities which is neither that of domination nor, at the same time, of the substitution of one with the other.

Thus Rosenzweig, having reached a point in the autumn of 1913 in which Judaism comes again to be important for him in his relation to the world, will reflect in the following period on how man can assert his entire being, prayer and action, faith and reason. The purpose will be to avoid remaining torn between a contemplation of God condemned to powerlessness, and action in time or history condemned to being devoid of ultimate meaning. His search for the ideal man, which he had begun to pursue from his very first meditations, will address itself in such a way towards a new, and this time, final goal.

3.2 Revelation and philosophy in the texts between 1913 and 1917 and in the *Star of Redemption*

The principal object towards which Rosenzweig addressed his reflections in the period between the winter of 1913 and 1917, is the question of the relationship between revelation and philosophy. If, in fact, human life must be conceived as both being tied to God by pure love, and as operating in the world in order to carry out what such pure love indicates in the moment in which it is passed on from God to human beings, does not revelation then already have within itself an invitation to thought and thus to philosophy, as a necessary tool which allows human beings to act in finite, daily reality? Certainly, Judaism and Christianity can be conceived in their polarity, as forms of life in conflict with each other – one centered on the faith which puts man and God in immediate relation, the other on thought whose implied reference to God begins from the immanence of God in history and in the world. However, if the two religions are conceived in their complementarity, because of the roots they share, is not then revelation, which addresses itself especially to God, closely connected to philosophy, which looks particularly to the world? Is there not in Judaism itself, as upheld in history by a people that makes itself visible and enters into relationships with other peoples and cultures, a thrust towards the world, and thus also towards philosophy, besides that towards revelation? And, with regard to Christianity, is not there in it as well, besides the thrust towards the world, and thus towards philosophy, with which it establishes a dialogue weaving its history with that of the nations and of the States (especially after 313), a movement towards revelation, as is proven by those Christian currents that are in conflict with the world or political power?

Rosenzweig was drawn, in this period, to focus his attention on the problem of the revelation–philosophy connection, in part by the difficulties inherent in his position in the autumn of 1913, of which he himself was gradually becoming aware, in part by reading new books and having new experiences and intellectual exchanges.

The difficulties regarding the point of view he had expressed in his letters to Rudolf Ehrenberg of October 31, and November 1, 1913, are already pointed out by Ehrenberg in his answer of November 3. Ehrenberg, in fact, expresses his doubt both that the Christian should need the Jew so as not to lose the sense of his mission in the world, and that the Jew should find meaning in his existence by carrying out a task which refers to the destiny of Christianity – things Rosenzweig had just stated in trying to define the functions of the two communities.

> Are the people of Israel still close to God? – he writes in his reply – [...] If God's anger is upon Israel, how can Israel have a function like that of the Christian Church? [...] From all of the duties within the Church do you not take one and give it to the people of Israel, which in this way should rise up? [...] Is it possible for Judaism, and is it permitted, to base its Jewish conscience on the relationship with the Christian Church in the world?

Rosenzweig admits – in his letter of November 4, 1913 to Rudolf Ehrenberg answering these comments – not to have yet really found a solution to the question. He intends to find a deeper base from which Synagogue and Church can both originate and through which they can take on a rôle in human history.

Between the winter of 1913 and the spring of 1914 Rosenzweig makes some remarks, in his diaries as in his letters, referring to the history of philosophy within the medieval Christian sphere and within the medieval Jewish sphere. His interest in the Church Fathers and Scholasticism appears in the letter to Hans Ehrenberg of December 11, 1913, and in the letter to Eva Sommer, translator of the *Divina Commedia* into German, of January 28, 1914. Reflections on the principal themes of the Jewish thinkers of the Middle Ages – such as miracles, the conflict between astrology and revelation, the connection between natural law and revelation, the rapport between

Torah and philosophy – appear in his diary entries of May 24 and June 14 and 26, 1914. A comment of June 23, 1914, within this context of study, "The difference between revelation and reason is absolute while the difference between writing and interpretation, therefore the difference within revelation, is absolutely relative," demonstrates how the author accepts, from the medieval Jewish thinkers, both the theme of the radical contrast between revelation and philosophy from the point of view of what constitutes for them the premise of thought – divine word to man in the first case, autonomous reason in the second – and the theme of the necessary connection between revelation and philosophy, once the priority of the former has been asserted. Rosenzweig is led thus, through his study of the Jewish thinkers of the Middle Ages, not only to consider the question of the revelation–philosophy connection important within Judaism itself – and not only in the history of Christianity – but also to define such a connection giving priority to the immediacy of the relation between man and God over the relation between man and man in the world. In fact, while the first relation depends on faith considered as the elevation of the whole soul towards the supersensible, the second depends on an attitude in which the human being, moved already by the divine spirit, acts in the world through reason. Rosenzweig also feels that the peculiarity of Jewish revelation – which implies distance between a God who gives the law, and a people who as its chosen people receives it, and proves with its own religious existence the truth of such a law, as is said in the note of June 23, 1914 – in contrast with Christian revelation which cancels the radical difference between the divine and the human, is that it avoids that dissolution of revelation in philosophy which, through the interpretation given by Thomas Aquinas of Maimonides' *Guide of the Perplexed* and the various events of European rationalism up to the Enlightenment, finally finds its completion in Hegel. In the notes of July 1 and 11, 1914, Rosenzweig gives a general outline of the history of European philosophy which, via Maimonides and Scholasticism reaches Hegel's doctrine and ends with the triumph of reason no longer limited by elements external to it, and thus founded on itself.

Between the winter of 1913 and the spring of 1914, Rosenzweig also met two philosophers who would be important for his life and thought. The first was Hermann Cohen, whom he met in Berlin at the "Lehranstalt für die Wissenschaft des Judentums" at a course Cohen dedicated to the relation between religion and philosophical system, as he reports in a letter to Rudolf Ehrenberg of August 2, 1914. The second was Martin Buber, whom he visited with his friends Bertha and Bruno Strauss at Heppenheim, not far from Berlin, as he tells the same correspondent in a letter of April 1914. Of the relations that he developed with these two representatives of Jewish thought more will be said later. His examination of their works from 1914 on – as will be seen further on – led Rosenzweig to reflect on the way in which Judaism and philosophy can come together. He felt that neither Cohen nor Buber had known until then how to reconcile this double aspect of their personalities.

In a text dedicated to the close scrutiny of Cohen's essay on the relationship between German culture and Judaism,[9] Rosenzweig notes that Cohen reduces to abstractions the two terms that he wishes to compare, and that furthermore he never presents with deep awareness the Jewish idea of God in its effective differentiation from and contrast with the principal ideas inspiring philosophers, poets and German intellectuals. This is due to the fact that Cohen carries out his own meditation on the relation between Judaism and German culture basing himself on a philosophical system which is already built on the notion of the spirit's autonomy. The problem of such a relation is placed at an already advanced phase of the development of Cohen's doctrine, although it should have been a focus from the very beginning so that its real solution could have been possible. In an essay dedicated to some of Buber's works, in which Buber wishes for a renewal of Judaism from the most internal forces in the people's life,[10] Rosenzweig points out that Buber simply gives up considering as a central element, the pact between God and Israel in the way in which it is asserted in the Jewish sources – that is as a relationship between two terms which remain completely distinct – and that therefore the revelation is completely set aside to the advantage of philosophy and of human liberty as autonomy. Neither philosopher appears, according to Rosenzweig, to have solved, up to then, the question of the relationship between Jewish religion and philosophical thought, the culminating expression of European culture.

The period between the autumn of 1914 and the autumn of 1917, during which Rosenzweig was involved in military action, first in Belgium and France and then in the Balkans, produced his most intense intellectual work – as can be seen from the diaries and letters – aimed especially at closely examining the theme which he had outlined, the connection between the point of view offered by faith in revelation, and philosophy which implies reasoning about historical and political events.

In the correspondence with his parents in the years 1916 and 1917, Rosenzweig reflects on the cultural history of Europe and on the Jewish situation of the time, and once more examines the figure and the writings of Cohen, as representing both German liberal Judaism's best points – the universality of culture, rationalism, the defence of the ideals of liberty, equality, and brotherhood – and its deepest limitations – the inability of really showing the meaning of Judaism in the modern age, and as a consequence Jewish subordination to a German culture seen only as the bearer of cosmopolitan values, and not of irrationality and mysticism as well.[11]

In the correspondence carried out between Rosenzweig and Eugen Rosenstock, initiated by the latter with a letter of May 29, 1916 and brought to conclusion by Rosenzweig with a letter in December 1916,[12] it is not so much the definition of Judaism or Christianity which is at stake (Rosenzweig sees the first, because of its pure monotheism, as the most definite enemy of a paganism, that is to say of an annulment of human freedom radically opposed to nature and history, which would not be avoided by the second because of its trinitarian monotheism; Rosenstock, for his part, sees Christianity, because of its pure universality, as the most fearsome enemy of paganism, that is to say of the assertion of a particularism of individuals and nations, which Judaism would not overcome because of its principle of election). At stake in this correspondence is not so much either the definition of the relationship between Judaism and Christianity (Rosenzweig underlines how Jewish revelation implies prayer, concentrated study, and walking in the world, regardless of the fact that Judaism from the Talmudic age has above all upheld the Synagogue, and thus how Christianity should look at Jewish revelation so as not to lose the meaning of its action in history; Rosenstock, however, points out how Judaism's function of maintaining in time divine transcendence became unnecessary after the advent of Christianity, which accomplished what Judaism had introduced in an imperfect manner and only as an announcement) but, rather, the determination of the possibility of a new philosophical system based upon revelation, substituting the old philosophical system built on human reason. Both authors describe the crisis of philosophy centered on that *Logos* which from the Greeks reaches Hegel through Kant's *Critique of Pure Reason*. Rosenzweig, however, sees Christianity, in the form reached in the modern age, as also involved in this process, and thus indicates Jewish revelation, also necessary for the revitalization of Christianity, as the new basis for the system. Rosenstock, by contrast, holds that Christian revelation alone, having surpassed the Jewish one, can at this point fulfil the task of constituting the premise for the system. He also remarks, mentioning Zionism, that extant Judaism follows the modern spirit. While Rosenstock reproaches Rosenzweig, who is convinced of divine intervention in the world, for being an obstinate rationalist and for this reason unable to enter the Church, Rosenzweig reproaches Rosenstock, who is convinced of the need to offer a new philosophical system, for his individualism and ingenuousness. Although the two rivals and friends conclude their discussion without reaching an agreement, they share the need for a universal way of thinking, based nevertheless on faith, and on the heart and the existence of the individual.

In the letters written to Gertrud Oppenheim on May1, 30, and 31 and August 2, 1917, Rosenzweig deals with the problem of the relationship between revelation of the divine word and philosophical thought: from the point of view of judging contemporary Judaism, divided between the orthodox and liberals who look to the Diaspora, and the Zionists who look to the return to the land, and from the point of view of the relation between the decision to live in freedom as responsibility, which takes place directly at a certain point of one's existence, and the labor of carrying on day after day in the mediations and necessary compromises with the world, which involves the use of reason. In both situations the author maintains the necessity of keeping both the first and the second attitude together, and of giving precedence to the first view. In fact, if non-Zionist Judaism were not completed by that Judaism which is turned through action to the realization of the Messianic goal, by means of returning to the land, it would limit itself to waiting in hope; if, however, the Zionists did not have as their base and origin the Jews of the Diaspora, who are "strong" in their patience, they would lose the sense of their work, even if they are the "best" – as Rosenzweig himself puts it. In the same way, if the choice of one's life were not accompanied by the journey in time, it would remain internal and devoid of efficiency, not implying, in and of itself, any real redemption. If, however, the journey were not preceded by a reflection in which the "Self" becomes aware of itself and of its task, it would no longer have any defined direction. In the letter to Gertrud Oppenheim of May 1, 1917, based upon exactly these considerations, the author envisions the plan for a book he believes will be "posthumous." "In the book there will be nothing more than this, that Jewish duty (*müssen*) and Jewish will [...] are one, mysteriously one; that everything that is called history, happens in such a way that a will rises above duty and so becomes at the end a new duty. [...] Here in fact a piece of eternity has burst into history." Eternity and history remain separate, however, for although contact between finite and Infinite is possible, it is not so between uniqueness and mediation.

One can thus understand, keeping in mind the evolution of Rosenzweig's thinking from his *Teshuva*, or return to Judaism, up to the summer of 1917, how he was able, in the months immediately following, to quickly develop the project of a work which would express his vision of the connection between man's relation with the eternal and his proceeding within boundedness – a work outlined not only in its whole structure, but also in its articulations. In as much as the central idea – that of the necessary connection between the individual's acceptance of revelation and his thinking while acting with others in the world – had already been circumscribed, the matter was to develop it and realise it in a planned exposition, dealing with the various themes implied. Autumn 1917 was the period in which the author finalized the layout of his book.[13] The book had a Jewish form – as it presented revelation the way the Jewish sources, liturgy and Jewish life had transmitted it, and drew from it a doctrine of the being of God, man and the world – and at the same time was universal – for such a revelation and doctrine were only the means through which light was shed both on human existence as immediately connected to a transcendent God who gives man his spirit, and on the philosophical system regarding the whole of reality, no longer, however, enclosed within itself. From the Jewish condition as it encompasses both faith and knowledge, so that, in any case, the second never opposes the first, Rosenzweig derived the human condition. However, since the Jewish community had also assumed throughout its history a specific appearance, distinguishing itself from the Christian one, as being the protector more of the moment of faith addressed to God than of that of knowledge addressed to the world, then the Jew witnessed in his life the one truth he saw in the one God in a specific way. The Jew upheld, in fact, the one truth as an individual dedicated to study, prayer, or contemplation, carried out however by the whole soul and not only by pure reason.

The Star of Redemption is the title the author gives the book in which he develops his system of philosophy centered on revelation, indicating with this term different things: the Jewish symbol of the star of David; the image composed of the two triangles formed in the human face by tracing lines between the eyes and the chin, the center of the forehead and the corners of the mouth; finally, the ultimate figure produced by drawing a triangle between the three points indicating God, world, and man, understood as single and separate existences, and another triangle formed by the lines having as their points creation, revelation, and redemption. The fire of the book is, as said, revelation.[14] Rosenzweig presents in the pages dedicated specifically to this subject – the second book of the second part entitled in fact *Revelation* – a phenomenology of the immediate contact between God and the soul in the moment in which it is awakened by divine love: this love expresses itself by giving the soul commandments to guide it on its journey through the world. The spirit in man comes about from revelation and brings about a sensitivity which is neither animal nor selfish: this sensitivity identifies with reason or the whole complex of moral and intellectual forces. It is in the fault of selfishness, for the mere fact of existing only in the world, that the soul has to face God; the soul frees itself completely of its selfishness in the moment in which it responds to divine love by loving in turn. The entirety of the spiritual forces is characterized by Rosenzweig as pure love. This love, aroused by a loving God, and thus absolute, infinite, and completely unselfish, like God's love, does not remain enclosed within the "self." This love moves within the world in which the soul lives as a single entity, towards the present or what is close, towards the past or what is distant, and towards the future, transforming itself in pity and compassion towards everything there is in the world, and particularly towards human beings. These are in fact either one's neighbors or those called upon in one's affection (affection as the complex of human faculties), i.e. those who lived in the past, the past generations, and those that will live in the future, the generations to come. The "self" which is moved by the love for another human being – at first the closest – coming about from one's love addressed to God as a response to the divine love towards oneself, feels only in this way the reality and strength of this intimate experience:

> The authentic profession of faith – Rosenzweig writes – is always the witness that one's own lived experience of love (*Liebeserlebnis*) must be more than one's own lived experience, that He whose soul, in its love, has experience, is not simply an illusion or self-deception of the soul loved, but really (*wirklich*) living.[15]

The pure affection that the "self" takes as a model, at the time in which it addresses the world, is that of a "Self" that expresses to it every time anew in every instant its love for the very existence of the soul in the world as a free personality: thus the love of the soul loving the world is always fresh and new; having its roots in the non-earthly, this love renders time possible. The encounter between the soul and God mediated only by this type of affection, which does not allow their fusion as they are manifested in different ways – infinite activity of divine love and awakening of love in the soul which is the object of divine love – in fact places the human being on a plane which is not that of existing in time, but of existing in the world in an instant which is in contact with the eternal (this latter understood, however, not as substance but as infinite action on behalf of a transcendent God). Time originates in the moment in which man, thus loved, addresses his pure love, which gathers up in itself all of its energy, to the outside world, coming in contact with what surrounds him and in which he sees the sign of the God he has known in his own intimate experience. Rosenzweig characterizes man who is led by such love towards God and, beginning with Him, towards all human beings, as the "saint" or the "suffering servant," using the Biblical terminology. This individual is characterized not only by the virtues of humility and charity, but also by those of loyalty, justice, and courage – the last three necessary for his action in a world that does not everywhere show the signs of divine presence and which he cannot bring back in its totality to a God who would show

Himself completely as love: God is not, in fact, for him love; he only experiences a love that comes from a God which is beyond him and which he cannot reach.

Now, it is starting out from revelation conceived in this manner – revelation orienting the "self" from the immediate relation with God, which takes place through the spirit, towards the present of the encounter with one's neighbor, towards the past of creation, and towards the future of redemption – that in the *Star of Redemption* arises thinking of being, proper to philosophy. Thinking which originates from the pure love of the "self" which formed itself in revelation, makes itself independent of such love, as the whole of the faculties of the "self." Thinking turns from God, to whom it first addresses itself, to the world which it conceives as what has been created by divine action, and which will one day be redeemed through divine action. Philosophy, which defines being through the work of reason, is thus directed by those categories of revelation, creation, and redemption which have at their base revelation itself as an event not to be included only in being. This event is, in fact, even before it has been thought of, an immediate fact, to be recognized as such only by a "self" which experiences it. Thus Rosenzweig sets up the philosophical system (which now no longer appears closed) by abandoning the old premise of thought founded on itself, for a new premise: this coincides with a fact, which is no longer the fact of reason, but of a directly lived experience which does not take place within the soul, but rather consists in contact between the finite human being and the Infinite. The Infinite remains external and can never be fully encompassed within the human horizon.

The *Star of Redemption* is divided into three parts. The first is dedicated to the description of what is called the "prior" or "primogenital world" (*Vorwelt*) which has different aspects: this world is at the same time the world of the elements – God, world, man – produced by the loss of the idealistic totality which philosophical thought reaches in its path, from Parmenides to Hegel (a totality not really contrasted with any theological rebellion that would be addressed to the defence of the individual, or of life, feeling, or faith as opposed either to universality or philosophical reason); the world of myth, with its gods subject to fate, its ever-changing, and nevertheless immutable cosmos, its tragic heroes; and the world of the abstract language of mathematics and of the original words of "yes," "no," "and." The second part is dedicated to the description of what is simply called "world" (*Welt*), which is at the same time: the world of living relationships between God, the world and man, in creation, revelation, redemption; the world of revelation, understood as the true "miracle" in being, and identified with Jewish revelation – because considered pure and original, the root of Judaism as well as of Christianity according to their historical development; and finally the world of spoken language in its liveliness and variety of forms, from epic, or narrative, or representation, to lyric, or expression of the "self's" feelings in dialogue with the "thou," to the *pathos* of hymns, exhortations, or appeals pronounced by human beings united in nations, projects, or enterprises for social and political transformation. The third part is dedicated to the description of what is called the "supernatural" or "superior world" (*Ueberwelt*) which encompasses: first, the world of that tension towards the final unification between God, the world and man which is expressed both through prayer and action, to which the Synagogue and the

Church are respectively dedicated as historical institutions – in fact, humanity and the world are not yet redeemed in history, while they are redeemed in the moment in which, even within time, they connect with the Infinite; second, the world of philosophy or knowledge of an Absolute which is certainly beyond man, but does not deny him access to truth, first given in fact to everybody directly through revelation under the form of pure love as a synthesis of the commandments, and then thought out and rendered alive by each individual as applicable to his own individual situation; third, the world of liturgical language addressed to God, which comes close to the silent language of sacred art, dance, glance, and gesture. The movement that leads from revelation on high, which is dealt with in this third and final part of the *Star of Redemption* – once the "self" has reached the Infinite towards whom it aspires with all its strength, addressed either to theoretical or to practical effort – is then followed by a new movement: this leads from on high towards revelation, that is to say downwards towards the world of the living relationships which the "self" holds with the other "self," with the world, and with God. And addressed towards the center of revelation is also that movement proceeding from below, from the *Vorwelt*, that is to say from the sphere of the absolutely separated or coincident elements (in fact, absolute separation and identity call each other forth). Finally, it is only the subsistence of such a center which allows one, according to Rosenzweig, to triumph over both the abstract truth of the pure philosophers, who look only above, and over the obscurity of the life defended by those who appeal against philosophy to pure existence, looking only below. The nocturnal mythical world of the simple elements is nothing but the *pendant* of the dazzling world of pure philosophical ideas. They are the two symmetrical sides of that paganism which ignores the true reality of human beings: only through their pure spiritual strength, the love which connects finite and Infinite, are they able to relate each with the other in the world and to think on the ground of this spiritual strength. Human language which – according to Rosenzweig – can originate only in this way, has already been able to express and represent this reality. Rosenzweig often refers in the *Star of Redemption* to Jewish sources too – from the Pentateuch, to the Prophets, to the Song of Songs, the Psalms, the rabbinical literature, and on to the liturgy and the medieval thinkers – in order to analyze the various aspects of such a human reality. Thus the word of the philosopher can appear as a continuation or a development of the word that, according to Jewish tradition, is inspired by God himself. Just like the language of the Bible and Jewish sources, however, the language of the philosopher cannot but be metaphorical when referring to God; the metaphor, in this case, is not the mere perceptible wrapping for a determined meaning, but is allusive in as much as it is a sign for a meaning which is never exactly definable. Thus, Rosenzweig concludes his book not with the exaltation of a God directly named, but with an appeal to each man that he choose that path indicated to him with simplicity by revelation, that is to say that he opt for the freedom from the laws which rule the cosmos and pure historical temporality.

So Rosenzweig who, since the period immediately following his return to Judaism, had reflected on the possibility of establishing a connection between faith in Jewish revelation and thinking, later amplifies his ideas about this perspective to every human being. If from a faith and a way of thinking originating within Jewish history, he reaches a faith and a way of thinking which are universal, it is also true, conversely, that he presents these universal elements using Jewish expressions. Years later, he liked to present the fundamental work of his life, either as a Jewish, although philosophical book, especially when addressing a non-Jewish audience,[16] or as a philosophical system, expressed, however, using Hebrew words, when addressing a mostly Jewish audience.[17] But this philosophical system, which contains, according to the Kantian model, a theory of knowledge, an ethics and an aesthetic, is no longer founded on the theory of knowledge, as a doctrine which emphasizes the action of the *Logos*, but on ethics as a doctrine based on the awakening of the spirit in the contact between human existence and the Infinite, transpiring through the face of one's neighbor, before this existence assumes temporality in the world. Thus, the particular and the universal in Rosenzweig's orientation cannot be separated: every individual existence, placed at a particular point in space and time and having specific characteristics, can reach the truth through the pure affection of love in the moment in which it meets another individual existence, and be a witness of this truth in the world in the way which is peculiar to every human being.

3.3 The question of Jewish and human essence in the writings on education and history

In 1917, before Rosenzweig had outlined in detail the *Star of Redemption* and had started its composition, a text of his dedicated to education became known.[18] Here he deals with the question of Jewish education, proposing on one side that the participation of the young members of the community in the life of the Synagogue be promoted throughout the liturgical year, and on the other side presenting a detailed program of readings from Jewish sources for them, from elementary school up to secondary school. These readings were to be led, after the German school day, by Jewish teachers who were also researchers at a Jewish scientific institute, and to be financed by Jewish communities themselves. These Jewish teachers should also hold a rôle external to the rabbis and the presidents of Jewish communities, in non-Jewish culture. They were to be recruited amongst members of the various contemporary tendencies, ranging from the wing closest to religious observance of the precepts to the non-religious Zionists. In this text, Rosenzweig certainly presents Judaism as a living reality to be transmitted from the past to the future; he presents it, however, as if it consisted of a set of traditions, practices, and texts which the new generation had to make its own. The theme of Jewish *Bildung*, which Rosenzweig makes urgent claims for at the conclusion of this text, is presented at first as a determination of the essence of Judaism, found in some actions pertinent to the celebration of the divine law and in concepts expressed in some texts (which he encouraged to be read in the original languages) – from the Bible to the interpretations of the Bible, to the Talmud and texts of philosophy and mysticism – and then as the acceptance of this essence by the Jews. In this text Rosenzweig wanted the universal idea of Judaism to precede the living experience of the Jewish people: certainly, he was aware of the great differentiations existing in the situations of single individuals in the Jewish world of his time; but he was also convinced that the universal idea of Judaism shaped their lives.[19]

Later pedagogical writing, likewise directed to emphasizing the necessity of a Jewish return to learning and living one's religiousness, stresses the fact that life cannot do without knowledge and culture.[20] The Jewish world should thus – Rosenzweig comes back to this point – give greatest priority to the creation of a core of Jewish scientists and theologians, also with teaching functions, with the purpose of giving life itself a way of finding the right tools necessary to provide its sense of direction. Even in this case, however, the Jewish essence, found in religious tradition and religious literature, was presented as preceding Jewish existence, even though it was this existence that was the purpose of Jewish science and theology. As a model to follow in order to carry out this project, Rosenzweig referred to the work by Adolf Harnack *The Essence of Christianity* which, highlighting the essence of the Christian religion, had succeeded in rekindling the religious feeling of the members of the Christian community.[21] This is how Rosenzweig concluded his text:

> Finally science can, if necessary, come about even without life. Precisely its greatest results have often originated, as experience teaches us, beyond their own century; and exactly the principal works of our Jewish science have always searched and found their audience less in the horizontal line of the surrounding world, than in the vertical one of the centuries to come. Science, if driven by necessity, can renounce life; life for its part cannot renounce science.[22]

Thus the author, while having as his goal the development of knowledge not so much for erudition or technical ability, but as an instrument for the formation of man, nevertheless maintains the ideal of a theory, at first detached from life, but later to be introduced into life so as not to abandon life to itself. Like the theologians and historians of religions of the nineteenth century, who were influenced by idealism, he felt he could give a definition of Judaism as being a specific direction within human culture.

After having written the *Star of Redemption*, Rosenzweig faces the problem of Jewish education in a different way than that presented in his previous writings dedicated to this subject. On one side, in fact, Rosenzweig no longer makes any distinctions between the Jewish problem and the human problem because he has identified, through the analysis carried out in this book, the story of the soul in its relation with the world and God, as described by philosophy, with the story of the soul as described by Jewish sources. On the other side, he no longer considers it possible to determine the Jewish or the human essence through thought detached from revelation, and to render Jewish or human existence dependent on such an essence: in fact, he has indicated revelation as the point in which human existence opens itself to what transcends it which is no longer essence, but a distant God that manifests itself. Although God, while remaining hidden, gives each individual human being a truth that is universal and immutable, this truth is understood in one's love for it only in the form peculiar to every individual: the truth is rendered living and actual – because at first it is not an ideal being, but a complex of commandments expressing the divine attributes of action – only through the existence of the individuals that witness it. Thus Rosenzweig on one side identifies the education of the Jew with education towards humanity, through his becoming aware of the universal human meanings which his experience and the specific sources of his tradition express in an exemplary or original manner. On the other side, the point of departure for the knowledge of truth becomes the existence of the Jew: as being simply human or as someone who keeps in touch with Jewish experience or sources, the Jew is already open towards the truth, directly intuited through moral connection with other human beings and with a non-incarnate God. In two texts, in which he lays out the program of the "Lehrhaus" which he directs in Frankfurt beginning in 1920, this new direction he gives the pedagogical problem within Judaism is perceptible.[23]

The starting point of Jewish education – as Rosenzweig states in the first of these texts – cannot but be the Jew himself, in whichever way his being Jewish is rendered visible. As such, however, all he does is to express his being human: "As a Jew he is a man, as a man he is a Jew."[24] Jewish literature and culture belong to Jewish life. They do not form a separate sphere which one enters only by putting one's existence between parentheses. The books can lose their character of dead word only if they enter the live current of the spoken word. Jewish *Bildung*, as any *Bildung*, must start from the present moment and from the given situation. Starting from the present, the *Bildung* turns necessarily towards the past, necessitating science, and towards the future, requiring teaching and learning. "Only from the 'spirit' of the present moment, free from the 'letter', can strength and life reach the worlds that touch its borders, that is to say the world of research and the world of teaching, science and instruction."[25] But this happens because the present moment itself in Jewish life – as in human life – is the point of contact with what is beyond time: the present renders the past and the future alive because it is animated by an eternal which does not identify itself with a being which has always been and always will be, but with an active God who bursts into finiteness. Truly, Rosenzweig admits, in the life of the modern Jew, the family, the law, the Synagogue, through which in previous ages and in the most varied historical circumstances, contact with the eternal thus conceived was maintained, have almost disappeared; and yet, it is only with the fragments of these realities which still survive that it is possible once again to establish a Jewish science and a Jewish teaching. It is not a matter of setting up detailed programs of research or instruction. Science and teaching will be defined by being oriented towards the sources or by the exigency of the hour, only once the attitude of trust (*Vertrauen*) is reached, for solely from this can they acquire meaning. "To have trust," Rosenzweig notes, means "to be ready," each one for his own part and in the situation in which he finds himself, to deal with what is "at hand"; precisely because "to have trust" regards what is "next," although considered in the light of the "distant," it brings the "whole" closer. Nor should teachers in this type of Jewish education be seen as if they had the duty of transmitting to the students an already established doctrine of which they are the bearers: they themselves learn, teaching what they as individuals have elaborated, through contact with other individuals who are active in assimilating, each in his own way, what is communicated to them. What is important in the end is not so much the "what" that one investigates or teaches as the "how" one decides to investigate or teach.

In the second of these texts Rosenzweig considers as the common core of the directions into which the Judaism of his time divides itself – Jewish orthodoxy, Jewish liberalism, nationalist Zionism – what he calls "the heart of life," that is to say the trusting attitude of openness towards the outside. This must be the starting point so that a Jewish knowledge be developed which is more than a science for specialists: certainly, in this development there will be oppositions; however, these will find an agreement in the "unity of fire," which is the Jewish existence itself. Thus all those who will study Jewish knowledge, notwithstanding the variety of the positions that they can take with regard to the three directions, will in this way simply come back to themselves, remember the past, even though lived again in a new form.

Whenever Rosenzweig, in the twenties, found himself once more having to face the problems of *Bildung* within Judaism, he always insisted on the necessity of taking as a starting point the life of pupils and teachers in the dimension of the spoken word: only an existence willing to welcome the truth contained in the Jewish sources and experience, in order to witness it or confirm it in one's own specific ambit, could be the base of a significant knowledge and culture. As there is no abstract Jewish essence, as thinking connects itself to life and this cannot be reduced to an essence, likewise there is no abstract Jewish existence: life opens itself to thinking and this leads to a universality transcending existence. So, Jewish essence and Jewish existence cannot be isolated from each other; and they are connected to each other in such a way that the first can never become a pure object of thought, nor can the second ever be considered in and of itself, unconnected with what is beyond the simple life. And what counts, according to Rosenzweig, for the connection between Jewish essence and Jewish existence, counts also for the connection between human essence and human existence.

Rosenzweig also deals with the question of essence in some of the texts which he dedicates to the evaluation of the Jewish situation of his times, to the reconstruction of Jewish history, to the clarification of the relationship between Jewish history and human history, written after completing the *Star of Redemption* – and not only in his writings on the problem of *Bildung*.

In a text entitled *Essence of Judaism*[26] he states that the problem being discussed can be solved only if one finds in what is individual that which permits the universal to exist. The division of Jewish life into various currents cannot be cancelled by finding that the definition of Judaism, maintained by one current, can be complementary to another definition, maintained by another current: rather, the selfsame definition of being Jewish either in the exclusively religious sense, of observing the law, as orthodoxy upholds, or in an exclusively spiritual sense of adhering to certain universal rational ethical principles, as the liberals feel is right, or in an exclusively national sense of being part of a people, as the Zionists say – this is already the sign of a rupture within living Jewish existence which does not tolerate these separations. Only returning to this status – which was present at Sinai when the law was given to the people in spirit – would it be possible to unite each Jew with the Jewish community: "The objective is not the essence of Judaism, but the whole of Judaism; not the essence, but the life."[27]

In the text entitled *Spirit and Ages of Jewish History*,[28] what is placed at the root of all the phases of Jewish history – from the age of the patriarchs and Moses to the period of the judges and the kings, and then the Babylonian exile, the Hellenistic and Roman era, the Diaspora and the various Diaspora currents – is precisely the connection between the law, the people and the spirit: this is the universal element which survives in a permanent way throughout the different forms of Jewish existence succeeding each other in time. The Jew is from the very beginning, with Abraham, what he will be also in the following phases until the modern era. The tie with God and, through Him, with human beings, for the Jew, precedes the tie he has with the land on which he lives, or with the land promised to him, although he necessarily lives on the earth. This explains why none of the currents into which modern Judaism is divided, truly intends to abandon what is held by the other currents: just as there is an orthodoxy not inimical to the rationalism of the liberals, so is there a Messianic Zionism. The universal unification of the three moments which characterize the Jewish essence, and the human essence as well, will take place in history only at the end of times, although such a unification will never imply annulling the distinction between them: "The Jewish spirit goes on intact through history. [...] Through its simply existing (*Dasein*), free from connection with the epochs, it preaches one word only: to hope!."[29]

In *Jewish History in the Framework of World History*[30] and in *The Jew*,[31] a connection is outlined between the divisions characteristic of European culture in the nineteenth century – man and citizen, individual and universal, Church and State, life and philosophy, connection with the past with no criticism and destructive criticism of the past without any faith – and the divisions the Jew finds in himself after emancipation. The question was then for the Jews of the twentieth century, to accomplish in their existence, each one in his own way, that unified Jewish essence of law, nation, and spirit, which in the past was there within Jewish history itself, and however fragmented, was still present. They would thus prove to Europe, and from there, to the world, the possibility of redemption, consisting in the universal unification of man with other men assembled together in nations through the divine law and in freedom.

Thus Rosenzweig thinks that the solution of the question of the relationship between essence and existence, for and mankind, requires a "messianic theory of knowledge."[32] There is between these two terms a necessary relation which, at the end of time, will appear in the world as universally realized, although it will never be possible to establish an identity between essence and existence. The actuation of redemption is thus definable, for Rosenzweig, not simply as "God in All," but as "God in All and above All."

3.4 Faith in God and the concept of God in the comments on the poems of Yehuda Ha-Levi

In 1924 Rosenzweig published a collection of hymns and lyrics of the medieval Jewish thinker Yehuda Ha-Levi, translated from Hebrew to German by himself, each one accompanied by a comment, and followed by an "Epilogue."[33]

In the pages which accompany his work as translator and commentator of Yehuda Ha-Levi, Rosenzweig develops a theory of translation and translating in which, as in his previous writings on education and history, he underlines both the close relationship between what is Jewish and what is human, and the non-separability of essence and existence. In fact, in these pages he first explains how a particular text belonging to a specific culture of the past should not be considered by the translator as being close to his own context, but should be seen above all in its distance and specific physiognomy with regard to the present; and that because only this way of considering it truly allows one to comprehend both the permanent meaning of the text one is translating, that is to say what constitutes its "classicism," and thus also its value for the present day, and the original way in which this meaning was expressed. When there is this respectful comprehension, in dealing with the text the translator renews his own language, finding in it unsuspected possibilities, as each language, while distinguishing itself from every other language, has within itself a structure which is identical to the structure of all the others. Second, the author reflects on the fact that the history of the Jews in particular manifests in an exemplary way – notwithstanding the fact that it is certainly not without crises and divisions – how each new generation has a relation with the tradition. Yehuda Ha-Levi himself saw in his poems a way of offering his contemporaries and posterity the world of the Bible, fruit of the Jewish experience through the centuries; in them he uses expressions and terms taken directly from the Biblical texts, while at the same time not renouncing expressions of his own feelings and thoughts. And the Bible was the instrument giving his feelings and thoughts a point of reference. The Bible allowed their precise and personal form: it was where the experiences of the forefathers had been collected. Judaism thus acts as nucleus or model for other traditions or cultures, while not losing its own specific being. Rosenzweig shows in this way how on the one hand, the translatability of different languages is the premise that permits us to think of humanity united in the messianic era, when individuals, still remaining individuals, will enter into universal communication with each other; and on the other, how the Jewish past, although occurring in a particular way, indicates that which constitutes the essential, and gives the Jewish present its order and measure, notwithstanding the fact that each age presents itself, time by time, in different guises. Thus Rosenzweig effectively expresses his first point: "There is only one language. [...] On this essential unity of all languages and on the commandment based on this unity, of universal comprehension, the possibility and the task of translating are founded, its 'can', 'is permitted' and 'must'."[34] He expresses the second point as follows:

> The lie has many possibilities, the truth only a few, fundamentally always only one. That the truth never tires of repeating this same one always in a new way, proves its strength of making true (*wahrende*). In the mouth of the lover the word of love is not old which, in the mouth of he who feigns love, withers already when it is said for the first time.[35]

On one side Rosenzweig attributes to translators the rôle of those who, through their daily work, speed the realization of the kingdom on earth; on the other he thinks that the truth has already been said by all cultures and in various ways, although he feels that the ability to say it before others and in the simplest and most direct way was granted to the Jew. Mediterranean and European civilizations have drawn from the Jews that which constitutes their true base, as demonstrated by the translation of the Bible into the most diverse languages; it is from this base that the sciences, philosophy, and cultures acquire meaning.

In the comments which Rosenzweig places after each of Yehuda Ha-Levi's hymns or lyrical poems, he particularly highlights, among many different subjects, that one truth, which coincides with awareness of the meaning of what is human in the world, founded on the immediacy of revelation. Thus faith in God and the concept of God, which originates from such a faith, without which the soul would not be able to grasp the meaning of its being in nature and in history, are very often discussed by Rosenzweig in his notes. He groups together the translated poems under four different headings, which read "God," "Soul," "People," "Zion"; but the theme of believing in God and of thinking of God constitutes the underlying theme of his activity as exegete. In fact, all the events of the human soul – the formation of its identity, its hoping and despairing, its guilt and forgiveness, its being able or not to gather the signs of divine grace in its own time, the relationship with its community, its venturing through the world, its aspiration of reaching the place which God indicated at the beginning as the land in which to settle, the vicissitudes it encounters in its desire for the Infinite, the conflict it feels between love and the suffering of evil or death and, at the end, the victory over this suffering, which remains nevertheless something obscure – are all enclosed in this theme. Rosenzweig pursues it in the entire poetic production of Yehuda Ha-Levi that he translates and comments on in his book.

This is how Rosenzweig comments on, for example, the poem belonging to the first group, entitled *At Night*,[36] in which he uncovers in the medieval author a feeling of the divine presence revealing itself, and which inspires the remembrance in thought of what happened at Sinai:

> What has been seen has happened. A nocturnal scene brought the poet the live experience of the divine intuition. In the state between dream and waking, which derives from the first its peculiar legality (*Eigengesetzlichkeit*), and from the second its validity (*Gultigkeit*), meditating on the connection of body and soul, he has the intuition of God, as if it had also been permitted to his heart 'to hold on tightly to Sinai'. The experience lived today confirms and repeats historical revelation.[37]

Revelation – it is observed further on – is not a dogma or a formula: it remains a "miracle" in which God shows himself in an action which becomes a model for human behavior; the thinking of God in this way has therefore its roots in the most intimate part of a soul awakened by an external call.

> God – Rosenzweig writes – reveals in revelation always only – the revelation. In other words: he always only reveals Himself to man, to man Himself. This accusative and dative in their connection is the only content of the

revelation. What does not immediately follow from this connection, thus founded between God and man, what cannot prove its immediacy to this connection, does not belong to this ambit. The problem is not solved for the man who sees (*Seher*) the view (*Gesicht*), but – it is passed. The miracle does not become for him a non-miracle (*entwundert*), for intuition has given him the courage to bow before the source of the miracle. From a question of thinking it has become a strength of the heart.[38]

Of revelation, in relation to its immediacy and the need to return to thought – not so that the object thought of can be grasped or understood, but in such a way that it appears as the inaccessible origin of things – Rosenzweig says this in the comment to the lyric, belonging to the second group, entitled *This Soul Here*[39]:

The soul is not a thing. [...] The appearance that it should be a thing, a "substance," a "something," is brought about by the fact that it, like things, is "here." But things can certainly be "here," and just as well "there." The soul can only always "be here." A soul "there," a soul in the third person cannot be. It is always present – my, your, our soul, thus always: this soul here.[40]

The soul is in fact a "self" in revelation. But it is also in the world, towards which thinking necessarily addresses itself: however, not in the sense that, in nature or in history, the soul loses its character of "self" transforming itself completely in an object – which would happen if thinking of being were to detach itself completely from its foundation, which is trust in God. The "self" always remains an individual, even when it is related with the universal; the "self" always remains in contact with the Eternal, even when it is seen in its belonging to the world of things or of social or political events.

In a note to a poem which Rosenzweig includes in the third group and entitles *Looking Upwards*,[41] in which the situation is described of a human being who, at first, no longer sees any trace of God in the world around him, and later, because of a change in perspective, caused by a change of heart, finds it again, the author states:

The question has often been asked why the Jewish people have preserved themselves through all difficulties, and to this many more or less intelligent, thus more or less stupid answers have been given. The true foundation, which in fact does not allow any plural form "foundations," may be taught through this poem. It starts out with a cry from an abyss of difficulties, which is so deep that He who is appealed to, addressed in the cry, at first can only – be addressed, doubted, accused. But almost while still in this scream of doubt and blame [...] the eye recognizes (*erkennt*) in the One who is addressed the One around whom the stars turn, and the mouth, which now resumes breathing, witnesses (*bekennt*) the power of the One who rules the armies of the skies, and the heart enraptured plunges into the intuition of divine glory – and forgets any need.[42]

Revelation implies having a faith in God which leads one to see the world itself in the light of his holiness and power, while it still remains mysterious from the point of view of its course and its directions.

Finally, in the pages where the fourth group of poems is arranged, there is a commentary dedicated to the composition entitled *Premonition*[43] which, in the most penetrating way, analyzes the human condition. This commentary, in fact, highlights the connection existing between the immediacy of the present day, in which one experiences the presence of a transcendent God, and the thought of the future, connected to redemption. Yehuda Ha-Levi – thus one can deduce from this poem – still needs to make one last decision before taking the step which will lead him on the journey to Zion: this decision, towards which he feels compelled because of his fear of death, and which he takes only moved by the love of God, is an ultimate decision which will give his action a messianic effect.

> God – Rosenzweig writes – gives man freedom for the ultimate decision, in fact just for it, only for it [...]. He invests man with a today, and renders him thus master of his tomorrow. Man thus must tremble for his today as long as another tomorrow will come; and if at the beginning of the realization there was a constriction sent by God, thus fear as coercion will be at the end [...], fear aroused by God, that this today might not be followed by any tomorrows. Finally, however, from this fear arises the action which elevates the today to an eternal tomorrow.[44]

So, the author finds in Yehuda Ha-Levi's *Diwan* a source in which he retrieves that same way of setting up the relation between revelation and philosophical system, believing and thinking, faith and reason, which he had formulated in his previous writings. One can assume furthermore, that the *Kuzari*, the prose work of this medieval Jewish thinker, had already been considered by Rosenzweig when he had discussed this central point in the *Star of Redemption*. The symbols of the "seed" and the "tree," which in the *Kuzari* indicate Judaism and Christianity, transformed in Rosenzweig's book into the symbols of "fire" and "rays," are one of the forms in which Yehuda Ha-Levi had characterized the relation between the pact occurring immediately between man and God, and philosophical thought requiring deductions and argumentations. In fact, deductions and argumentations are worthy not when resulting from the strength of human thought alone, but if they are based on that spirit – which is at the same time sensitivity, passion, reason, and word – which already constitutes the connection between the first human being and his creator.[45]

3.5 The Bible as expression of the heart in the last reflection

Between 1925 and 1929 Rosenzweig worked with Buber on the translation into German of the Hebrew Bible.[46] He accompanied this work with some essays and letters written and published in those years, regarding his reflections on the content, language, style, influence on culture, and the different possible readings, of the Bible.

Already in 1921 Rosenzweig had commented on the language of the Bible and the particular type of contents it expresses. In a text which was perhaps the outline for a series of lessons he held that year at the "Lehrhaus,"[47] he underlines how Hebrew has never been for the Jews a dead language, but – being the means of expressing their faith – a language considered as familiar and present in every day life. Onto Hebrew, which is the language of faith, the Jew, throughout the course of history, later grafted Greek, the language of science or knowledge. Whereas the first is prophetic, and thus characterizes the course of time in the sense of past, present and future, the second is descriptive of things and events and inserts things and events into a sphere which is beyond space and beyond time. Biblical language, inspired by God, coincides with that human language which first expresses subjective feelings and then connects them with the understanding of being as creation and messianic journey. Thus, the individual who philosophizes, makes a connection between the Greek language – the language of reason – and the Hebrew language – the language of feelings and his point of departure. In a letter sent to Rabbi Benno Jacob on May 27, 1921,[48] Rosenzweig exalts the Bible as the work in which, with infinite variations, the essential aspects of human life are contained:

> All other books are learned by reading them. What is in the Bible can be learned in two ways: 1) listening to what it says; 2) noticing the human heart beat (in both cases by induction). The Bible and the heart say the same thing. Therefore (and only therefore) the Bible is revelation.

Furthermore, in another text written the same year,[49] Rosenzweig states that although it is true that the Bible, like any other book, needs science and philology, it can be truly understood only by those who approach it with the "right frame of mind" (*richtige Stimmung*); this implies recovering in one's own living experience that experience of meeting God which those who wrote the Bible had, albeit each individual in a different time, place and way.

In 1926, Rosenzweig wrote two essays in which he discusses the question of the Hebrew language, in the first case in reference to the translation into Hebrew of Spinoza's *Ethics*, carried out by Jacob Klatzkin,[50] in the second in reference to the translation of the Bible accomplished by Luther.[51] In the first case, he points out how Hebrew, even while becoming the language of a work which proceeds in a geometric pattern, as it does in Spinoza's *Ethics*, maintains such echoes so as to bring to mind Biblical images and situations: so the Hebrew language also confers on what is secular, a sacred aspect, and therefore distinguishes itself, as the original language of revelation, from other European languages. In the second case, he comments on how in Luther's translation, the Hebrew of the Scriptures is rendered in German, not so much in a direct manner, but through the Latin mediation of the *Vulgata*; and how this does not render superfluous a translation into German, such as the one he is at that time carrying out with Buber, since this translation intends to respect the construction of sentences, the roots of words, and the specific tone of the Biblical text.

In 1927, Rosenzweig gives his opinion on the Bible with regard both to Goethe's language,[52] and to the relation between the spoken word, which is always part of one's existence and implies the presence of the speaker's subjectivity, and the written word, which runs the risk of stiffening itself into monologue and system, and of drawing away from its author.[53] Goethe's language, according to Rosenzweig, authentically echoes Biblical expressions both because of the Judaic studies he first pursued in his youth, and because of his own particular reading of Luther's version. With regard to the second theme, he remarks how only by returning to spoken language – regardless of the ways in which this may occur – can writing avoid transforming itself into objectivity with no soul. For this very reason, in fact, the disquisitions of the Talmud, Christian Scholasticism and modern discussions being carried out either in universities or in scientific and religious institutions, are the authentic "redemption of Man," as they are exchanges of ideas between living human beings. Nevertheless, writing is necessary so that thought may have order, structure, permanence in time. Although they are the expressions of one's thought, the descriptions and stories which appear in the Bible more often than the poetic compositions, do not imply however an absolute separation from the author. The dialogue between the soul and God – that is to say the lyric – remains in this case the premise for prose, even when this becomes the listing of arid genealogies.

1927 was also the year in which Rosenzweig, in a letter to Gertrud Oppenheim of May 25, reflects on the connection between the way in which the authors of the Bible lived and perceived their relationship with God, and the forms in which Kafka portrays such a relationship in his novel *The Castle*.[54] In 1927 Rosenzweig also describes, in a letter to Jocob Rosenheim of April 21, his own way of translating and interpreting the Biblical text as equally distant from that of Orthodoxy and that of the Liberals;[55] and furthermore reflects, in a letter to Martin Goldner of June 23, on the translation of the verse of Exodus 3:14, where the name of God appears, in the sense of indicating the rescuing divine presence towards those who invoke it rather than the Eternal Being.[56] Between 1928 and 1929 Rosenzweig published his last commentaries on the Scriptures. Reviewing the volumes of the *Encyclopaedia Judaica*, first of all he expresses his hope that in the future of the Jewish community there will be a close unity between traditional commentaries, inspired by faith, and those brought about by scientific interest; then, that there will be clearer consideration of Biblical anthropomorphisms as originating from the living perception of God and, therefore, as being foundations of divine qualities pertaining to God as an object of thought; and, finally, that there will be a better in-depth study of the Jewish Bible as the center of a culture having a multiplicity of facets and developments, for, if it is true that this book is the "secret center of the created world," it is not true that it is "the totality."[57] In another essay, he discusses the different ways in which the various Biblical names of God have been translated and interpreted in both the Jewish and the Christian world: in this context, he gives particular attention to the German version and to the commentary by Moses Mendelssohn, a personality in which he finds a contrast between his "philosophical formation," carried out on the works of Christian metaphysicians, and his "Jewish instinct."[58] He returns once more to the lyrical or dialogical base – Psalms, prophecies, laws – of the narrative or epic parts of the Bible, and thus to the precedence of the ethical element, that is to say what has directly to do with human actions, over the aesthetic one, that is to say human images of things or of the world.[59]

Two of his witnessing statements in the years 1928 and 1929 are important in order to clarify the extent to which the philosophical thought of Rosenzweig is built upon the Bible, or upon faith – a faith certainly not understood as subordination without freedom to some absolute norms or dogmatic statements considered as divine revelation, but as trust in the ethical spirit given to man by God. In the first, a letter to Richard Koch of September 2, 1928, he recalls that the principal work of his existence, conceived between 1916 and 1917, should have had, according to his initial intention, the form of a commentary on the Bible, and how the *Star of Redemption*, which was suddenly substituted for this project, is therefore nothing else but "a commentary with omission of the text;" moving the polemic to the "philosophy of life," he also holds in this letter that thought necessarily originates with faith.[60] In the second witness, an essay dedicated to the historical and universal meaning of the Bible, he declares that the Bible will never lose its function of being a guide for man, even when the law and the dogma, the Synagogue and the Church, because of the process of "secularization," should no longer be the guardians of the "portal of the journey of humanity": the Bible would continue to indicate the way to humankind and be a model for all of those writings whose purpose is the foundation of community.[61] Thus Rosenzweig, in these last witnessing statements, clarifies how his philosophical research on man, beginning with his return to his community in 1913, has been led by the Jewish Bible.

4

MARTIN BUBER (1878–1965)

4.1 The refusal of Transcendence between 1900 and 1919

Buber was well known to Jewish and non-Jewish publics, between 1900 and 1919, as the author who was a member of the Zionist movement, the defender of a profound and necessary renewal in Judaism and the popularizer of Jewish and non-Jewish mystical texts and currents.[1] What gives this multilateral activity unity is his criticism of Transcendence, and therefore also his defence of human freedom as spontaneity, or capacity for autodetermination.

In 1916 Buber published a collection of texts, written between 1900 and 1915 in his role as a spiritual leader of Zionism, whose title is *The Jewish Movement*.[2] The oldest text in the collection was written in 1900 and is called *Jewish Renaissance*. It does not refer to Jewish sources, or to the past, but to the strength of the people and to the future, being concerned with resuscitating Jewish life and culture. The Jewish people is that part of the "race" (*Stamm*) which "feels itself" as a "race" and intends to free itself from all those customs and ideas which the ghetto (segregation from the life of other peoples, and the exclusion of the Jewish people from history), and the *golus* (the exile) gave to its appearance, and to find again the path of its independence. Buber emphasizes not so much external liberation from the past, as internal liberation. He does not want an organization to be constituted aiming at this objective, but rather a large movement: this movement had to permit the arising of the "whole, unitary feeling of life (*Lebensgefühl*) of the Jews." This movement had to give the Jews the simplicity and truth of a "free active life." The renewal had to come from the rest of Jewish life, still present in the soul, rather than from the study of Jewish traditional sources, for they no longer held a true meaning. Buber does not separate this emphasis on the vitality of the Jews from an emphasis on the solidarity of Jews each with the other and on the friendship between Jews and humankind. The Jewish renaissance seems to him to be only an aspect of the universal awakening of all nations to the free expression of their needs and values. Another text of this collection, written in 1901, whose title is *Feasts of Life*, ponders the Jewish festivals: they are not signs recalling the covenant between Israel and God, but celebrations of the living unity of the Jewish people. Buber does not deny that science and culture are important for the constitution of a nation. But he thinks – as he says in two texts of 1901, entitled *Jewish Science* and *Jewish Art* – that the roots of science and culture are in deep impulses, whose vitality is the necessary ground for Jewish scientific and artistic institutions. In another text, written in 1902, *A Spiritual Center*, Buber becomes a supporter of Ahad Ha-am – the leader of the cultural Zionism which defended the gathering of a Jewish population in Palestine in order to spread a Jewish culture rooted in the existence of a community. In this text Buber criticizes the intellectual works of the Jews of the Diaspora because these were the result of the activity of Jews as individuals and not as members of a living people. In a text, written in 1903, whose title is *Renaissance and Movement*, Buber connects the Jewish Enlightenment, or *Haskala*, inspired by Moses Mendelssohn and his circle in Berlin, Hasidism and Zionism: what is common to these three trends in Jewish history is, according to him, criticism of the law as a passive obligation for the believer; these trends exalt a new type of Jew who has self-determination as the center of himself, and therefore sees Spinoza as his precursor. The value of Zionism consists, for Buber, not so much in the fact that this movement wants to create a "State of Jews" (*Judenstaat*), according to the program of political Zionism, as in the fact that this movement presupposes a spiritual transformation of the Jewish world. Whence Buber's evaluations in this book in 1904 and 1907, of Theodor Herzl, the founder of political Zionism: Buber criticizes Herzl, because he was mainly interested in politics and diplomacy and realizing practical things, and celebrates him, because he was a charismatic leader of the Jewish people who, under his direction, had become active in history. In another essay, in this same collection, firstly published in 1912 with the title *What Gives Form* (*Das Gestaltende*) – which clearly shows the influence of Wilhelm Dilthey and Georg Simmel on Buber – the author emphasizes that in the dialectic between "life" and "form," that is to say how an objective work arises from a living subject, "life" only has a role. The life of a people is not created by the past culture reproducing itself, but by the people's internal forces; these forces always produce a new culture when the old one ceases to correspond to the exigencies of the present. The life of the Diaspora Jew – so Buber writes in this essay – has lost its creative force because this life is no longer organically tied to the life of other Jews: what in the past was the common element, the law forming their existences, does not now have a unifying meaning.

And so Buber's point of view is modern in the Judaism of his time. He rejects the model of a Jew who finds God at the center of his life, God who gives law and therefore freedom, thinking instead of the Jew who builds with his own forces his specific culture, in relation with the life of his community, and so finds his place among the nations.

In Buber's articles published between 1916 and 1919 in *Der Jude* – the Zionist journal he directed – the same call is evident: a call to the immediacy of feeling as the ground from which one acts freely according to the rules which the subject himself gives to his life. Where there had been the concept of an infinite distance between man and God, notwithstanding their dialogue – and this is typical of Jewish tradition – Buber substitutes the concept of creation, by Jews themselves, of the religious culture of the past, and of their new culture in the present. This new culture should clarify the history and the existential situations of the Jewish people, and therefore should be oriented towards the future.[3]

In 1916, Buber published some contributions about Zionism as a reply to Hermann Cohen's anti-Zionist criticism.[4] They were published in *Der Jude*, a journal that was more successful with young Jews than the other German Jewish journals of the age. Cohen, in his polemics, made evident the affinity between Jewish orthodoxy and Zionism, and their alliance against liberal Judaism, which was trying to establish a relationship with European culture. He accused Zionism of preferring the "cynicism" of Spinozist pantheism to the religion of a transcendent God, that is to say that religion which Jewish sources for very many centuries had defended. He felt indignation for the Zionist equivalence of Jewish vital force and Jewish ethical force. He recognized the distinctive quality of Jewish "nationality" (*Nationalität*) in religion as the only constituting force of the Jewish people's life. It was not to be identified with the "nation" (*Nation*) because this was formed by the State. He criticized the Zionist reduction of the Messianic idea to something abstract and void. In his defense of Zionism, Buber accused Cohen of maintaining an idealism which was indifferent to existence and history. He defended his thesis of a living Jewish people before and beyond religion. He did not consider meaningful Cohen's distinction between "nationality" and "nation" (and in fact: does not the dominant "nationality" in a State, where different "nationalities" coexist, have the tendency to transform itself into a "nation" and therefore into a State?). Finally, he denied that Zionism wanted to cancel the Messianic idea in Judaism: on the contrary, Zionism wanted to connect this idea to the Jewish return to the land, and therefore to make this idea practically realizable. In the conflict between Cohen and Buber about Zionism there were some misunderstandings: for example, Cohen reproached Buber because, in his opinion, he did not separate Jewish nationality and the Jewish State, while Buber actually separated them; and Buber reproached Cohen because he transformed Judaism into a rational idea while Cohen actually celebrated a living Judaism. But the root of their conflict is deep: it depends on fundamental aspects of the philosophies which they were then defending (later, as we have seen, Cohen would accept Buber's demand of a philosophy which does not forget the drama and suffering of individuals; and, as we will see, Buber would come to accept Cohen's idea of religious love as a force of the spirit which involves all the faculties of the individual). In fact, while Cohen exalted, in his writings, the value of ethics as the ground of social and political relations, Buber described a living society as the basis of law and State. Cohen made the particular dependent on the universal and identified the universal with a humanity unified by spirit or culture; Buber, on the contrary, emphasized the concrete relations, grounded in feelings, which exist in particular communities, and thought that only from these communities could the unification of all men arise. While the first loved what he himself called the "classicism" of European culture and art, the second preferred the "romantic" or "expressionist" style, that is to say that style expressing the passions of the individual not through a clear and well-balanced form, but in a dramatic way. Moreover, the first considered that keeping their unity in history, especially after the destruction of the second Temple, only through moral and religious ties, was a peculiar force of the Jewish people, and he thought that this fact was precious for all peoples. The second considered Jewish life weak if it was not autonomous in relations with other peoples, and he thought that only if the Jewish people renounced Diaspora existence could there be a real Jewish participation in world history. Finally, while the first believed in the virtues of patience, fidelity and hope as the means of preserving Jewish community, the second believed in their capacity to act in time. Cohen and Buber were at that time the most important representatives of German Judaism in the philosophical field, and their conflict about Zionism awoke a strong interest and had a great influence: such themes as the behaviour of German Jewish soldiers during the war, or the participation of the Jews in German culture were discussed in this debate together with larger topics – such as examining and evaluating Jewish history from the Patriarchs to the age of emancipation, or determining the meaning of Jewish existence in history, especially in modern times.[5]

The writings pointing out the necessity for a radical renovation of Judaism, published by Buber in his youth, are collected in two books, entitled *Three Discourses on Judaism* (1911) and *On the Spirit of Judaism* (1916).[6] The author describes the Jewish situation of this age as deeply unhappy and without perspective, and shows the path to take to leave it. He emphasizes how the return of the Jew to himself, *Teshuva*, involves the recovering of an essential human dimension, almost forgotten by European people because of their history, and therefore how Jewish redemption could produce a human redemption.

The essay *Judaism and the Jews* – the first in the first collection – ponders the relation between "life" and "memory" in a Jewish milieu: while in the past there was an "actual Jewish religiousness" (*wirkliche jüdische Religiosität*), from the beginning of the nineteenth century there was only memory and no connection with the present; therefore, in the present age, it is absolutely necessary to emphasize the "here" and the "now," giving new obligations to the Jew. So Buber writes poetically: "At the nod of the other peoples, his Judaism was no more a living substance, only a memory of suffering, and a memory of images, like the traces of the years and destiny in our faces."[7] But, as the Jew also participates in a non-Jewish culture, he is torn between the past and the present: he will "master" this "mixture" in his soul only if he gives primacy to his Jewish side – which he has to transform into the feeling of belonging to a nation. Once the Jew recovers his unity through contact with his true inner life, he will identify his being with the being of his people: "Not: my soul is near my people; but: my people is my soul."[8] Only in this way will the Jew make his contribution to general history. In the essay *Judaism and Mankind*, included in the same collection, Buber again emphasizes the Jew's inner return as the only ground which could allow the rest of his Jewish life to bloom, when he could then be rooted in the world; but he also points out what he sees as the universal human meaning of such a life. In fact, in Judaism "a fundamental form of human life" came about in a more energetic manner than in other peoples: "this original element in the human soul" is that immediate unity between the "high" and the "low" which was at first given by the connection between man and God found in the Prophets or the first Christian communities still influenced by Judaism, and then – in modern times – is realized through creativity. The results of creativity become distant and alien from their source. But creativity is itself the means that allows those products to be continuously reappropriated. Spinoza – once again a model for Buber – and all those Jews who are his followers when they defend human rights through democracy and socialism, prove, according to the author, the truth of this position. Buber qualifies as "oriental" this pull towards the unification of two contrasting elements produced in action. In the last essay of the first collection, *The Renovation of Judaism*, the ideas of unity, action, and future, are considered as oriental characters of Judaism – because Judaism, in modernity, is centered on the idea of human activity as the means of unifying the opposites: and it is for exactly this reason that Buber sees human activity as absolute.

The essays in the second book – entitled *The Spirit of the East and Judaism, Jewish Religiousness*, and *The Myth of the Jews*, deepen the subjects already sketched in the previous essays: like these, they point out how Jewish communities could supersede their spiritual crisis and flourish. The first essay opposes East and West: the representatives of the first are the Chinese, the people of India and, especially, Jews; the representatives of the second are the Greeks in the age of Pericles, the Italians of the Trecento and Quattrocento, and the Germans of the century of Goethe. The "oriental" principle is "movement," that is to say to act and transform; the "western" principle is "intuition," that is to say to look at an objective form. This text also says that the "western spirit" needs the "oriental spirit" if it is to lose its fixity in the contemplation of a given being or thing. A Jewish life in Jerusalem could once again build a link between East and West, as happened in the past. The second essay opposes "religiousness" as a producing force and "religion" as a totality of forms, ceremonies, and doctrines, grounded on this force. While "religion" represents in Judaism the continuity of tradition – the father who communicates faith in God to the son, rabbinic rules and commandments, and the formulae of philosophical rationalism – "religiousness" shows an individual choosing and making decisions, and the son's self-liberation: the son finds the Absolute in acting according to his own rules and norms; that is also meant to realize the Absolute in the world. The third text introduces myth among the Jews: myth expresses the immediate contact between man and a God who not only is beyond imagination, but also beyond any possibility of determination. Therefore in myth man celebrates his freedom. Myth, in Jewish history, was kept alive by the people, women, heretics, mystics, as an "esoteric" or "secret" current against the priests and intellectuals who formed an elite. Myth shows a vision of reality which is deeper and more authentic than the vision of the world according to causal connections.

So, in these essays Buber invited the German speaking Jewish world to take its destiny into its own hands rather than to resist in a passive mood, in the defense of an old legacy perceived as an indestructible value for the Jews and for humanity. He maintained the necessity of abandoning not only pre-modern Judaism, centered on the respect for rabbinic legislation, but also liberal Judaism, grounded on the faith in reason. Certainly, Buber continued to affirm the idea of redemption for all human beings in history as well as the idea of a Jewish role in the redemption, like an orthodox Jew, or like the liberal Jew who in the age of emancipation identified the modern idea of progress and the Messianic ideal. Buber changed these ideas, however, in the light of his refusal first of the concept of Transcendence (Transcendence either of the God of the Bible or of reason beyond the life of the philosophers), and second of the concept of the Jewish people as a people formed either by divine revelation or exclusively by rational and moral principles. In two texts published in 1919, *The Holy Path* and *Heruth* (*Freedom*), these theses of Buber are backed up with a lot of evidence.[9] In these essays, the author exalts the end of dualism between the divine and the human, truth and reality, idea and fact – dualism affirmed continuously by religion and philosophy – through the exercise of human freedom: Jews must look at this idea of freedom in order to abandon their subordination to the law and the abstractions of Enlightenment and idealism, and therefore to exist as an independent community in their own land; and in this way the community and the land could immediately assume a spiritual meaning, and the holy and the profane could have a real connection between them.

In the years 1906–17 Buber published a number of writings on Hasidism, which he introduces as a form of Jewish mysticism,[10] on oriental, neoplatonic, gnostic, medieval, and modern Christian mysticism,[11] and on some particular mystical experiences which also appear in the life of a modern man.[12] These writings expound – in brilliant and suggestive forms, in language that is allusive and poetic – that human attitude which the author offers in his writings on Zionism and fundamental aspects of Judaism: in the Jewish soul returning to the unity of life, where the divine itself is present, through an "ecstasy" which does not mean self-negation, but the conquest of eternity, Buber sees the model of a universal quality of human soul; and this quality is its highest and deepest character. Certainly, Buber does not deny that in reality there are many forms of life, the peculiarity of individuals, the variety of natural phenomena and social relations; but he emphasizes that interpenetration between the human and the divine which allows the mystic to find God in his life. Jewish experience, if seen in this way, clearly and effectively expresses an original aspect of human experience: this aspect is alive also in other religions and cultures with less purity and vivacity with respect to Judaism.

In the years of the first world war Buber himself would criticize such a vision of man: this vision would seem to him too far from the real existence of human beings and too weak to resist the gravity of historical events.

4.2   The lyric-dramatic moment of reality in *I and Thou*

The book entitled *I and Thou*, published in 1923, but meditated and sketched in the years of the war, as Buber himself would later recall, is only a fragment of the project of a very large work. To this work Buber assigned the task of describing not only the fundamental forms of human reality, but also the different ways in which such forms are alive in the different religions.[13] The author published only that part of his project, in a form that was not definitive, which he could expound in a series of lectures at the "Lehrhaus" leaded by Rosenzweig between January and March 1922.[14] Later, as we will see, he used the results of *I and Thou* as an outline for other investigations, which in turn articulated, enriched, and made more profound the concepts first introduced in this book.

The first part of the text makes clear – through an analysis grounded in language – two fundamental attitudes which man is able to have when facing reality. As he uses two "fundamental words," which actually are each a couple of words – "I and Thou" (*Ich und Du*) and "I and It" (*Ich und Es*) – there are thus in his dealing with reality two types of approaches. The first refers to "relation" (*Beziehung*), in which the "I" enters with its whole being, and what is in front of the "I" in this case is a "Thou," not a thing or an object, but a living and acting being. The second refers to "experience" (*Erfahrung*), in which the "I" is involved only with a part of its being, and what is in front of the "I" is instead an "It," a thing or an object which could be perceived, wanted, represented, or thought. Both attitudes happen in time because they are characters of the "I" as a finite being. But the attitude, which expresses itself in the couple of words "I and Thou" also leads the "I" beyond time. Whereas things limit each other and therefore appear to the "I" only as finite, the "Thou" which certainly is part of the world, nevertheless appears to the "I" as infinite. Only the "relation" allows the entrance of the "I" to reality as the "world" because in the "relation" only the "I" approaches what is and remains different. On the contrary, in "experience" the "I" is closed in on itself because it appropriates what is at the beginning external and alien. So Buber writes: "The 'I' who has experience (*der Erfahrende*) does not participate in the world: experience is 'in' him, not 'between' him and the world."[15] In "relation" the being is more solid, firm and stable than in "experience": this involves the "I" in many connections which ultimately become only contents of its own consciousness. The word "Thou" does not need to be said in order to transform an element of being into a "Thou": the "relation" between two human beings implies language, but the "relation" which connects the "I" with a natural element (plant or animal) or a spiritual essence (image, idea, poetic vision, ideal program to be realized) as a "Thou" happens in a silence which is "at the limit of language." However, in each one of these three types of "relation" (the "Thou" as human being, nature, or ideal form), the "I" feels itself as called or invited to a reply. The "Thou" who makes such a request, certainly appears to the "I" placed in time and space, with a silhouette or precise features; but, through and notwithstanding this appearance of objectivity, it is nevertheless a "Thou." "Experience," once implied as a whole in "relation," suddenly loses this quality of "experience," in spite of its permanence. The "Thou" who comes to the "I" is immediately perceived as a totality of elements which however keep their distinctiveness. Buber underlines the necessity of the difference between the "I" and the "Thou," in spite of their reciprocity, in the three cases of "relation" he describes. He tries to accurately elucidate the way in which the "relation" takes place in reality: in "relation" the "I" is active and passive at the same time; it chooses and is chosen; it is consistent with himself and every time again becomes different. In "relation" there is no element which could represent a middle between the "I" and the "Thou" such as memory, imagination, thinking; therefore, the "present" (*Gegenwart*) is its dimension. The world of "relation" is formed by essences; however, "relation" is an "event," the "between" which is able to give a unity to different elements, what really makes life "effective" (*wirklich*). The term of "love" – interpreted not as a "feeling," nor as an "idea," but as "responsibility" or "worldly act" (*welthaftes wirken*), is used by Buber in order to express the immediacy of the "relation." Hate does not allow a "relation" because it transforms the "Thou" into the "It": the "I" does not see what is in front of it as a living whole, but only as an instrument or obstacle. Buber discovers the "relation," which he sees as the original attitude or the a priori in human beings, in infancy and at the beginnings of civilization: first of all, there is the "relation"; once the "I" and the "Thou" are formed within the "relation," the connection of the "I" with the "It" grows. But finally – as Buber recognizes – "relation" has a minor presence compared with "experience" in human life: the first is the lyric–dramatic moment, the second the customary or usual moment. However, it is the first which makes man human: "Without the 'It' man could not live. But whoever lives only with this, is not man."[16]

In the second part of *I and Thou*, Buber on one side gives an analysis of the human condition in that society and civilization where the field of the "It" (i.e. the utilisable or manipulable) is dominant because of the development of science and technology, and almost makes the event of "relation" impossible. On the other, he underlines the need to rediscover this essential dimension of man in order to avoid his reduction to an abstract, unilateral, egoistic "I." In this part, Buber identifies the field of "relation" with that of the "spirit" (*Geist*); therefore he connects "spirit" and language. "Language is not in man, but man is in language; he speaks through language – so all words, so all spirit."[17] Buber makes the sphere of the "It," which certainly is absolutely necessary to "spirit" when this produces or knows, dependent on the sphere of the "Thou." He attributes the separations between interiority and exteriority, feeling and institutions, freedom and mechanism – which he considers typical of western society in his time – to the weakness of the original a priori of the "relation" or "faith" (*Glauben*). He makes a distinction between the "subject" (*Subjekt*), that is to say the "I" in front of the "It," and the "person" (*Person*) or "subjectivity" (*Subjektivität*), that is to say the "I" in front of the "Thou": only in this case can a true identity come about for the "I" and the "I" as an individual arise. In the last pages of this part there is a severe criticism of Spinoza – as if Buber intended to criticize his earlier ideas. In fact, the "conversion" or "return" (*Umkehr*) from the impersonality of being, produced by modernity, to the true being of the "relation" presupposes a will which refuses the formula "One and All" and accepts instead the concept of a clear difference between the soul and the cosmos. Once the soul does not have the cosmos inside, or cannot find itself in the cosmos, then the soul will discover the almost forgotten sphere of the "Thou," or the "person." Buber had all along identified Spinozism as mysticism, but now he does not celebrate it. Spinozism does not recognize a true exteriority, and therefore reality as effective.

The analysis in the first two parts of *I and Thou* already evokes the problem of the "eternal Thou," whose "breath" we feel in every meeting with the "Thou," which is the "centre" of the "relations" of human beings, when they are in a "community"

(*Gemeinschaft, Gemeinde*), and allows that every "relation" is lived by every "subjectivity" as a victory over death. But the third part in particular deals with the "eternal Thou." Buber follows different paths with regard to this point. On the one side he does not separate the "relation" of the "I" with the "eternal Thou" from the "relation" of the "I" with the finite "Thou" because he identifies the "eternal Thou" with the a priori of the "relation" or the point of confluence of all human relations (the fire in which all the rays converge). On the other side, he considers the peculiarity of the "relation" between the "I" and the "eternal Thou": this "relation" – in praying or in religious ceremonies – is never transformable into "experience," as is the case in all the other "relations." Exactly because the "eternal Thou" can never become an object or an "It," its name always sounds as an invocation or a cry, even when it appears in a discourse that is not a lyric poem or a drama, but a description or a tale. Buber thinks that it is absolutely necessary to keep the finitude of the "I" in the encounter between the "I" and the "eternal Thou": the encounter can only happen in the world. Therefore he now criticizes all those mystical currents or mystics – be they Oriental, such as the *Upanishad* or Buddha, or Western, like John the Evangelist or Eckart – which have not given enough emphasis to the distance between the finite "I" and the infinite "Thou." This "eternal Thou" is the "totally other," the "totally present," "the most original." The antinomies – between the "eternal Thou" and the world, the "I" and the world – preserve the finitude of "subjectivity," and it is this finitude which permits the "I" to make contact with the Infinite. The encounter between the "I" and the "eternal Thou," which the author also calls "revelation," does not involve any knowledge: neither the origin, nor the end of being is known in this event because the encounter happens beyond things or objects. Beyond "revelation" that happens "here" and "now" there is the mystery of being and of the human role in being. So Buber interprets Exodus 3:14: "I am here as the here I am (*Ich bin da als der ich da bin*). The being who accomplishes revelation is the being who accomplishes revelation (*das Offenbarende ist das Offenbarende*). The being (*das Seiende*) is here, nothing more."[18] "Revelation" is what keeps religions alive: if "revelation" does not take place, and is substituted by the knowledge of God through images and doctrines, then religions become rigid and have no more meaning. "Revelation" is what permits society to be a living "community" of members unified only through the "spirit"; "revelation" makes possible "relations" and therefore the redemption of human beings.

Thus, in *Ich und Du*, Buber abandoned the celebration of mysticism, the idea of the "One and All," the call to the entire and full life, without inquietude, which had been the main characters of his previous reflection. Buber himself at some points of this work criticizes his previous pantheistic theses.[19] Now he connects the Transcendence of God as a "person," present in the world, with his idea of man. Now he considers the different expressions of religiousness – such as, for example, holy books or ceremonies – as forms which have their model, in different ways, in Judaism because this is grounded in the idea of the "relation." The soul of Judaism is the "I and Thou": this is the origin of that religion which is the presupposition of other religions and present in each one.

In the *Preface* (1923) to the book entitled *Discourses on Judaism*, which collected all the texts previously published in *Three Discourses on Judaism* and *Spirit of Judaism*,

Buber himself pointed out how Judaism now was for him that "phenomenon" which had discovered "religious reality" (*religiöse Wirklichkeit*): this is not a "lived experience" (*Erlebnis*) which is able to embrace the divine, but an "event" (*Ereignis*). In fact, "religious life" is nothing else than that "full human life" which is existence in the sphere of the "between." "All men – so Buber writes in his Preface – [...] somewhere come to God; there is no invulnerable pagan. But the Jew, who is in the world, stands towards God in the immediacy of the 'I' and 'Thou'."[20] Therefore Jewish religious texts should be considered neither as a human work, nor as a divine gift, but as the word which is the result of the encounter between man and God. In this *Preface* Buber invites the reader to read his contributions, already published, from the point of view of the new dialogic perspective. The main theme he defends is not more human autonomy, but God who is beyond man and nevertheless produces human self-consciousness.

Although in 1923 Buber is more careful than in his youth with regard to the difficult and problematic aspects of human life, there are also in the writings of this period some points which need clarifying. If the "relation" only happens in the present, because it excludes memory, imagination and thought, is the risk of the indistinction between the "I" and the "Thou" really avoided? If the "Thou" is perceived as a "whole" in immediacy, is the "Thou" still distant and independent from the "I"? Is time not a necessary element in thinking the "relation"? In *I and Thou* and his preface to *Discourses on Judaism*, Buber himself alludes to "creation" and "redemption" as dimensions connected with "revelation."[21] If, then, the "eternal Thou" is not only called by the "I" in the "relation," but also expressed as a third person in a story or narration, is this not a sign of a human need to think God? Is the possibility that the "eternal Thou" becomes an "It" really excluded, even though the "relation" is the presupposition of such objectification? Buber himself says, in these writings of his, that talk about God through metaphor is an essential part of religions.[22] Finally, is "love" – which immediately connects the "I" and the "Thou" – able to create those obligations between them which alone produce the reply of the "I" to the call of the "Thou"? In *I and Thou*, Buber himself criticizes the reduction of love to a subjective feeling, and grounds the social sphere of reciprocal duties and rights on this affection.[23]

These objections were expressed to Buber by Rosenzweig in a letter of his in September 1922.[24] Only through a long reflection on difficult Biblical texts and on the various, ambiguous, and subtle forms in which the "relation" really occurs, could Buber elucidate these questions and find answers to them. Thus, the lyric–dramatic moment of reality and its connection with the sphere of objective being were again discussed in the following writings.

4.3   The analysis of human existence in Biblical exegesis between 1926 and 1945

Between 1926 and 1945 Buber published several writings on the Jewish Bible, whose German translation he had begun with Rosenzweig in 1925.[25]

On one side Buber, as observed in our examination of his *Preface* to *Discourses on Judaism*, reads the books of the Jewish Bible according to the point of view of the philosophy presented in *I and Thou*: as they are the results of the encounter between man and God, they have their origin in "faith" (*Glauben*); it is from here that they draw their character of holy texts which then subsist in history. On the other side, it is through the interpretation of these books that Buber deepens his idea of human beings as open to the encounter with the "Thou" or the "It." Analyzing the Jewish sources allows Buber the possibility of pondering the various conditions, situations and aspects of human nature.

Among these writings there are those concerning questions of language, style, rhythm, composition, and types of Biblical exegesis.[26] In these contributions Buber explains that the language of the Bible must be considered first of all as a poetic language, because it expresses the "relation" between man and God; and, second, as a means of narration. Certainly, Biblical language is a reproduction of the spoken word, expressed by the persons who are the protagonists of the different accounts before an audience; but Biblical language is also a written word which presupposes separation of the "I" and other communicating persons. So according to this approach – which is different from that maintained in *I and Thou* – lyricism and drama join epic and history in the Biblical books. The spoken language, however, continues to be for Buber the ground of the written language in the Bible because the word itself of the author was inspired by God. It is precisely because of this primacy of the oral over the written word that the Biblical text must be inserted in time, and seen as a book open to different interpretations by different subjectivities in history. In these essays of his Buber also emphasizes the unity of the different books of the Bible, consonant with his peculiar reading: the same attitude connects the various redactors, the various books, the various parts within a particular book; there is a continuity in the Jewish way of reading the Bible – every commentary goes back to ponder the earlier commentaries – in spite of the ruptures and crises of Jewish history. Buber does not reject the results of Biblical criticism, grounded on historical, philological and archeological research, which had produced remarkable works especially in his times.[27] But he inserts the results of this criticism, mostly concerning the ages and external causes of the redaction of the Bible, in the context of a hermeneutics which is more interested in the meaning of the texts than in their genesis. Science and objective data are for Buber important in Biblical exegesis; however, more important is the approach grounded on "faith" (*Glauben*) because only the interpreter who shares the attitude and affection of the author of a Biblical source is able to truly understand its meaning and message.

Thus Buber – in his essays on reading the Bible and on its literary forms – explains how in human existence, besides the "relation" between persons and the present, loneliness and the connection with past and future are essential: without loneliness the author of the Biblical texts could not objectify his subjective "faith"; without an interest in the past and future, Jewish transmission of the Biblical sources would not be possible. Certainly the first moments – "relation" and the present – are the basis for the second ones – loneliness and continuity in time; but the first moments, if devoid of the second ones, would be unstable and volatile. Thus, reflection on the writing of the Bible and on the history of Jewish reading, makes Buber conscious of some aspects of human beings which he had not considered in his previous philosophical or Jewish writings.

There are then, among Buber's essays on the Jewish Bible, those where he clarifies the great importance of this Book for contemporary man.[28] He thinks that between human nature described by the Biblical dialogues and tales, and human nature in contemporary times, the distance is not insuperable: what is essential, that is to say the encounter between one man and another or between man and God in justice and love, is their common element. In this sense not only the Jew, but also every man, if he really respects and understands the fundamental Jewish sources, can become a "man worthy of the Bible." This man knows that the "eternal Thou" is secret and unimaginable and still not inaccessible: He shows him the path to be walked through the simple effects of his action in the world; the "normative," which permits the distinction to be made between right and wrong, truth and falsehood, is the content of divine revelation; the Biblical world is nothing other than that world of our daily experience in the light of eternity (although this light is never perfectly clear and evident) which every man should long for, in every time and place.

Thus Buber, in these writings of his on the perennial value of the Bible, emphasizes the element of the "norm" or law together with the element of the "spirit" between man and God. Now he underlines how between freedom and obligation, both perceived as God's gifts to man when man is able to keep contact with Him, there is no contrast. The link between man and God is represented by both love as "event" – and Buber, as seen, had maintained this in his previous writings – and the divine commandments. Reading the Jewish Bible teaches Buber the value of the rules which govern human life.

Some other writings, among those which Buber writes on the Bible in this period, refer to Biblical themes or figures.

In the essay on the concept of the imitation of God,[29] Buber explains how this concept has a special meaning for the Jews: for the Greeks God is an "image" which is worth imitating; for the Christians God is imitated through Christ as the "mediator"; for the Jews there is the paradox of taking as a model a God which is not imaginable and beyond man. For the Jew, the imitation of God means "keeping his paths, walking his paths," that is to say accomplishing in the world actions which have the same qualities or attributes of divine actions, perceived by man, although God remains beyond his actions and therefore covered with obscurity. So Buber, in his interpretation of the Bible, now considers God not only as the "eternal Thou" in contact with man through the "relation" – this was Buber's thesis in 1923 – but also as the "He" (*Er*) whom man cannot immediately comprehend and of whom man can only understand the works, or traces, in the world.

Another essay, about the Ten Commandments, clarifies some moments which are essential to the "relation" between man and God, but not mentioned by Buber in his previous texts.[30] These moments are: the asymmetry of the "relation," because at the beginning only God gives, and man receives; the nexus between divine love and commandments; human freedom as choice; and the link between the original spoken word or the dialogue and the writing of law.

The essays on the Biblical concepts of election, history and prophecy[31] describe, in a different vein, how not only the present is implied in revelation – as Buber had underlined in his earlier writings – but also the past and the future: in fact, faith in the event of revelation, which occurs at a precise hour, gives sense to historical time, from creation to the Messianic times. They also describe how the heroes of the history of redemption acquire their identity through humility and suffering for the love of God, before they act in history, rather than in an attitude where passivity and activity are inseparable; and how the human action effective in this history is very often not so much that of the political leader who longs for justice, but that of the common man who resists evil and firmly keeps the divine law. Certainly, redemption is not an object of knowledge: we can only trust that every action really inspired by a good will produces – now or later – a good result. Besides, these essays describe how prophecy, that is to say contact with the Absolute, and election, that is to say the obligation to affirm the content of revelation among other peoples, were and still are the foundations of the survival of the Jewish people, before this people acts in the fields of history and politics. Buber expresses this theme thus:

> What does it mean to teach the peoples an unconditional faith? [...] Two things. [...] The first: to show as relative all that is falsely considered absolute. The second: to point out the true Absolute so that the difference between this and every relative becomes perceivable. The first is, according to its sense, the result of thinking: investigation, analysis, criticism. The second, according to its sense, cannot be the result of thinking.[32]

So Buber deepens his analysis of human being also in these texts about the concepts of election, history and prophecy in the Bible: now he is aware – unlike in *I and Thou* – of all the difficulties with which man lives, when he connects his "relation" with God to his walking in the world, his faith with his thinking, the immediacy of affection to its necessary mediation in reality. But Buber's most important books on the Bible between 1926 and 1945, are *The Kingship of God, The Messiah, The Prophetic Faith* and *Moses*.[33]

What I wish to bring out, through this context for Buber's exegesis, is not so much his dialogue with Jewish, Christian, or scientific Biblical interpretation of his times, his ties with traditional or liberal Jewish exegesis, the nexus between this side of his work and the Jewish or non-Jewish contemporary situation – all these themes have already been objects of criticism.[34] Rather, we intend to emphasize the fact that Buber, in these books of his, offers complex and extremely subtle analyses of human beings. In fact, through his reconstruction of the history of Jewish faith, he not only enriches his idea of the fundamental aspects of human life – "relation" and "experience" – but also reproduces a great variety of human characters and situations. As a Jewish interpreter of the Bible, Buber fully becomes a philosopher of human condition.

Besides, there is a central theme which Buber develops in these books: the fact that the Jewish community – and, through this community as an example, every human community – can be truly formed only by the leadership of God who gives its members laws, rules, precepts. Certainly, this leadership can also be realized indirectly or by a prophet who at the same time is a statesman, or by other figures, sometimes in conflict with each other, such as judges, kings, prophets. The authority of these men is nevertheless always grounded in their respect for the divine law. Buber calls this theme the "theopolitical idea." The "nomadism" of the Jewish people – that is to say their living first of all in a sphere which is not being in the world, a field of reciprocal limitations of egoism, a region of violence and power, but the reality of ethical "relations" – is pointed out as the root of social and political coexistence for every people. Buber thinks that the Jewish people has always affirmed this "nomadism," including during the ages in which they had precise borders, and a centralized administrative and military organization. This explains why the heroes of Jewish history were not only leaders of the people, be they prophets, judges or kings, but also and mostly those human beings who, hidden and despised by the majority, suffer in silence for the love of the divine commandments. Buber thinks that this form of human life – which he clarifies in his analyses of Isaiah, Job, the Psalms – is the highest point that men are able to reach.[35] But Buber places other forms of humanity near the "suffering servant" in his Biblical books: the rebel, the doubter, the man who fights divine "demonism," the man who tries to avoid the divine voice calling, the courageous, the coward, the man who is not able to find traces of God in this world, the man who is potentially an idolater, the man who breaks the law because he is weak or excessively proud....[36]

Thus, many are the characters who act in the human drama and comedy Buber describes in his Biblical books. The "I" in "relation" with the "eternal Thou" and the human "Thou" takes on new and various aspects in Buber's teachings. As philosophical considerations lead him in his Biblical exegesis, so this exegesis affects his philosophical point of view, centered on the peculiarity of the "relation" in human existence.

4.4 Education, social philosophy, Hasidic studies between 1926 and 1945

Between 1926 and 1945, Buber not only translated and commented on Biblical texts; in other writings of his he also deals with pedagogical problems, social and political questions, and Hasidic tales and legends. The leitmotif which appears in all these writings is the theme of the "relation" between a "person" and another "person" as a reality that grounds the connection between the "I" and the world, and gives this connection sense and direction. So Buber develops his *I and Thou*.

Between 1926 and 1939, the author writes three pedagogical essays.[37] In the first of these contributions, he expresses his perplexity faced with an education whose main aim is the development of creativity. First of all Buber points out the romantic roots of the concept of creativity; then he makes this concept dependent on the idea of a common working expressing the freedom of everybody (a freedom which is not so much about choice as responsibility); finally he gives some advice about educational method. This method should exclude from their relationship the attitude of power and control of the teacher over the pupil, as well as excessive proximity of the second to the first. Buber's pedagogic ideal is sober, classical, temperate: he thinks that for the relationship of "feeling together" or "sympathy" (*Einfühlung*) between teacher and pupil it is necessary to substitute the relationship of "enlargement" (*Umfassung*), which implies a common participation in reality. "Dialogue" is the term that Buber also uses for this relationship, which does not exclude silence or distance between the partners. But "dialogue" presupposes, in any case, "trust" (*Vertrauen*) between them. The author thinks that "dialogue" has a full and pure form not so much in education as in friendship: in fact, it aims at the equality and reciprocity of the persons involved. The formation of man is the most important objective of education – of the man who longs for the "imitatio Dei absconditi sed non ignoti," as it is written at the end of this essay.

The second pedagogical contribution discusses how what unifies human beings, beyond their different *Weltanschauungen*, must be at the same time the basis and end of education. This "unique truth" is nothing other than what allows them to live, work, stay together. Their differences are the necessary elements of an education which first aims at the constitution of a common context.

The third essay, the most disturbing, tackles the problem of how the teacher can oppose the negation of a truth beyond time – an attitude particularly present in the twentieth century because of the influence of vitalist and historicist doctrines – when this negation is shared by the pupil. Buber describes, in dialogue form, a dramatic situation in which a young Jew vehemently objects that the Decalogue has no remaining value faced with the necessity of Jewish survival, and the teacher tries to reply to this objection. Certainly, one can remind this pupil that past Jewish generations lived and survived hearing the "you shalt not kill." But the youth could reject such an answer, opposing to a "life in exile," that is to say formed by the commandments, another kind of life, or just "life." So Buber writes: "There is here a conflict – not only between two generations, but between a world several millennia old which has believed in a truth beyond man, and a world which does not believe this any more – it does not want, or cannot believe this."[38] The teacher, according to Buber, cannot lead the pupil towards his position through the demonstration of eternal truths – which are not demonstrable – nor through pointing to them. In fact, it is not only a theoretical position he opposes, but also one which has deep roots in existence. He can only prove those truths by his way of life, awaken the "nostalgia" for the eternal or the longing to be a "person" in his pupil. But, in order to achieve such an aim, first of all it is necessary to invest the "I" with a sense of responsibility: this affection does not express itself in obedience to pre-defined rules, but in the intuition and understanding of one's own path, albeit not without an orientation. Only from existence can the contemplation of the "divine face" spring up. The "community" can be formed only through this attitude of the "I."

Among Buber's contributions to a philosophy of man in society and in his ties with other living beings, there are a reflection on the different situations in which authentic or inauthentic human contacts take place;[39] an analysis of the situation of the individual in modern society;[40] the introductory lecture to his first course of social philosophy at the Hebrew University in Jerusalem;[41] and his account of the various doctrines of man in the history of philosophy up to his times.[42]

In the first of these writings the author first of all evokes those impressions, feelings, and perceptions – of which it is difficult to give a definition – which are the necessary ground of an encounter, exchange of ideas, communication. Sometimes it happens that one awakes in the night in vague distress, and then finds the certainty of a reply which almost "waves in the air"; or one meets an unknown woman or man with whom, however, one establishes a silent agreement; or precisely during a passionate discussion between representatives of different religions, all the members actually build up a sincere and true friendship. There is, according to Buber, an immediacy at the ground of social relationships that only can be pointed to and described: this immediacy cannot be explained by a reduction to other attitudes of the "I," nor exactly defined. We are in this case, in the presence of a phenomenon which characterizes what is human. Second, in this essay, Buber ponders this immediacy: we must distinguish between "to observe" (*Beobachten*), "to consider" (*Betrachten*), and "to be involved" (*Innewerden*). The first verb means to have an objective experience of the world; the second to have a subjective feeling together with this experience, as in art; the third to perceive what is encountered as what interests and concerns. In this case, perception has a peculiar form in respect to the other two perceptions. With this perception the "sign" (*Zeichen*) is associated: the "sign" troubles, exposes, breaks our customs. Although Buber gives the name of "knowledge" to the first two forms of perceiving, he gives the name of "faith" to the third one. So, the "concreteness of the world" opposes the "space and time continuity of the world" which refers to "knowledge": the first suddenly interrupts the second and opens a breach. Perception of the "other" that enters into my life, does not depend on analogic procedures, but on a particular kind of sensitivity. Buber also connects what he characterizes as "faith," and "religiosity" or "religion": every encounter between the "I" and the "Thou" necessarily refers to God. Therefore, "religion" in this sense is nothing else than living with others in daily life in immediacy. God as the unique is pointed out by "signs" which are perceived by the "I" when the "I" has "faith." "Responsibility"or "morality" is essential to "religion": these concepts refer to the concrete engagement of everybody in the world. Ethics without "religion" – Buber observes – only has a relative value because it is in time and history; but "religion" without the immediacy of the "I"–"Thou" relation becomes a dogma and loses vitality and freshness. Finally, in this essay, the author describes some attitudes which do not allow authentic social relationships: self-closure, separation between thinking and living, mysticism, "eros," when it is not unified with respect or "responsibility" for the other, emphasis on the individual – as happens in liberalism – or on society – as happens in movements inspired by the idea of community. It is necessary to call attention to the "relation" to guard against these dangers, which could lead a society to "chaos" or "abysm." This entering into "reality" (*Wirklichkeit*) can also occur, according to Buber, in the complex social organization of modern times. The task of the philosopher who, in his or her life, perceives this extraordinary moment, is to point it out and keep it: "I only try to say that there is something, and to show how it is; I inform."[43] Thus the author concludes his phenomenological account.

The essay on the problem of the individual first of all compares Kierkegaard and Stirner. Buber maintains that the second who destroys the idealistic concept of truth – that is to say universal and objective truth, produced only by reason – opens the path to the first who connects truth and individual existence. There is no longer any separation between living and thinking in Kierkegaard. "There is this human side of the truth: in human existence" – so Buber writes – "God is the truth because He is; the individual is the truth because he finds himself in existence."[44] The believed truth which Kierkegaard looks at, is a truth which should be confirmed, witnessed, realized in the individual's existence, and in this way also communicated. However, according to Buber, there is in Kierkegaard a unilateral emphasis on the relationship between the "I" and God beyond the relationship between the "I" and society, although sometimes in his books "religious" and "moral" are interconnected. This gives Buber occasion to reflect on "theology": this abstract and impersonal science expresses the same loneliness which the idealistic philosopher suffers. Kierkegaard, like the idealistic philosopher, is not interested in those social "relations" which form a community or people. Second, in this essay Buber observes that the individual as such arises only through these "relations." The "moral," if thought together with the "religious," is no longer the field of abstract and impersonal laws, but a region where the individual himself can take his decision in contact with the Absolute and other individuals. In this case, the certainty of moral commandments does not exclude uncertainty, due to the peculiar situation of the individual. The separation between religion and society as a consequence of Kierkegaard's separation between the nexus individual-God and the nexus individual-world is, according to Buber, the most important cause of the separation of ethics from politics. So it happens that ethics, once reduced to the sphere of intentions because ineffective on exteriority, loses all value for concrete human life. Buber considers and criticizes the works of three authors – the first, Oswald Spengler, a philosopher of history, the second, Carl Schmitt, a political philosopher, the third, Friedrich Gogarten, a theologian[45] – which show this extreme dissolution of ethics: they transform man into a being devoid of reason or spirit, dominated by biology, or dependent on his egoistic impulse, or irrational choice. Hence their consideration of history, State or God as the Absolute with regard to the individual, who is unable to be free because affected by his natural violence or bad disposition, and is therefore without dignity or value. Against these theories of his times, Buber defends the Biblical idea of man as an "image of God." Finally, in this essay the author once again points out that "person" and "truth" cannot be conceived as separate. Buber neither follows those philosophies of existence which make truth dependent on the individual, in his peculiar situation, nor those philosophies which identify truth and essence and have no interest in the individual. He tries to take an intermediate position between idealism and existentialism, convinced as he is, that only through their convergence would it be possible to renew the individual and society.

The lecture which opened Buber's academic activity in Jerusalem is important because it deals with a central topic: the dialogue between the social reformist and his ideas on society, and political authority in a historical situation. Buber deals with this topic with regard to the similarity and difference between Plato and the Jewish prophets. He observes how modern sociology, whose founders are, in his opinion, Saint-Simon and Comte, was born on the basis of a will for social regeneration. Although the movements influenced by naturalism and objectivism in the human sciences have tried to transform sociology into a value free science, this criticism of actually existing society was kept in the history of this discipline. The social philosopher should share this attitude: he should formulate a theory of society which should not be grounded on requirements of the "spirit," but on what the entire man – aware of the immediacy of social "relation" before the "spirit" begins to work – requires. Asceticism, necessary to "spirit," does not in fact imply the negation of life. Plato and the prophets show it; both give to their defense of justice the aim of influencing the actions of the political leadership. But, between Plato and the prophets there are also deep differences. So Buber writes:

> The prophetic spirit – unlike Plato – does not aim at a universal and eternal, conceptual truth. It only receives a message for a situation. But precisely for this reason the prophetic word still speaks to the changing situations of the people after millennia. The prophetic spirit does not show a universal image of perfection, a pan- or u-topia, to men. Nor does it have a choice between its own land and another, more "appropriate" land; it is assigned to this *topos*, place, people for realization. [...] Nor can it – unlike the Platonic spirit – retire to calm contemplation, when it feels like somebody in the midst of wild beasts; it must say the message. And this message is not understood, not known, badly used, even strengthens the people in their distrust. But its stimulus remains in the people in every time.[46]

Now – Buber explains at the end of this lecture – the peculiar position of the critical social thinker, is the following: in one way he is not a prophet, but a philosopher, because he does not express a message, but a doctrine, through description and analysis; in another, he is not a philosopher, but a prophet, because he has "faith," is in a particular situation, is attentive to the "here" and "now." He intends to prepare and educate for the future. The impossible will be possible if the spirit works in this sense.[47]

Buber's book on the problem of man develops two main themes: it is a reflection on the reasons giving rise to this problem at certain moments of human history; it is a synthetic review of some answers to this problem from the Greeks to the twentieth century. The question on man – Buber notices – was always asked when man had lost a home in the world, and therefore when a civilization had a crisis or there was a passage from one civilization to another: Plato, Augustine, Pascal, Kant, Hegel, Feuerbach, Marx, Nietzsche, are examples of thinkers who reflected on man. But at the beginning of the twentieth century there are three new elements which introduce a deeper crisis than those man had lived in the past: the rupture of family, economic, traditional religious ties, and, therefore, the reduction of man to an individual without roots and identity; the uncontrolled independence of political power, economic mechanism, and technical development; the conception of time and space no longer absolutely grounded on sensibility, in the theory of relativity, and therefore an idea of man as a being looking at another, supersensible world. Husserl – Buber writes – tried to give a solution to the problem of man in the form it took in his times. Consequently, in his 1935 lectures on the crisis of European sciences and phenomenology, he particularly emphasized the connection between the human being and society, human capacities before or beyond reason, the subjective aspect in philosophy. He thought that if man could bring to light the deep strata of his consciousness, then he also could establish new social relationships, dominate his own culture and find a new position in the cosmos. Buber accepts this Husserlian program of research on man. He did not believe that Max Scheler, or Martin Heidegger, Husserl's disciples, were able to follow his path: the first because, in his meditation on the position of man in the world, he radically opposes "life" and "spirit," although human language itself makes evident their confluence;[48] the second because, in his analysis of human being, he does not describe man in the multilaterality and richness of his faculties, but only a "homunculus," the result of a specific age and situation.[49] Buber believes, instead, that his own "philosophical anthropology," built on the idea of immediate social relationships as the basis of the sciences, arts, and culture, has a Husserlian inspiration. "Trust" (*Vertrauen*) – the affection which permits the event of the "between" or "man with man" – is for Buber an attitude that contemporary societies must nourish. "Trust" is not for Buber a mere feeling, but something which happens in being, and therefore can change social intercourse, and finally the entire social structure.

The writings on Hasidism of this period[50] – unlike those published from the beginning of the twentieth century to the 1920s – deal particularly with social, historical and political matters. The author explains the Hasidic intuition of the role of the individual in his community; he tells how the Hasidim lived the events of the French revolution and Napoleonic wars in their expectations of the Messianic era. He freely expounds Hasidic written documents or oral accounts.

Thus Buber, in his Biblical researches between 1926 and 1945, makes his concept of the "I" more complex and articulate: its distinctive character is longing for the encounter with the "Thou." And in his non-Biblical writings, in the same phase of his activity, he deepens this concept in thinking about society and politics. He also tries to place his teachings in the context of the problems and doctrines of the past and present.

4.5   The problem of evil in the writings 1945–65

If one carefully considers the writings published by Buber after the end of the Second World War, what is evident is their aim of pondering everything that makes it very difficult to realize the "relation" in history and society as the specific a priori of human nature. Certainly, this a priori, according to Buber, is not destructible in man because it does not depend on exterior events, or a psychic and contingent mechanism. This a priori is innate in human beings: not in the sense that it is native in the psycho-physical organism, but as a universal and necessary principle without which it would be impossible to understand social and cultural phenomena. Although it is in embryonic form, there is this a priori at the beginning of civilization; and it is the ground and origin of religion, ethics, and politics as well as of the arts and sciences. However, according to Buber, this a priori could be concealed either immediately by the tendency to rebel against the "I"–"Thou" relationship (a tendency typical of the human heart, although not necessarily and essentially connected with it, unlike the innate a priori); or in a way due to some contingent elements, like forms of life or thought maintained by a specific religion or culture. Certainly, these elements could be seen as the results of such a tendency; but, according to Buber's interpretation, they are more the effects of confusion and disorder than the works of a bad will. These elements are the solipsism of the "I" or the incapacity to think of God as a "person."

Some of Buber's writings of this last period of his life and intellectual evolution refer to the first difficulty in realizing the a priori of the "relation." Therefore, they discuss the problem of the different forms of moral evil – that is to say the evil which implies the negation of the dialogic principle – and the problem of the means of opposing this evil. Other writings refer to the second difficulty. Therefore they describe the events which led modern Western culture, as result of various religious and philosophical influences, to lose what is the essential moment in human existence; or they oppose this to another type of culture.

The interpretation of the chapters 3–4 of Genesis belongs to the first group of writings through the comparison with some old Persian religious texts,[51] along with the exegesis of some Psalms,[52] the drama *Elijah*,[53] and some essays which refer to both the tendency to evil and the disposition to good, that is to say original sociality in human beings.[54] Belonging to the second group are the texts on Western social and political thought,[55] the lectures collected in *Eclipse of God*,[56] the book which offers a description of Judaism and Christianity in history and their situation in modernity, entitled *Two Forms of Faith*,[57] a contribution to psychotherapy,[58] and the last texts on Hasidism.[59]

In the analysis of the chapters 3–4 of Genesis and some myths in the *Avesta* Buber makes a distinction between two types of moral evil: the first arises from the chaos of the passions and is the result not so much of choice as of lack of decision, lack of resistance to the natural egoism of the soul; the second arises from an act of will in which what is formless is concentrated in a direction which then becomes the motor of the action. Both the Bible and the *Avesta* describe these types of evil. But the Bible, according to Buber, gives more emphasis to the first type than the second, and so Genesis attends to evil as it is carried out by the majority of men. The *Avesta*, by contrast, emphasizes the second type more than the first, and so makes evident that evil which is the limit, carried out only by a minority. In both cases, however, the root is the loss of contact between a man and other human beings. But while in the first case the "I" is confused, unsure, and lives between reality and dream, in the second the "I" has a dangerous consistency, although internally split up, and intends to substitute reality with an imaginary world. Buber outlines moral evil, in analyzing both forms through his exegesis, as an element which is not the symmetrical opposite of good. Only because of good can man have a unified personality: this also happens when those inclinations which in themselves are certainly motors for evil, such as hate and aggressiveness, are dominated by "trust" or "faith," and transformed into energies to act well. But the good direction always requires a choice, an understanding which only arises from the heart, an immediate awareness of what is already in the human soul.

Buber's commentary on some Psalms and the drama *Elijah* deal precisely with the choice of good in the presence of evil: the soul which chooses good is aware that the mysteries of the suffering of the just and happiness of the unjust do not contradict holiness, benevolence and divine justice. There are no steps before this choice, nor a profession of faith, nor counsellors for the "I": freedom is the only ground of the encounter between the "I" and the "divine sanctuary" or "voice of subtle silence"; and only from this encounter can the "I" establish peaceful and true "relations" with another "I." Buber's exegesis of the Psalms is "existential": he sees the story of a soul in some Psalms (he reproduces them in a different order from that of the Bible). And this soul from trust arrives at desperation, and from desperation again at trust. The story of Elijah too is represented in the drama as if it were the story of a man who from perplexity arrives at a new certainty, although aware that as a human it is not possible to understand the workings of God on earth. Thus, in these works of his, Buber proposes a solution to the question of theodicy through a "faith" or "trust" in God which does not depend on the world, but gives a meaning to the world, in spite of the obscurity of some events.[60]

In the essays mentioned on the theme of "relation" published in the 1950s and the 1960s, Buber describes how some attitudes inspired by moral evil endanger the possibility of sincere human intercourse; and how there are in human nature itself powerful remedies against these attitudes. The first theme appears in the pages of these essays in which Buber, in dialogue with Sartre and other existentialists, ponders the phenomena of vanity, egocentrism, lack of loyalty and self-closure, which make what he defines as "authentic" human connections impossible. These attitudes are typical of an "I" which considers himself as the centre of being and places all the others in this totality. This theme also appears in those pages of these essays in which Buber explains how in "relations," despite the openness of the "I" and the "Thou," misunderstanding, reticence, or falsity are always possible. The second theme appears where these texts deal with language, art, or human peculiarity with regard to other living beings. Research on these aspects, according to the author, proves – in spite of everything – how the disposition to live in a common world through sincere inter-subjective ties is natural to human beings.[61]

If we consider the second group of Buber's writings of the last period – the group which does not deal with moral evil, but with the forms of religion and culture in a sense inspired by it, and not so much with the original apriority as with the forms of life and culture that this apriority produces – we notice how they discuss topics concerning political philosophy, psychology, and history of religions.

In the book *Paths in Utopia* Buber gives a positive evaluation of that socialism which Marx and Engels called "utopian," and of other "utopian" ideas in the twentieth century; and he proposes to revive the Messianic ideal according to the form and presuppositions affirmed by the Prophets. European history – Buber remarks – has gradually lost the meaning of original Jewish Messianism.The teachings about building a society where freedom and justice could be realized were gradually emptied of their original elements, between the Middle Ages and modernity: no longer living were the religious element, because only man's energy was trusted; the element of faith, because only science was exalted; the element of time, because only the actuation of a new society in a specific space was considered important; the element of love for the other man as a living subjectivity, because more and more only the future was seen as meaningful and the near was seen only as an instrument for the far; the element of social emancipation, because only a minority had to act and to program the transformation of the economic and political structure. The influences in this separation of the social ideal from the intentions and grounds of Jewish Messianism, according to Buber, were on one side Greek thought, for its ideas of image and cosmos, rather than of infinity and time, and on the other Christianity, in which the divinity of man is energetically maintained. Certainly, Buber is sympathetic to "utopian" socialism, which intends to transform society through a change in the social cells rather than to take political power. In his book on "Utopia" he carefully considers those authors of the nineteenth century – Saint-Simon, Fourier, Owen, Proudhon – who thought about, and sometimes realized, social organisms on the basis of equality and solidarity; those figures – Kropotkin or Gustav Landauer – in which the socialist ideal is interlaced with federalism or anarchism; and finally, those socialist experiments which the socialist Zionists built in Palestine from the beginning of the twentieth century onwards. However, Buber thinks that the necessary social change in the capitalist as well as communist countries – out of the crisis after the end of the Second World War – does not need "utopian" socialism, but a call to "trust" in social "relations." The renewal should be realized at the same time in the heart, in spirit or culture, and in society: a change in the intersubjective "relations" could lead to a new economic or political life. This renewal should be grounded precisely on the reappropriation of the fundamental themes of Jewish Messianism.

Buber's essay on the original sense of the Evangelical dictum "to give Caesar what is due to him, and God what is due to Him," entitled *Validity and Limits of the Political Principle*, also makes social and political renewal dependent on the awareness that social and political problems cannot be separated from moral ones, and moral problems from religious ones. In the history of European political thought, especially in modernity – from Hobbes to Heidegger – the State was separated from Transcendence, and introduced only in the fields of nature and history. It is necessary, according to Buber, to reaffirm again the old connection between politics and the field of human relationship with God as the Absolute. Certainly, politics requires compromises and mediations: when one tries to realize moral principles, it is necessary to take account of the situation. But this does not mean negating these principles. Those who agree about these principles, meet in the one truth, in spite of their distance in their economic or social programs. So this essay ends:

> Human truth [...] is nothing else than man's loyalty to the one truth, to that truth that he cannot have, but only serve, his loyalty to the truth of God. In remaining loyal to the truth, so far as he can, he tends to his aim; the aims are different, but the lines towards them meet, if prolonged beyond the aims, in the truth of God, if the path was walked in truth.[62]

In *Eclipse of God* and *Two Forms of Faith* the same project appears, although expounded in two different ways. Both books describe the genesis of a crisis in the contemporary world – a crisis of philosophical thought and culture in the first case, of Jewish and Christian tradition in the second. In both books, the cause of the crisis is identified with the loss of contact with the original perception of God, which also means the loss of contact with other human beings. Philosophy, according to Buber, has not taken account of these original perceptions in its history, because it has mostly followed the Greek orientation, grounded on the autonomy of thinking. It is also true, however, that philosophy has sometimes not ignored this dimension of man – for example in the Platonic idea of the good "beyond essence," in the Kantian formula "you should," in the Spinozian concept of "intellectual love of God," in Hermann Cohen's idea of "religious love." Christianity, for its part, has not emphasized original perceptions of the Other in its history because it was influenced by Hellenism in its concept of faith: this is more *pistis*, that is to say a "belief" in some aspects of being, rather than *emuna*, that is to say "trust" in God and man, according to its Jewish meaning. It is also true, however, that Christianity has not completely denied this Jewish root – especially in those sources which are far from Paul's idea of redemption through faith or *pistis* in the event of the Incarnation. Buber thinks that Judaism too, which originally was the pure expression of perceiving the divine and human "Thou," runs the risk of losing its ground: Judaism sometimes no longer recognizes it. Faced with such a dramatic situation Buber invites us to pay attention to that daily reality which is still untouched – like the simple facts of sincere language, reciprocal engagements, solidarity in suffering. Judaism, precisely because it is very close to this ground, has the task of reviving it and pointing it out through keeping its religious tradition. Certainly, Judaism could only be a source or a basis for philosophy and for Christianity as well; these should have the task, in the future, of communicating originally Jewish contents to all the world. Philosophy and Christianity, through Judaism, could better clarify that original moment of encounter between the "I" and the "Thou" which, although sometimes recognized by them, has almost been forgotten in their history. So they could rediscover that contact with "reality" which they had almost lost – philosophy, because it had exalted the "I" only as the pure subject of science or knowledge; Christianity, because it had celebrated the "I" who finds God in his interiority through knowledge or feeling. Awareness of the "Thou" could lead philosophy to consider the "I" of science as a secondary element, and Christianity to see the "I" of faith in the sense of *pistis* as grounded on *emuna*. Both these "I"s, in fact, had become primary elements after "egoism" had wrought victory over the disposition to "relation." The return of Judaism to its sources and its alliance with Christianity and philosophy could be the means to come out of the crisis.

In the article on the problem of guilt in psychotherapy, Buber remarks that psychotherapists' inability to understand the reasons for the feeling of guilt, and the wish to free the patient from this feeling, are alarming signs of the crisis of society and contemporary culture. This incapacity expresses a crisis in the very concept of moral obligation. It is necessary, then, to go back to the connection between guilt, remorse, atonement, and new life, which in the past was well known not only to religious personalities, but also to writers and poets.[63] It is precisely this connection that is necessary to moral life.

Buber's last investigations and reflections on Hasidism have the goal of opposing the gray West and the lively, fresh, immediate Jewish East. He knows that the Hasidic world cannot be re-established in modern society and culture; but it can be a pointer to them of a way of life where there is, first and fundamentally, what is essential. Certainly, Buber is aware that he idealizes Hasidism; but he thinks it is justified to follow a subjective approach, as he does, in examining a religious or cultural fact. Another approach to Hasidism is possible, one that is grounded on richer documentation than is given in his interpretation and on more impartial research.[64]

Thus, at the end of his intellectual evolution grounded in existence – as the author himself recalled[65] – Buber pointed out the dangers menacing the world after the war. He was also convinced, however, of the impossibility of silencing that force – vital and spiritual – which he had discovered in man during his long life and work: only by means of this force can man, as a finite being, have contact with the Infinite, which is not a substance, but an active personality.

5

LEO STRAUSS (1899–1973)

5.1 Subjectivism as a characteristic of modernity in the book on Spinoza

In 1930, when he published his book *Spinoza's Critique of Religion as Basis of his Biblical Science*, Strauss was already well known in the German Jewish world. He had participated in the activities of the "Lehrhaus" founded by Rosenzweig, published contributions about Zionism, anti-semitism, and modern Judaism in the journal that Buber directed, *Der Jude*, and cooperated in the edition of Moses Mendelssohn's complete works.[1]

About three decades later, in publishing the English version, Strauss clarified the reasons for his interest in the figure and doctrine of Spinoza. And so in a long preface he referred to the historical and cultural situation of Germany in the twenties. He also sketched the main theme and result of the book, and explained why it became the ground for other investigations, only seemingly very remote.[2]

This *Preface* will be quoted again later, because it is one of Strauss' few writings where he says what he thinks directly rather than by interpreting texts, and has therefore a special meaning.[3] It is recounted there that the book on Spinoza was written between 1925 and 1928: in this period, the author remembers, he "found himself in the grip of the theologico-political predicament."[4] In Weimar Germany – as Strauss describes those years – there was a struggle between the defenders of those liberal and democratic institutions which made the political constitution of the Republic close to that of France or England, and the defenders of a tradition, considered typically German, which was grounded on Christian faith, immediate knowledge, or poetic imagination. These defenders found Nietzsche useful as the philosopher who had criticized reason through the exaltation of naturalism and the will to power. Certainly, according to Strauss, it was not as if the supporters of liberal democracy intended to abandon German culture. In fact, unlike the French or English Enlighteners who celebrated reason, which does not accept what it cannot reduce to its criteria, they upheld the balance between faith and reason: German idealism, whose climax was Hegel, had maintained just this ideal of equilibrium and compromise. However, these liberal democrats – led by a logic immanent in their position – were actually followers of a movement of ideas not originally German. Once reason was chosen as the principle of their theses in political philosophy and politics, they could not be tolerant of the concept of faith as the ground of human life and, therefore, human political life. Thus, the defenders of the liberal and democratic institutions of Weimar Germany considered faith as a private sphere, belonging to individual conscience and interiority. They readopted that distinction between "citizen" and "man" which the modern State had introduced; they exalted the equality of all citizens as rational beings before the law, and recognized their differences as men or concrete living beings. In the polemics of this time those who supported theology or faith, convinced as they were of man's incapacity to live in independence and freedom, opposed those who supported politics or reason or man's capacity to be autonomous. Certainly, the conflict could appear as a struggle between the pre-modern and the modern. Strauss recalls, in his *Preface*, how those who defended theology or faith had the aspiration to reestablish Christianity as the public religion recognized by the State, and were nostalgic for medieval works and institutions. But this was only an appearance: behind such aspirations there was the figure of Nietzsche and Nietzscheanism. So Strauss writes:

> All profound German longings – and those for the middle ages were not the only ones nor even the most profound – all these longings for origins or, negatively expressed, all German dissatisfaction with modernity pointed towards a third Reich, for Germany was to be the core even of Nietzsche's Europe ruling the planet.[5]

Therefore, the contrast between faith and reason referred not so much to the relation between the past – when religious feeling was the origin of every aspect of culture – and the present – when reason had become the instrument of scientific knowledge and, consequently, of all human activities, as to the relation between two aspects of the present. The first aspect is the exaltation of natural elements in man: passions, instincts, tendency to acquire power. The second aspect is the celebration of non-natural elements in man: reason, culture, morality. When theology and politics could no longer find a point of contact, these two aspects of modernity began to clash.

In his *Preface* Strauss also deals with the Jewish situation in the Weimar Republic. In the Jews' life and culture – he thinks – there was that same separation of reason from faith and naturalistic elements characterizing the age, but in a more dramatic form. Of course liberal Judaism praised Jewish participation in the modern State, even though aware that this participation had destroyed neither social differences between Jews and non-Jews nor anti-Jewish prejudices. Anyway, to liberal Judaism the pre-modern era was much more sombre than the age of emancipation because in this era public life was identified with Christianity: "The action most characteristic of the middle ages is the Crusades" – Strauss observes in this writing – "It may be said to have culminated not accidentally in the murder of whole Jewish communities."[6] Although medieval anti-semitism, grounded on faith, was still present at that time, it assumed a more dangerous and sinister aspect than ever before in its heir, anti-semitism grounded on naturalistic concepts. But liberal Jews continued to be strenuous defenders of reason: the "Wissenschaft des Judentums," expressing liberal Judaism in the field of culture, born at the beginning of the nineteenth century and still flourishing, founded its investigations into Jewish life, religion and thought on the utilization of rational instruments, such as philology, a critical and impartial reading of the sources and historiography. However, the "Wissenschaft of Judentums" was mostly maintained – as in the nineteenth century – by rabbis who did not intend to abandon their faith. The point of view of faith was, on the contrary, explicitly defended by those Jews who referred to revelation as an immediate encounter between the soul and God because this event was not refuted by scientific rationality: "It was granted by all except the most backward" – so Strauss writes – "that the Jewish faith had not been refuted by science or by history."[7] The author recalls that at that time Cohen was considered the most important representative of liberal Jews because of his defence of Judaism as a "religion of reason," that is to say a religion which scientific and philosophical reason itself produces. Rosenzweig and Buber on the other hand were seen as the modern defenders of faith. However, Cohen was also the philosopher who had defended the existence of a Jewish nationality within the German State; and Rosenzweig and Buber had not renounced the use of rational instruments in their reading of the Bible. Zionism, too, was internally split. In the past Jewish people had found their whole identity in obeying the revealed law. And they had lived almost as a phantasm among the nations for many centuries: Leo Pinsker and Theodore Herzl now invited the people to "self emancipation." But they could not help making an agreement with those who defended revelation and the idea – grounded on revelation – of a promised land in order to ensure the success of political Zionism. On the other side, the religious Zionists were obliged to entrust the realization of Messianic hopes to man rather than to God. Cultural Zionism intended to keep Jewish religious sources and tradition, and had the project of founding a spiritual center – and not a State – in Palestine. Although it considered religion as the Jewish people's work, it contained the conflict between the call to God, implicit in its concern for Jewish religion, and the call to man. Therefore, in German Judaism too, and not only in German society in the first decades of the twentieth century, theology and politics, revelation and reason, faith and knowledge constituted the poles of an antithesis: the oppositions referred not so much to the past of Judaism as to Jewish modernity.

Now, in the context of German and German Jewish culture of the twenties – as Strauss still recalls in his *Preface* – Spinoza represented the origin of all the directions which opposed each other and, just because of this opposition, were also complementary. Certainly, in the German culture, Spinoza's pupils were idealistic philosophers who had built their philosophical systems on reason, like Hegel; but they were also theologians who had identified religious feeling with the "taste for the Infinite," like Schleiermacher. In German Jewish culture Spinoza's pupils were liberal Jews (because Spinoza had defended reason in man), Jewish supporters of a God beyond reason (because in his teachings Spinoza had also underlined God's free choice), and Zionists (because he had emphasized activity in man rather than the passive reception of revelation, and human passions rather than abstract metaphysical principles).

So for the young Strauss, Spinoza assumed the aspect of a central figure in modernity. There were different themes in Spinozian philosophy which modernity had developed. The "theologico-political predicament" found in Spinoza both its centre and its different aspects. If the contents and meanings of his doctrine could be explained, then this "predicament" could be precisely understood: perhaps from this analysis of Spinoza's thought some indications could arise which could give a direction to thought for the future beyond the actual German and German Jewish crisis.

Strauss, in the *Preface* mentioned, also remembers his debt to Cohen as mentor of his book on Spinoza: Cohen was the only one, among the German Jewish intellectuals of his times, who not only dared to criticize Spinoza and his work, but also expressed a moral judgment against them. Cohen paid attention to the *Theologico-political treatise*, instead of *Ethics*, because he thought that Spinoza's criticism of the concept of God's transcendence, defended by the Jewish sources, in the first book was the basis for the identification of justice with necessity in being, present in the second book. Strauss asserts that he had taken from Cohen, at the time of his research on Spinoza, the attitude of detachment towards him and the concern first of all for the *Theologico-political treatise* as well. Strauss also asserts in his *Preface* that he had not shared at that time all aspects of the criticism which Cohen had referred to Spinoza and his theses.[8]

So, the book *Spinoza's Critique of Religion* arose from the consideration that the central problem of the age was the conflict between reason and irrational forces. These forces were partly elements which had been exalted before reason could establish itself in the history of European thought, partly new elements which derived their threatening energy from still deeper strata in human nature. In Germany these two types of elements – the first ones represented in the historical and social field by classes connected with a feudal economy, the second ones by classes connected with an out-of-control capitalist economy – would stipulate an agreement only three years after the publication of the book. They would produce the defeat of liberal democracy and of the philosophical ground on which it had been founded.

The leitmotir of the book is the fundamental conviction that the opposition between faith and reason certainly depends on two different attitudes, but that these attitudes are the results of a free choice. Man can choose between two directions: to trust reason alone, thus assigning only to reason the role of leading knowledge, judgment and action, or to have trust only in God as the giver of a specific revelation. Spinoza, according to Strauss, opposed reason, as man's fundamental force, and what is not reason; he affirmed a principle, chosen and transformed into a norm by him, against another principle, equally legitimate because equally chosen and transformed into a norm. Hence the non-refutability of faith by reason, and of reason by faith. Therefore, Spinoza's Biblical criticism arises from his lack of faith in the holiness of the Biblical text, and can only persuade somebody who already shares this lack of faith. It is not Biblical criticism which led Spinoza to his critique of religion; on the contrary, it is the latter which produces his Biblical criticism. But the believer in a specific revelation, indifferent to Spinoza's philosophical criticism, cannot demonstrate his certainty with regard to the divine inspiration of the authors of the holy books. The rationalist and the believer do not have common ground allowing dialogue, and so they struggle: their points of view are not compatible, or cannot be brought into accord, because they presuppose radically different choices that are not justifiable.

This is a main theme of Strauss' book, and already appears in the *Introduction*: Spinoza, according to Strauss, began the "radical Enlightenment" maintained by Bayle, Voltaire and Reimarus, and is preceded by other authors in his critique of religion. These founded their trust in human reason on different non-rational motives: Epicurus thinks that philosophy, which shows the non-interference of the gods in the human world, is the means to a serene life; Bruno and Machiavelli see the choice of virtue as the strength of the soul at the root of that philosophy which abandons revealed religion; Uriel da Costa and Isaac de la Peyrère place the defence of social peace, human unity, perfectibility and cultural progress at the base of their scientific and historical thought about Biblical tradition. Spinoza, according to Strauss, shares the motives driving these authors to criticize traditional religion in their different milieus, and hence every religion as a sphere where man abandons his autonomy. Spinoza – Strauss claims – develops his criticism in two directions: on one side he contests those who deny man the capacity of knowing and acting by means only of reason, and who therefore follow Scripture or have faith; on the other, he contests those who, rather than being led only by reason in their reflection on being, are led in this reflection by Scripture. So, the first group of adversaries are Jewish orthodoxy and Calvin; the second are Maimonides and his followers. Spinoza defends two positions – only seemingly contradictory, according to Strauss – in his battle against these figures: on one side he makes a radical distinction between theology and philosophy, maintaining that affections and morality belong to theology, and the whole field of knowing the truth to philosophy; on the other, he thinks that only philosophy, which allows man to know the truth, also gives him the true laws of his actions. In fact, Spinoza identifies theology with a non-systematic and non-grounded science, appropriate for human beings not able to be philosophers (for him the majority), and useful only from the social point of view in order to ensure peace and harmony. Hence – as Strauss writes at the end of his *Introduction* – Spinoza's two attitudes towards Scripture: for Spinoza, the holy books are a source of moral teachings, on the grounds of critical thought arising from the holy books themselves; he also criticizes these books, however, through a rational investigation, relying on reason's main theses.

In the chapters of his book where Strauss considers in detail Spinoza's enquiry into Jewish orthodoxy, Maimonides and Calvin, the ineffectiveness of Spinoza's criticism is underlined. He would win his enemies only if he were able to demonstrate that reason – grounded on human longing for autonomy – comprehends the whole of being in all its particulars, including miracles or action derived from a free choice. But reason is incapable of this. Hence the lack of success of Spinoza's enterprise in the *Theologico-political treatise* directed towards freedom from religion. Faith and rationality remain the two forces in the human soul: the first cannot contradict the results of the second, when this operates in the fields of physics or history; nor can the second interfere in the field of the first which is that of the Absolute and individuality.

Thus, the result of Strauss' book on Spinoza was the awareness that in modernity the conflict between raison and faith had no real solution. In the Weimar Republic the conflict paired liberal democrats with pre-modern or Nietzschean thinkers, and humanist philosophers with believers in God and human finiteness. There was, however, a difference between the two parties. Unlike the rationalists, those who fought reason in the name of the irrational were well aware that the ground of their ideas was non-demonstrable and they indicated just this ground in their propaganda. In the diffusion of their doctrines they elevated elements in the human soul which were much more effective than reason detached from passions and feelings. Strauss, in the *Preface* in which he recounts the genesis of his book, sets out this relation between the Spinozist and the anti-Spinozist side: "On the whole – he writes – the Weimar Republic presented the sorry spectacle of justice without a sword or of justice unable to use the sword."[9] Certainly, rationalism and irrationalism met in subjectivism as a characteristic of modernity. But this had a consciousness of itself and an energy towards action which the other did not have.

This fundamental result of *Spinoza's Critique of Religion* – very sad for those who understood how a crisis of German idealism and European rationalism was then incumbent and menacing – was followed however, as Strauss goes on to recount at the end of his *Preface*, by other investigations: precisely because of such a result he was led for one thing to reflect on the concept of reason developed by modern political thought to provide a basis for liberal democracy; for another, to ask the question if the rationalism which appeared as the antithesis of faith, was the only possible rationalism, or if it could allow – alongside itself or as a substitute for itself – a different rationalism.

5.2   The research on the grounds of liberal democracy between 1932 and 1936

In 1932 Strauss published a review of Carl Schmitt's work called *The Concept of Politics*.[10] In this review he shows the roots of the concept of reason as an autonomous force in man. Although in his book on Spinoza he had recognized this concept of reason as what characterizes modern in contrast to medieval civilization, mostly oriented by revelation, the origins of this concept of reason were in Epicurus or in Machiavelli.

Strauss begins his review by clarifying how, contrary to what the author himself thought, Schmitt's theory was not radically opposed to the political theory of modern liberalism. Schmitt, in fact, described his concept of politics, grounded on the conflict between friends and enemies, as antithetical to the liberal concept of politics, on one side dependent on ethics – the sphere of human rights protected by the State – and on the other on economics – the sphere of free market relations of which the State is the guarantor. In fact, according to Strauss, Schmitt and modern liberal political theory both consider a pessimistically evaluated human being as being at the base of society and State: a human being whose aim is self-conservation, that is building his power, security and happiness, and who is violent against all those who menace these tendencies of his. The difference between them consists in the fact that the first considers this egoistic human nature as a means to immediately define the very concept of politics, and the second thinks that this concept needs the prior transformation of the natural man into a social and civil man. For modern, liberal political theory, man transforms himself – as Hobbes teaches, whom Strauss identifies as the first and most rigorous representative of liberalism – in moving from an individual at war with all others to a member of a common body. However, also in this case, there is not a true de-naturalization of man within the civil state: civilization is only an instrument to satisfy natural impulses and needs in human beings in the best way. Reason is only the means to make it possible to realize his natural aspirations to security and happiness. Strauss then, discusses another important point in his examination of Schmitt's thought: it refers to the subjective base which inspires his research on the characteristics of political life. From the Christian vision of man as originally sinful, he takes his idea of human beings as immediately moved by violence and aggression towards others: these are identified by a community as enemies when they organize their social and political life according to different or opposite values from their own. The Christian vision of man is not rationally justifiable. In this case too, there is a similarity between Schmitt and modern liberalism. Certainly, this theory begins with man as a natural being who spontaneously and innocently wants to be the master of the world rather than with corrupt man; and chooses civil man, with values of concord and peace, once given the existence of the State. But this theory too chooses its practical values without demonstrating their truth. Therefore, beyond their different models of humanity, Schmitt and modern liberal doctrine meet in subjectivism.

Thus, in his review of Schmitt's writing Strauss points out the permanence of a naturalistic concept of man in modern liberal theory of civil society, the modern instrumental or anti-metaphysical concept of reason, and modern subjectivistic values. At the end of his review Strauss declares his agreement with Schmitt about the necessity of abandoning modern liberalism; but he thinks that Schmitt has not really superseded this modern political theory. In his review Strauss emphasizes that politics implies public norms and obligations, and therefore an objective concept of justice as principle of the State. It was indispensable and urgent to think about politics according to this old–new form.

Strauss' book on Hobbes, published some years after his dialogue with Schmitt, is dedicated to the detailed examination of just those grounds of modern political thought indicated in this dialogue.[11] In the *Preface*, written in 1936, Strauss points out with great clarity the fundamental point of his research on Hobbes. He intends to dramatically emphasize this point because he considers the political evolution – or involution – of some European countries in the thirties no accident in the context of the history of Western politics from the middle ages to modernity. This point concerns the idea of "natural law." Strauss writes:

> Traditional natural law is primarily and mainly an objective "rule and meas-
> ure," a binding order prior to, and independent of, the human will, while
> modern natural law is, or tends to be, primarily and mainly a series of
> "rights," of subjective claims, originating in the human will.[12]

Because of this fundamental difference between natural law in the past and natural law in the present, Strauss opposes Hobbes, the establisher of "modern political philosophy," and Plato and Aristotle, the establishers of "traditional political philosophy." Therefore, Strauss adds in his *Preface*, the book tries to clarify in particular Hobbes' concept of human life: this concept is the basis of Hobbes' political doctrine beyond the forms – often ambiguous because they are dependent on classical sources or on modern science – in which he expressed his idea of man.

Strauss' book makes explicit all the elements involved in the naturalistic and vitalistic idea of man, which Hobbes maintains in his work: the concept of reason as the means to find a way out of the danger of a violent death, the subjective experience at the roots of this idea, the negation of another world after life and the concept of temporality as the unique dimension of man, distrust as the fundamental attitude of the soul, the view that only history – and not philosophy whose object is the ideal – allows knowledge of man, the emphasis on action, the future, progress, and social relations grounded on art rather than on nature. Strauss also shows how far the Hobbesian idea of man is, not only from the Biblical and classical idea of man, which establishes a connection between humanity and the Absolute, but also from the idea of man maintained in everyday life, where moral distinctions are immediately perceived and recognized. As Strauss writes: "Political philosophy as Hobbes understands it is opposed to pre-scientific morals and politics, i.e. to everyday praise and blame."[13] In Hobbes' philosophy human reason does not refer to that objectivity which appears in daily language: therefore, according to Strauss, this reason is not really a true reason, that is to say the organ of the truth. Hence the necessity – for a political philosophy intending to sustain an objective moral order – to have as the point of reference the common language, that is to say the living morality present in a human community.

In this way, in his book on Hobbes, Strauss outlines the main features of a critique of modern political thought and of a renewal of the pre-modern that he will elaborate in his following work. In this book the pre-modern has simultaneously the form of classical Greece, the Biblical world, and human relations in which the individuals appear as both sensitive and rational beings, and are therefore able to have the intuition of some already given laws. There are, in this book, implicit references to Heidegger and Husserl – the first as the climax of modernity, because his concept of human life deepens the Hobbesian concept; and the second because, by highlighting the world of life, he shows a path out of modernity. These references will be made explicit – as will be seen – in some of the following writings.

5.3 The rationalism of medieval Jewish and Islamic thought in *Philosophy and Law*

The research in the thirties on the principles of Hobbes' political theory developed what had only been indicated in the book on Spinoza, that is to say the necessity of uncovering the roots of the modern State through a reflection on the beginnings of liberal democratic thought. The research on the medieval Jewish and Islamic thinkers, which engaged Strauss in the same years, developed the second indication, that is to say the necessity of finding a rationalism that was not modern in some authors of the past through a new interpretation of their works.

Now, in Western culture between the last decades of the nineteenth century and the first decades of the twentieth, medieval Jewish and Islamic thinkers were regarded as figures who had set an example of dialogue between religious sources and philosophy for Christian scholasticism – and who therefore prefigured the metaphysical systems of the seventeenth century and Hegel;[14] or, through a philological–historical approach, as figures who had been part of the Arabic language civilization that flourished in Spain between the tenth and the thirteenth century.[15]

If, however, these thinkers are considered beyond their traditional reception – as the most innovative philosophical historiography taught in the thirties[16] – do they not seem different from the Christian Scholastics' view of them, who grounded their philosophy on a doctrine of being communicated by holy books? In fact, unlike Scholasticism, they had not developed their philosophy from a doctrine concerning reality, but from the Torah or the Koran, that is to say from the law ruling humanity and particularly the Jewish or Islamic community. The rationalism of the Scholastics, continued by modern metaphysics, through Kant and Hegel, had arrived at Nietzsche because its base was the dogma that reason could embrace the All: at the end of the history of this metaphysics reason had been capable of a self-foundation through an ontological argument whose model had been the Christian idea of the mediator, that is to say the person in whom essence and existence coincide. Instead, the rationalism of Jewish and Islamic medieval thinkers was grounded on a base – the law given to man by God – which always remained external to reason because this base never was completely transformable into simple content or into an object of reason. But just this situation – according to Strauss – was a guarantee for reason. In fact, the self-foundation of reason had dissolved reason itself: reason had shown that at its roots there was a subjective choice – man's decision to trust only in reason – and therefore an irrational element. Instead, the dependence of reason on the revealed law gave reason the possibility of continuous critical work on the law itself, in spite of the persistent tension between law and reason. In his essays on medieval Jewish and Islamic thought, written between 1931 and 1935, Strauss made this second type of rationalism clear. Here too, as in the case of the previous research on Spinoza, he was inspired by a contribution of Cohen, where Maimonides was interpreted in the light of his relation not with Aristotle, but with Plato's *Republic*, with an ethico-political approach.[17]

The book where these essays are collected is called *Philosophy and Law: Contributions for the Understanding of Maimonides and his Forerunners*.[18]

The first essay – chronologically – in this collection, analyzes Maimonides' doctrine of prophecy and its philosophical sources.[19] This doctrine, in the essay, is not considered in all its aspects, but only as a teaching whose aim is the rational examination of the law as the main result of prophecy. Maimonides's doctrine of prophecy, according to Strauss, first of all intends to provide a philosophical foundation for the law. The discussion of this theme is introduced by some remarks which refer to the similarities and differences between modern enlightenment and the "religious enlightenment" of the medieval Jewish and Islamic authors. Certainly, both enlightenments exalt reason as a critical instrument with regard to history and tradition. But, while the first intends to enlighten the whole of society, has a public or exoteric character, celebrates practical reason, and mostly considers itself as a guide for action, the second makes a distinction between those who can acquire wisdom, and those who cannot, has an esoteric character, exalts pure contemplation, and mostly considers itself as a guide for theory. The modern enlightener keeps himself apart from the laws ruling the life of that society of which he is a member, in order to criticize the grounds of these laws. The medieval Jewish or Islamic enlightener remains – as a common man – in the context of a society ruled by laws; certainly, he examines the rationality of these laws, but as a faithful member of his religious community he does not intend to comprehend the Absolute, who is the revealer of the laws, in his philosophical knowledge. This situation could seem somehow paradoxical: the first, who certainly exalts active life, does not consider himself primarily as a part of his community; the second, who certainly celebrates pure contemplation, considers himself first of all as a member of his people. But the paradox has a solution: in the case of the modern enlightener the law is not binding, and therefore autonomous reason has an orientation first of all towards the free field of politics and history; in the case of the medieval enlightener, the law binds, and therefore reason has an orientation first of all towards the Absolute who is the origin of the law and of being. Then, in this essay, Strauss analyzes Maimonides as the most important representative of medieval Jewish enlightenment: "For Maimonides two things are sure – he writes – the first, that revelation is absolutely binding (*verbindlich*); and the second, that in order to be perfect man should absolutely live in theory."[20] The life of the philosopher in his community is tense: on the one hand he obeys the law, on the other he reflects on the law in order to find the truth. However, this life is not irremediably dualistic. Strauss examines in detail the subtle, tortuous, and ambiguous paths of the *Guide of the Perplexed* in dealing with the theme of prophecy: this event is characterized as an encounter between divine action and the prophet who first of all has moral qualities and then imagination and intellect (in the case of Moses, however, only intellect permits the encounter); from this event arises the law which first gives man rules of action, and then the commandments of knowing the law itself and the Revealer of the law. For Maimonides, according to Strauss' interpretation, God first of all has moral qualities or attributes of action: they are manifest in his act of giving the law to men and the Jewish people through the prophet. Second, God is the Creator of the cosmos and man. Strauss also considers the sources of Maimonides' doctrine of prophecy and prophetic faculties. These sources are classic, Hellenistic, and especially Islamic: for example, Plato's *Republic* – which Cohen already mentioned, as above observed – through Arabic mediation, Philo, Al-Farabi, and Ibn Sina.

The second essay in *Philosophy and Law* deals with "The legal foundation of philosophy."[21] The theme is – as the subtitle indicates – philosophy as grounded in the law: on one side the law itself commands us to philosophize, on the other philosophizing, if free from every control, produces the danger of introducing radical doubt about the law and the revelation of the law. The second essay completes the first: in fact, if philosophy understands the law as the result of prophecy – although not completely because autonomous reason is inferior to prophetic capacity moved by

God – and can therefore show the rationality of the law, then the law itself not only allows, but commands those who are good, wise, cautious, and intelligent to philosophize. However, the law also imposes a limit to philosophizing: this cannot enlarge its field to the point of problematizing the divine origin of the law, that is to say the base itself of the activity of reason. Actually, Strauss remarks, all the medieval Jewish and Islamic philosophers derive the obligation of philosophizing from revelation: in this there are rules and teachings which should be elaborated by reason in order to be meaningful and truthful and to be communicable. These philosophers are well aware of the fact that, when the philosopher denies revelation, he destroys not only what allows social relations, but the possibility of philosophizing. Revelation – which first of all is "revealed law," and then includes principles about the being of God, cosmos, and man – is always a "reality" (*Wirklichkeit*), although it can assume two forms: revelation as a present, immediately perceived fact, or revelation as a mediate fact, given by tradition. With regard to this doctrine of the dependence of philosophy on law – like with the transformation of law into an object for philosophy, the topic of the first essay – Strauss refers to Maimonides in particular. For Maimonides activity aiming at knowledge of the law and of God, through the utilization of reason and the rational sciences – mathematics, physics, astronomy, medicine – is commanded by the law and, therefore, by God himself. However, he knows first that to think about revelation could be dangerous for those men who are disposed by their rebellious and undisciplined natures to free themselves from it, and second that to think has inevitable limits faced with revelation. Hence the complexity of the literal text of the *Guide of the Perplexed*: the author makes universally comprehensible some passages of Scripture in explaining some metaphors and meanings of terms; on the other hand, he does not intend to give the truth to those who are not perspicacious, and therefore inclined more to the sensible world than to the intelligible world and to God; moreover, he knows that the intellect and philosophy cannot comprehend the totality of being in all its particularities or the ultimate mysteries such as creation or redemption. Maimonides, according to Strauss, in the context of medieval Jewish philosophy, is perhaps the most famous example of an author who writes in a very sophisticated manner and therefore produces ambiguity, texts having different strata of meanings. This art of writing is not at all a frivolous play or a rhetoric device, but is absolutely necessary because of the different readers for whom these authors compose their works.

These two fundamental essays are completed by two other writings in *Philosophy and Law*. The first has the aim of showing how Jewish and Islamic philosophy of the Middle Ages cannot be understood with modern categories and concepts; the second has the task of making a distinction between the faith–philosophy relation in modernity and the faith–philosophy relation in medieval Jewish and Islamic thinkers.

In the first essay, entitled *The Conflict of Ancients and Moderns in the Philosophy of Judaism*, the polemical objective is the reading and interpretation of medieval Jewish philosophy by Julius Guttmann in his most important book.[22]

The second essay – which forms the *Introduction* to the collected texts – energetically opposes Maimonides' rationalism, which is evaluated as a true rationalism, and modern rationalism, evaluated as an irrationalism. The explicit modern irrationalism which arises together with the supposed rationalism is therefore only another form, and not an enemy, of this rationalism. The supposed modern rationalism is irrationalism, according to Strauss, because after the exclusion of faith from the philosophical field, and the following transformation of faith into absolute belief, it deprives itself of an objective foundation. All that remains of this supposed rationalism is the trust of the subject in his rational faculty, detached from the living reality of language, tradition and custom. Maimonides' rationalism, on the other hand, is a true rationalism because it is grounded on a law in which there are objective social and moral rules (considered as God's words), and because it is critical of the law itself when this appears as contradictory to reason. Faith, in the modern sense, is a subjective attitude: this faith is also fundamental to the activity of reason when reason is made independent from all the other faculties of man. Faith, in Maimonides' sense, is rather the attitude of receiving a law which has a rational part; the law becomes the presupposition of a reason which is only one among all the human faculties.

In the conclusion of his *Introduction* to *Philosophy and Law*, Strauss points out how Maimonides' position characterizes the normal human condition: man cannot renounce his relations with his family and community nor his disposition to reasoning. He thinks that the departure from this human condition, which marked the beginning of modernity, was due to hatred of the obligations of the law. At the beginning Epicureanism – identified by Rabbinic literature as that philosophy which considers man as a being moved only by the pursuit of his happiness[23] – inspired modern political philosophy; but Epicureanism as a secret impulse continues to live throughout the history of this philosophy. According to Strauss, the duty of Judaism – because aware of the true human condition whose concept was maintained by its sources and religious and intellectual tradition – is to show the way back to this condition. Judaism should recuperate the orientation that it had particularly during the Middle Ages when it encountered philosophy. At the end of his *Introduction* Strauss defends an "enlightened Judaism" which could reconcile law and philosophy, as an example of a way of life and thinking that is pre-modern. Only through such a path could humanity evade a situation of open or concealed egoism and violence, a result as much of the rationalistic side of modernity as of the fideistic side.

5.4 The meditation on natural right between 1937 and 1966

Thus, the analysis of the *Theologico-political treatise* expounded in the book published in 1930 had brought Strauss, between 1932 and 1936, to follow two interconnected directions of research: the first, towards reconstructing the genesis of the political theory at the base of the modern State; the second, towards the reconstruction of the peculiar rationalism of medieval Jewish and Islamic philosophy, in order to show the possibility of a political theory grounded on the relation between the religious or traditional life of a people and reason that discovers the necessary and universal elements in this social and political life. The first direction had clarified the self-dissolution of reason when reason loses an external point of reference – public life and speaking which refer to God as the remote source of their objectivity. The second had showed the force of a reason which recognizes its own dependence on revelation: reason itself considers revelation as a living reality in society and history when it identifies with the critical capacity of a human being who is first a member of this reality, and then a philosopher. Modern political philosophy had come to a situation where every point of view – be it rational or fideistic – is finally grounded on a choice of the subject. Pre-modern political philosophy, however, had indicated how there are objective moral and theoretical principles, immanent in law as divine revelation, universally recognized by all human beings as rational beings.

Now, after 1936, Strauss reflects upon the effects that the pre-modern and the modern points of view have on the concept of natural right. Actually, the concept of man as a being able to bring his behavior and knowledge into conformity with objective criteria, with the good and with truth, which medieval Jewish and Islamic thinkers had defended, had been made problematic by the modern concept of man. According to this view, man as living in nature or history is not able to reach absolute norms or principles. Natural right, as the system of rules grounding human coexistence, had been considered by pre-moderns objective because identified with the rational part of divine revelation, that is to say with a supersensible element, independent from time and particular situations. The moderns had transformed natural right into an attribute of man, grounded on his nature or his autonomous, and therefore subjective, reason. In this way, the moderns had made natural right dependent on nature or history.

Between 1937 and 1966 Strauss discusses the problem of natural right in all his writings. The texts of this period expounding the modern concept of natural right have a critical and polemical aspect. The author in these texts criticizes and accuses those whom he considers responsible for the loss of objective morality. The passion which moves this criticism and accusation is not only not concealed, it is explicitly vindicated by Strauss: in fact, he knows that his own point of view has roots in faithfulness to a moral ideal; and he thinks that all men who live in the common world of moral distinctions expressed in religious traditions or language, share this ideal. Instead, the writings of this period dedicated to the question of pre-modern natural right have an analytical and constructive aspect. In these the author shows how pre-modern philosophers certainly affirm the truth of natural right with arguments, but on the ground of the consensus given to a specific law, already established and vigorous.

In 1953 Strauss published *Natural Right and History*, a book which collects lectures given between 1949 and 1953.[24] In this book he describes the path which brought modern philosophy – from Hobbes to Rousseau, Burke, Max Weber's historicism, and Hans Kelsen's positivism – further and further away from the idea of eternal moral truths as pillars of real political life. There is a line connecting Hobbes' idea of man as fundamentally egoistic – and this idea presupposes the destruction of rational theology, incapable of resisting the conjoint attacks of natural science and materialism against its presumptuous wish to give a teleological order to the totality of being – to Rousseau's thesis of natural man as devoid of any social instinct and intelligence, because they are nothing but the results of society. Hence Burke's celebration of historical customs and peculiarities; then Weber's opposition between ethics of pure intention, beyond social and political reality, and ethics of responsibility (as if the moral action of a man who has a "natural comprehension of the world" – Strauss observes – were not accomplished both with pure intention and the awareness of reality!); and finally, Kelsen's idea that there is not any norm, beyond the norms of positive right, which allows the establishment of a legitimate juridical order. In the passage from one to the other phase of the path of modern thought the concept of reason as a faculty which allows man to know an eternal and universal moral order is progressively cancelled. In the eighteenth century, there were still some Enlighteners who could hold onto this knowledge, although they did not keep the idea of divine transcendence, maintained by Biblical religions, and so made this moral order similar to a cosmic order. While describing the decay of ethics as a sphere of absolute principles and a guide for political theory in the history of Western culture, Strauss follows a non chronological order of exposition. His aim is to draw attention to the end result – nihilism – of a philosophical direction which dissolves ethics as data and is finally the distinctive sign of modernity.[25]

In 1958 Strauss published his *Thoughts on Machiavelli*, a book which enlarges a series of lectures held in 1953.[26] It is no longer Hobbes – as it seemed to Strauss in the thirties – but Machiavelli who is now the philosopher who represents the beginning of a modern attitude towards human nature. The author – he writes provocatively in the *Introduction*, if one considers the respect and admiration of some of the most important authors of modern times, such as Spinoza, Hegel, and Marx, Machiavelli's figure and work, and the imposing critical literature dedicated to them – shares "the old-fashioned and simple opinion according to which Machiavelli was a teacher of evil."[27] Strauss also thinks that what are generally recognized as Machiavelli's merits, for example the impartial and objective character of his description of social phenomena and his patriotism, is not blameless, built as it is on the base of his immorality and – given the connection between morality and religion which Strauss maintains – his irreligion. Therefore, one should not be afraid to read Machiavelli according to a point of view which seems naive and devoid of profundity. In fact, to neglect what is at the surface for the sake of what is deep and concealed, does not permit a precise comprehension of events. An example: those researchers who as historians renounce the expression of those immediate moral judgments of figures or events they admit as men because they suppose that in this way they understand history better than those morally engaged in life and social relations; but, for Strauss this supposition is a grave mistake.[28] In the book there is a minute and subtle analysis of Machiavelli's fundamental works *Il Principe* and the *Discorsi sopra la prima Deca dei libri di Tito Livio*. This analysis intends to clarify what is the fundamental point of Machiavelli's doctrine, according to Strauss, and the effects that this point has produced and continues to produce in history. In these works, Machiavelli has elevated to the dignity of political action that behavior which common opinion condemns; has made religion an instrument of politics; has considered the nation – including the Italian nation whose freedom and unification he has forecast – as a mere human society rather than a society grounded on a divine law independent from the authority of political power; while describing only violent or petty human passions, has defined man not in the light of what is superior to man, but inferior to him, that is to say the world of the animals, and especially wild beasts; has thought to substitute the moral code of the peoples who had recognized the Bible as a sacred text, with a new code. In the ancient Roman world, dominated by the ideas of power and conquest, according to Machiavelli, this code had vigor. Machiavelli has emphatically left behind classical culture, inspired by the idea of the existence of divine norms as criteria for humanity, as well as Biblical revelation, grounded on the relationship between man and God; has denied every idea of teleology in history, entrusting human things to *Fortuna* and free choice; and has seen no remaining shadow of a divine presence in the human world, painting man as a miserable, avid creature, terrorized by death or poverty. He has identified a certain form of man with human essence and destiny.

Two currents, which are typical of twentieth-century culture, attract Strauss' attention (and sarcasm) in his review of the different aspects modernity presents: they are philosophical historiography and social science; they are specifically discussed in two essays of his.[29]

The first contribution explains the historicity of the point of view which privileges historical research in philosophy without any reference to a metaphysical sphere. This point of view arises in the last decades of the nineteenth century, although anticipated by philosophers' interest in history during the ages of the Renaissance and Enlightenment. The idea that man lives only in time is an obstacle to understanding those works which their authors considered as eternal replies to eternal questions. Moreover, the concept itself of historicism is problematic: if historicism becomes philosophy, therefore knowledge independent from time, it contradicts its main thesis; if it admits a dialogue between different ages, then it supposes something common or universal in man. A consistent historicism destroys philosophy and condemns every age to solipsism. However, according to Strauss, the historiography of philosophy is important in an age, such as the twentieth century, which has lost cognition of the eternal order of being: through the reading of texts oriented by the idea of such an order, this age will recuperate a different perspective from that maintained by historicism. In this way Strauss justifies his own activity as a historian of philosophy.

The second essay, rather, invites those who investigate social or historical reality to reestablish a nexus between their sciences and common morality. This connection, according to Strauss, was considered obvious when in pre-modern times philosophy was a means to expound aspects of human existence – such as justice or piety – which were referred to an intelligible world or to God. In the seventeenth century this was still the case. Social science – says Strauss – should be founded on human knowledge of "what constitutes humanity," what makes man "complete," "whole," "truly human": founded, then, as "common sense" perceives, on "human kindness," "the betterment and opening of one's mind," a blend of "firm delicacy and hard won serenity."[30] Social science should abandon any "relativism" that hinders the immediate recognition of universal ethics or natural law: actually, this science itself never completely abandons this universalism. Heidegger is explicitly examined by Strauss – in the context of his struggle against those modern philosophical trends which deny metaphysics or absolute values, characteristic of this phase of his thought – in an essay which reproduces a lecture held at the beginning of the 1950s,[31] and in the *Preface* to the English edition of his book on Spinoza.[32]

Strauss recognizes Heidegger's philosophical originality and profundity, which he judges as superior to those of Cassirer,[33] Rosenzweig,[34] or Buber,[35] all superior to him however from the point of view of their defence of the disinterested sociality in man. He thinks that precisely in Heidegger's *Sein und Zeit* the modern negation of a universal ethics or natural right finds its most radical and clear expression. According to Strauss, Heidegger's criticism of reason which the Enlightenment and idealism consider the origin of civilization, is justified and reaches the objective: Heideggerian doctrine irrefutably shows how the root of pure reason lies in existence. However, in this doctrine reason becomes only a function or instrument to attain the subjective goals of individual existences. In *Sein und Zeit*, philosophy itself becomes only a function of the existence of the thinker, a *Weltanschauung*. Heidegger's description of human life does not have man's real social life as a point of reference; rather it expounds the loneliness, the closedness, finally the status of a man who belongs to a specific age, unhappy and devoid of any confidence. However, Strauss observes that after *Sein und Zeit*, Heidegger indicates a different direction for thinking from that which reduces being to the dimension of temporality: in Heidegger's last writings the longing for the eternal, transcendent, supersensible arises again with energy and intensity. On the one side, Strauss agrees with this Heideggerian quest, and he also shows how near this quest is to the metaphysical tendency of rational theology. On the other, he does not accept the concept of being proposed by Heidegger in his last writings: he points out how being, maintained by the late Heidegger, keeps deep ties with temporality, in spite of its appearance of identity with an eternal and divine sphere, because first of all this being is absolutely independent from creation, and second it has a mysterious and quasi-pagan aspect. Strauss connects Heidegger's late thought to myth: it seems to Strauss impossible to build political philosophy on this ground, which requires anchorage to universally valid laws.

Thus, in this stage of his thought, the author expresses his criticism of the evolution of modern thought: this thought first affirms the subjective natural right of individuals in contrast with the idea of natural right as an objective norm dependent on a transcendent reality; and then this thought also cancels subjective natural right because of the impossibility of defining human essence and the reduction of human being to existence.

Besides this criticism, Strauss clarifies the concept of natural right in pre-modern authors and texts. Between 1937 and 1966, he partly continues to develop his analysis of works of medieval Jewish and Islamic thinkers: through an ethico-political approach he reads them as defenders of divine law which, immanent in the revelation they profess, is clarified by reason. In this period he also analyzes the peculiar, enigmatic or equivocal ways they have of writing: this art of writing depends on their complex position in relation to religious tradition – accepted but also carefully discriminated.[36] Partly he discovers this same nexus – between the affection for a religious and moral legacy and philosophical critique – in some authors of the seventeenth and eighteenth century like Lessing and Spinoza himself (now no more considered, as in the book on him, the first of the moderns, but the last of the medievals).[37] Partly he finds in the figures and thoughts of Socrates and Plato the same type of attitude – divided between obedience to the laws of the *polis*, political myth, or ancient religion, and the rational critique of these very objects.[38]

In all the authors who are considered in this second group of writings – beyond the different ages in which they lived, and the different divine revelations to which they referred in their philosophies – Strauss finds a common orientation which he qualifies as "theo-political." Despite their deep differences, these authors share a common idea: they were deeply aware of the fact that man has a complicated and problematic nature, divided between respect for the fathers and the need to think, his belonging to a situation (also constituting the hard side of his existence) and his freedom (what exalts him beyond necessity), between the law and the rational application of the law in particular cases. Natural right is the result of the tension between these aspects of human nature. In the *Preface* to his book on Spinoza, after he has remembered how theology and politics opposed each other in his reading of Spinoza's *Theologico-political treatise*, Strauss explains how both elements characterize man. Therefore, that Jew who in his own personality and thinking divides himself between the memory of the Torah and an active life in the world, obedience to commandments and rules, and reflection and criticism on them, could be seen almost as the symbol or example of the human condition.[39]

5.5   The antithesis "Jerusalem"–"Athens," or fidelity–pride, in the last writings

In some contributions, written between 1967 and 1972, Strauss draws attention to the difficulty of establishing a tie precisely between those human directions – obedience and freedom, solidarity and loneliness – which from the 1930s onwards he had considered necessary, in order to avoid both an orthodoxy absolutely untouched by any light and a cold rationalism, destructive of social life. It now seems that it is almost impossible to make a connection between reverent listening to the words of the fathers concerning ethics and religion and rational research about the universal truth of these words, albeit inexhaustible. From the 1930s, the author had shown how there are both tendencies – the one towards the past, the other towards the eternal – as much in Greek culture as in Jewish religion: man's "heart" moves in the first direction because he is only a member of the chain of generations whose origin is God, the revealer of the law, therefore beyond being; man's "head" moves in the second direction because he isolates himself from time to reflect on the Absolute, although this Absolute as creator is only partially comprehensible to him. In both Greek culture and Jewish religion there are equally the concept of the divine character of the law – what makes the law holy, venerable, beyond any rational research – and the concept of reason as an essential capacity, a divine force in man, although finite. But, in some writings of the last phase of his activity, Strauss gives the name "Jerusalem" to that human disposition which consists in fidelity to the past, obedience to parents and humility in listening to divine commandments, and the name of "Athens" to that human disposition which consists in free research, the pride of independence and longing to know the divine and eternal.

In a lecture of 1967, the author ceases to underline the continuity, in spite of difference, between these two natural human attitudes: he shows their origins in two types of source, two types of civilization, two types of history evoked by the names of these towns.[40] "Jerusalem" – so Strauss explains – indicates the fear of God as the beginning of wisdom, prophecy as the means of contact between man and God, God as a person who enters into human history, the creation of the world and man, hope in the realization of God's kingdom. "Athens," by contrast, indicates astonishment as the beginning of wisdom, philosophy as the means to reach God, God as an impersonal idea, the eternity of the world, human action as the means of realization of political ideals. Therefore, love of God and knowledge of God, revealed wisdom and human wisdom, religion and philosophy radically oppose each other. Strauss quotes in this lecture the last lecture Cohen gave before his death, about Plato and the Prophets,[41] in order to remind us how the Prophetic attitude, concerning the realization of the Messianic ideas of human unification and peace, is very different from the Platonic one: Plato on one side accepts the particularism of the *polis* and war, and on the other maintains a methodical knowledge of being – first of all the being of nature, and then the being of morality. Unlike Cohen, however, Strauss thinks that Socrates, before Plato, is the figure who begins the Western philosophical tradition because of his investigation into the concepts and meanings of words. If the Jewish world looks at the Messianic future, the Greek world looks at cyclical time: this time is the reflex of that eternal truth of the intelligible world which science and philosophy permit us to reach and know.

In an essay, published in 1971 and entitled *Philosophy as Rigorous Science and Political Philosophy*, the conflict "Jerusalem"–"Athens" assumes the aspect of a struggle between the sphere of the *Weltanschauungen* – that is to say religious traditions, customs, forms of life in different civilizations – and the sphere of philosophy, where only reason has power.[42] While the *Weltanschauung* expresses that side of human nature which consists in its existence in time and history, philosophy means that side which consists in its longing for the eternal present or Absolute. The model for the first side is given by those who live according to the commandments of religious revelation; the model for the second by those who live in science, contemplation, or pure theory. In opposing the *Weltanschauung*, which man as a living and historical being professes, and philosophy, solely founded on human reason, Strauss is inspired by Husserl.[43] Certainly, Strauss thinks that one should not introduce a rupture between the first and the second aspect of human beings, as Husserl does, when he denies that a researcher is able simultaneously to offer analyses of historical situations and forms of "life" – which have only a relative value – and rigorous and scientific analyzes of pure "essences." In fact, if this were the case, political philosophy as a doctrine placed between myth and science, existence and universality, could not subsist. Husserl himself, who invites philosophy to pay attention to the most profound strata of consciousness, requires a thinking not detached from the concrete and actual world.[44] However, in following Husserl, at the end of this essay, Strauss only says that in human history there are two opposite ways of seeing the world – the way of the man who obeys religious and political authority, and the way of the man who is a free thinker and recognizes only rational principles and rules against this authority. Philosophical ethics requires the second attitude.

Strauss' *Introduction* to the English edition to Cohen's book *Religion of Reason out of the Sources of Judaism*, published one year before his death, also deals with both contrasting directions of religion and philosophy. It seems to Strauss that in this Cohenian work these directions do not have common ground, a space for cooperation. If religion drives Cohen to return to the sources of Judaism, philosophy drives him to use pure scientific reason. The two paths are parallel or, should they try to interlace, contradict each other because the first presupposes a fact not reducible to reason, and the second the complete idealization of the fact by means of the philosophical method.[45] So Strauss who in the earlier years had considered the need for philosophy to be built on the moral and religious traditions – expressed in daily language – of a living community, seems to have second thoughts at the end of his career. He seems to propose again the very same discordance between faith and reason, theology and philosophy which from the beginning of his reflection he had tried to supersede. Did he want to draw attention to the difficulty of his previous solution to the problem of nihilism produced by modernity? Was this solution no longer attainable by humanity in the last decades of the twentieth century?

Certainly Strauss, who as a young man had abandoned orthodox Judaism, thinks that only human action can produce effects in history. Still, Strauss – until his last years faithful to his community and a careful reader of the sources of his religion – says once that a non-believing Jew should also have trust in the Absolute, although beyond his reason, when he sees a non-redeemed world and is not sure of the human capacity to redeem it.[46] The late Strauss is a supremely ambiguous thinker who does not intend so much to give answers as to raise doubts and questions.

6

EMMANUEL LÉVINAS (1906–95)

6.1   The first contributions: beyond consciousness, existence, and the existent

The writings which Lévinas published between 1929 and 1949 could be seen as steps on a path starting with his adherence to Husserlian phenomenology (interpreted, however, according to Heidegger's approach) and ending with his attention to the theme of the Other (the Other as the other human being and also the Other than being because of his return to Plato's notion of the Good beyond essence). Lévinas expounds this theme of the Other, as we shall see, by means of a phenomenological analysis, but in such a way as to proceed beyond the field of Husserl's and Heidegger's phenomenologies.[1] Lévinas' writings of this period deal first of all with the problem of consciousness as the place where being appears in Husserl, then with the theme of existence as the place where being appears in Heidegger, and finally with the concept of the existent; this concept will be determined first of all in itself, that is, as an element which detaches itself from existence, and then, and above all, as an "I" who, in sociality, enters into a relationship with the Other.

In 1930 – after he helped diffuse knowledge of the philosophical movement which Husserl introduced to Germany, and of Husserl's works, with some articles, remarkable for their freshness and brilliance[2] – Lévinas published a book on Husserl's theory of intuition.[3] In this book he premises two considerations to his subtle analysis of the Husserlian texts published until then.[4] The first remark is that he wants to introduce Husserl's philosophy as a "living philosophy." Although references to Descartes, Kant and Bergson are found in this book, his aim is not so much to explain the link between this philosophy and other philosophies, or to make known specific areas of Husserlian research, for example, in logic or mathematics; rather, his aim is to understand the primary and original motif which characterizes this philosophy and therefore to place himself in the center of its becoming and development: one should comprehend Husserl's phenomenology not so much as a doctrine as a thought *in fieri*, paying attention not so much to its results as to its peculiar style. The second remark is that Heidegger's work *Being and Time*, published in 1927, helped him to catch this motif of Husserlian thinking. Thus Lévinas expresses this second point in the

Introduction to his *Theory of Intuition*:

> Heidegger's philosophy, so powerful and original, separates itself from
> Husserl's phenomenology in many aspects; but this philosophy is also, in
> a sense, no other than a continuation of Husserl's phenomenology. It seems
> to me – because of the spirit of my work which consists in taking into con-
> sideration the inspiration of Husserl's system rather than its history – that
> I am allowed to use the work of the Husserlians.[5]

The fundamental point of the Husserlian teachings which the author brings out in
his book is the concept of consciousness. According to Lévinas, Husserl emphasizes
the concreteness and multilateral quality of consciousness, and considers it as an
absolute and necessary existence – not in an empirical sense, but because it is given
with being itself: consciousness is at the roots of being considered as a whole, before
regional ontologies are built, it is immanent in living human beings as particular
"egos," and has intuition as the main feature of its life, no less when it becomes a
philosophical consciousness. Lévinas clarifies this point, which he considers the center of Husserl's thinking, through the explanation of certain themes. He observes that
the beginning of Husserl's meditation is the question of being, which he asks before
the question about particular or regional beings, and that this philosopher comes to
consciousness only in order to resolve the question of being: while determining the
concept and meaning of being, Husserl criticizes both naturalism and psychologism,
because the first identifies being with the world given by natural science, without
asking how natural science itself forms, and the second – in a similar way – examines
consciousness as a part of a nature whose principles and concepts it does not previously consider. Moreover, Lévinas notices how in Husserlian phenomenology consciousness – as an intentionality which is not only theoretical, practical and affective,
but also has other possibilities – has an absolute existence, that is, represents the universal and necessary moment within the empirical existence of individual consciousness. Consciousness, as an absolute existence, refers to a being which should not be
seen as its result or its correlative term; rather, this being coincides with consciousness' being itself because the division between subject and object is only the product
of a later abstraction. Lévinas remarks how intuition, as the only act which gives a
specific form to an object – even though this form can be different according to the
different sides of human experience – is for Husserl the introduction to being. Thus,
being has different strata of meaning. Intuition is also for this philosopher the
organon which allows philosophy to determine its object. And this object is no other
than the living flux of consciousness itself: intuition is able to make evident the
essences which are in this flux in a way which is not empirical or descriptive,
but ideal or universal: in fact, intuition itself is a kind of ideation or idealization.
Thus Lévinas clarifies these aspects of Husserl's phenomenology which he considers
as the most interesting and original with regard to previous philosophies: "The fundamental intuition of Husserl's philosophy is on one side the attribution of absolute
existence to concrete conscious life and, on the other, the transformation of the very

notion of conscious life."[6] "Conscious life [is] a life in the presence of transcendent being."[7] "Consciousness is at the roots of every being, which has a form through the intrinsic sense of consciousness itself."[8] "To exist does not mean for consciousness to be perceived in a series of subjective phenomena, but to be continuously present to itself – what the term consciousness itself expresses."[9] "Being is consciousness itself as it flows in all the richness of its details and sinousness."[10] "Only consciousness is able to make intelligible to us the meaning (*signification*) of the world's being – which is a certain way of meeting consciousness, of appearing in it."[11] "Existence is nothing other than the way consciousness meets its object, the rôle which this plays in the concrete life of consciousness, because it is in life that one finds the actual source of being."[12] And furthermore: "Phenomenological reflection is an intuitive look at life in all the fullness of its concrete forms, is an attempt to comprehend life, and from here to comprehend the world, its intentional object."[13] "In the reflection on consciousness, as in the direct intuition of the world, ideation is possible."[14] Thus, Husserl's phenomenology is for Lévinas, the living science of that living reality which is consciousness as the totality of human intuitions, as the connective element of consciousness of empirical individuals. Being can be enlightened only through this pure consciousness.

Now, Lévinas knows that in this interpretation of Husserlian phenomenology, influenced as it is by Heidegger, he goes in a direction which brings him very far from what he himself calls the primacy of knowledge, representation or contemplation in Husserl. It is exactly this primacy, connecting Husserl with previous philosophy, that stops Husserl catching the relation between the life of consciousness at the roots of being and the world of values or tools, beyond the world of things or objects; that drives him to suppose that consciousness without the world would be possible, that is, an intuition before it is filled with objective content – as idealism supposes, when it completely resolves being into the subject instead of considering the subject as indissolubly connected with being; that leads him to underline the intellectual aspect of intuition, that is, the objective knowledge of the world; and drives him to a *salto mortale* from life towards theory when he emphasizes the necessary connection between pure consciousness and being. So in his book Lévinas explains this last difficulty in Husserl:

> This reflection on life is too separate from life itself, and one does not see its connections with the destiny and the metaphysical essence of man. It seems that man whose natural attitude is not a mere contemplative attitude, whose world is not solely an object of scientific investigation – [...] abruptly realizes the phenomenological reduction, in the passage to reflection on life, a pure theoretical act; there is here an overturn that has no explanation in Husserl, and forms no problem. The metaphysical question of the situation of *homo philosophus* is not asked by Husserl at all.[15]

Nevertheless, Lévinas does not think that in his interpretation of Husserl's philosophy through Heidegger's reception of his teacher's phenomenological method – he has betrayed the spirit of this philosophy. On the contrary, it seems to him that he has clarified meaningful aspects which could eventually be developed.

It is, however, exactly to the problem of life, and of the passage from life to theory in Husserl's phenomenology, that Lévinas turns to after 1930: certainly, if empirical consciousness is understood only as a life in which pure consciousness is immanent, if existence is identified with the presence of consciousness as the intuitive ground for being, then this passage is not obscure at all. In fact, in life itself there is the moment of theory as the truth of life. If, however, one ponders life in itself – its flow-ing in time and history, that is to say its finitude – then the link between life and philosophy becomes problematic: philosophy itself, in this case, seems to assume a *status* different from that which Husserl gives it when he defines philosophy as the science of intuitions. Therefore, it is the concept of "existence" which one must reflect on, in order to show that it necessarily contains much more than Husserl discovers in it.

Heidegger showed the way to Lévinas for this concept. In the conclusion of the book on Husserl the author explains how for Husserl theory is independent from man's historical situation. But, are not temporality and historicity the substance itself of the human condition? Heidegger had asked precisely this question: he investigates the relation between historicity and the intentionality of consciousness. Thus, it is necessary to solve the problem of existence: this is where the phenomenological analysis, if seen as inspired by the argument of being, finally comes into its own. The essay published by Lévinas in 1932, whose title is *Martin Heidegger and Ontology*,[16] can be considered as the answer to the perplexity expressed by the author in the book on Husserl with regard to the Husserlian concept of life, which is too quickly reduced to a simple support of intellectual or ideational activity. Lévinas finds this answer in *Being and Time*. Existence as temporality is for Heidegger – so the author writes in this essay – where being acquires a sense, forms, and ends: existence is neither abandoned, when one looks at being, nor transcended by an act which originates in existence itself, as Husserl thought. Heidegger criticizes his teacher on precisely these points of his meditation.

Lévinas emphasizes at the beginning of this essay the fact that there is a profound continuity between Heidegger and the philosophical tradition. Like both Plato and Hegel, Heidegger considers as the object of his philosophy the connection between the truth of being and the subject – that is, ontology, which is for him, however, no longer grounded in man as a thinking being or provided with different spiritual functions. Rather – as Lévinas writes – "the comprehension of being is the charac-teristic and the fundamental fact of human existence."[17] Heidegger makes a distinc-tion between what is (*étant: das Seiende*), and the being (*être: Sein*) of what is, or entity: the being of entities – and not entities – is first of all accessible to human existence. Therefore, it is not consciousness – as separated and isolated from existence – but existence itself which is the ground for the comprehension of being: as Heidegger reduces consciousness to existence, so – Lévinas comments – he reduces human essence to human existence. In his "existential" (*existentiale: Existenziale*) analysis of existence (*Dasein*), which deals with the forms in which existence as the "fundamental event of being"[18] is open to the being of entities – different from the "existentive" (*existentielle: Existentielle*) analysis which ignores this openness – it comes out that time is the fundamental form of human *Dasein*. Hence Lévinas reviews the most important concepts of *Being and Time* through which the being of human existence is determined: care (*souci: Sorge*), to be in the world, finitude, the usability of instruments (*maniement: Zuhandenheit*), public life (*Oeffentlichkeit*), the condition of being thrown (*déreliction: Geworfenheit*), destiny (*destinée: Geschick*)...Lévinas remarks that all those elements which seem supratemporal are reduced to existence and time in Heidegger's thought: even the phenomenon of moral consciousness (*Gewissen*) is no longer an event which shows the connection between the sensible and the supersensible, but only a call within *Dasein* when it perceives its deep finitude. And – what Lévinas particularly emphasizes – in this manner philosophy itself acquires a status very different from that it had in the past: philosophy is no longer contemplation or theory, but one of the possibilities of a finite life. "*Dasein*" – so Lévinas expresses this Heideggerian theme – "is essentially fallen, and philosophy, as a finite possibility, starts from everyday life."[19] Whereas previous philosophies had underlined the separation between knowledge and the fact which knowledge refers to, Heidegger does not make any distinction between knowledge and the fact in which knowledge itself is involved: he substitutes a philosophy which allows the human being to escape its finitude, with a philosophy which makes man conscious of his own temporality, in an "anxious care." This philosophy is therefore not able to supersede time.

Thus Lévinas – clear and skillful – describes Heidegger's principal work in his essay of 1932: he points out its originality within the history of philosophy because of its problems concerning the relation between being and existence. He does not introduce any comment in his exposition of Heideggerian philosophy – one of the first writings on Heidegger and the phenomenological movement in French culture at that time.[20] Lévinas' laudatory mood when he shows how lucidly Heidegger analyses human existence's forms of comprehending being – among which the presentiment of death is the most important approach – gives the reader the impression that he shares Heideggerian feelings and perspectives.

The year 1933 was a turning point in the evolution of Lévinas' thought. After this date the philosopher again took up the theme of the infinite in human life as a central subject of his investigation: this theme was described in different ways in his subsequent writings.

In 1934 Lévinas published in "Esprit" an article which he ambiguously entitled *Some Reflections on the Philosophy of Hitlerism*.[21] In fact, on one side, the author shows how it is possible to describe the main characters of a philosophy which arises from Hitler's and the Hitlerians' peculiar being in the world, if one considers philosophy as a human project, a conceptual position grounded on a peculiar human form or way of life in history. On the other side, the author underlines how the concepts of Heidegger's philosophy (which he however does not mention) have affinities and correspondences with those concepts which are typical of Hitler's and the Hitlerians' intuition of the world. In this second sense, the philosophy of Hitlerism is a development of the philosophy of Heidegger. Now Lévinas no longer shares the idea of philosophy as a conceptual manifestation of how man lives in time, according to a certain choice – the idea he brought out in the conclusion of his essay of 1932. He adheres instead to the notion of philosophy which was affirmed in the history of Western philosophy, that is, as the result of a spirit in human beings which is independent from time, nature and history because it looks at a "beyond" them, at a pure ideal world. Nevertheless – as the article shows – he does not intend simply to reappropriate a tradition whose frailty and weakness he sees when attacked by its enemies: rather, he intends to renew, to re-elaborate this tradition. Lévinas explains not so much the doctrines as the fundamental principle of the history of Western culture, and he insists on the necessity of an obstinate and uncompromising defence of this principle against the attitudes and ideas which endanger it. This principle is human freedom, that is, the fact that human beings are not dependent on history, destiny, fate, or natural causes, but absolutely free when they choose to make their behavior correspond to ideas and laws belonging to a pure intelligible sphere. This is the reason which makes this text on the "philosophy of Hitlerism" a passionate defence of Western humanism as it was expressed, according to Lévinas, by Judaism, Christianity, Greek philosophy (when it opposed myth and Greek tragedy), the Renaissance, the Enlightenment, and idealism, up to those materialistic currents and that Marxism which – in spite of their emphasis on natural and economic determinism – had nevertheless recognized and honored free human action oriented by ideals of justice and peace. Lévinas calls on all the different forces present in Western culture for an implacable fight against Hitler, nevertheless knowing that the principle of freedom, defended by this culture, urgently needs a new foundation: in this new garb it could become the main idea of a new way of thinking beyond the perspectives generally maintained by the religious and philosophical movements of the past.

Particularly in his essay of 1934, Lévinas analyzes some experiences in which the human being seems "crushed" or "smashed" (rivé), and no more able to have a spiritual attitude. He shows how the Heideggerian concept of "being thrown" into the world becomes more radical, faced by the rise of the most elementary – and also destructive and autodestructive – forces in human beings, such as the will for power or hate against any moral rule. For example, he analyzes the experience of deep bodily suffering which does not allow a human being any other feeling or perception; the experience of being reduced to the status of members of a community unified only through blood; or the experience of brutal violence against the body without the possibility of defence or reaction. In all these cases, the "biological" substitutes the "spiritual." Because of this substitution, one could perhaps say that freedom is understood solely as the recognition of fate: but, as for this conception human beings remain determined by existence and thinking is only an expression of existence, in fact freedom is completely annulled. Certainly, with regard to the freedom of Western civilization which often becomes only a subjective choice – when freedom is independent from any universal ground or justification – the attitude which consists in abandoning freedom could seem serious, corresponding to the hardness of reality, authentic. In fact – as Lévinas foresees – this attitude will necessarily bring about the conquest of, aggression against, and the destruction of everything which attempts to escape from it because still animated by a breath, however minimal, of spirit. Therefore – thus Lévinas concludes dramatically, perfectly justified by contemporary times – racism is much more than a single doctrine which opposes Western culture grounded on freedom; it is rather a mortal danger for this culture: "What is at stake is not this or that dogma of democracy, parliamentarism, dictatorial regime or religious policy; it is the humanity itself of human beings."[22]

Lévinas' essay of 1935, *On Evasion*,[23] can be read as continuing the thinking of the previous text on the "philosophy of Hitlerism." Lévinas focuses two themes in this essay: the first is the identity between a philosophy which places man only in the context of time, natural necessity and economic and social relations, and a philosophy which certainly considers man as a free being, fighting against mechanism and determinism, but perceiving him as an "ego" without anxiety or divisions, at peace with himself, and grounded in himself, and therefore under that form of being typical of the being of reality, nature, or the world. The second is the theme of evasion: human beings long for evasion when they confront not only oppressive natural or social being, but also the eternal being of an ideal when comprehended as fixed, immutable, or motionless.

In expounding the first theme, the author clarifies how man in the philosophy of the past – Western wisdom from the Greeks up to modern idealism – certainly opposes the world, but never really opposes himself. He is not lacerated or tormented: the struggles which he fights either with himself or what appears alien to him always end in going back to the identity of the "ego." "He deals with business or science" – Lévinas writes – "as a defence against things and the unforeseen which things hide."[24] The secret impulse moving this "self" who after every struggle wishes to rest, to return to himself, is the desire for security, a quiet and satisfied appropriation of being. To be self-sufficient, this is the concept which defines such a form of the "ego": "This category of sufficiency is conceived according to the image of being as things offer it: things are."[25] This is the point shared by both Western philosophy – which "never went beyond,"[26] – and that philosophy which is resigned to cancel any sign of independence of the "self" with regard to the world, and therefore to shatter the "self" under the load of being. In both cases one affirms ontologism.

The second theme is presented through an analysis – inspired by past and present literature, but also attentive to everyday experience – of the different ways in which being can be evaded. In the past – Lévinas remarks – evasion assumed the form of asceticism, criticism of social conventions, and poetry against the prose of the world, but it did not take on the form of a radical negation of being; in modernity however "evasion is the need of an exit from themselves, of breaking the strongest and the least dissolvable chain, the fact that the 'I' is a 'self', an identity."[27] In this case, the "I" does not wish to become infinite in the universal, while breaking all the limits which connect it to finitude; the "I" wants instead to unfasten every bond with its own being, its own identity and substance. In a subtle way in his essay, Lévinas analyzes two forms of evasion from being, erotic pleasure and nausea: neither the first nor the second form really get what they aspire to, because erotic pleasure returns to being in the moment of shame, that is to say when the "ego" again closes in on its own "self"; and nausea, after the lightening of being – in a literal sense – caused by it, is inevitably followed by the permanence of the "I" in being. Therefore, in life as in the field of thinking, one should find a third path between the necessary being of the world and the being of the infinite, a type of evasion for the "I" different from both forms of eroticism and nausea, a real way out of being in all its aspects and forms.

In the conclusion of *On Evasion*, the idea of transcendence is outlined through the allusion to the concept of the Creator. Lévinas says that in his attempt "to exit from being in a new way," "at risk of overturning certain notions which seem most evident to common sense or to the wisdom of nations,"[28] he only intends to give new force to that impulse which inspires idealism beyond its real history:

> In the aspirations of idealism, if not in its practice – he writes – is found, without doubt, the value of European civilization. In its first inspiration idealism tries to supersede being. Every civilisation which accepts being, the tragic desperation which it involves, and the crimes which it justifies, deserves the name of barbarian.[29]

Defending the West's freedom requires the effort of discovering a new path – or of re-discovering an old and original path, now forgotten.

After 1935 Lévinas comes back to Husserl and Heidegger in a manner reflecting the point of view he had reached after 1932: after this year he is aware of the similarity between Heidegger's thought and the intuition of the world defended by Hitler and his followers, and of the connection between the problem of being and the "egoistic" concept of the subject in Western philosophy.

In the essay on Husserl published in 1940[30] an important argument is focussed: Husserl, according to Lévinas' interpretation in this essay, has renovated Descartes' and Kant's idealism when he maintains "pure thought" or "spirit" as what is essential in man, *Selbstbesinnung* or self-consciousness of man as "spirit" through phenomenology, consciousness as freedom, light and evidence, man's complete separation from nature when he appears as intentionality. Hence his difference from Heidegger: "For all this" – Lévinas writes – "Husserl's philosophy radically opposes Heidegger's philosophy where man is always submerged by existence."[31] Nevertheless, in this contribution too, as in his book of 1930, Lévinas recognizes great merit in Heidegger: he was able to analyze the non-intellectual aspects of human being, and therefore to extend the Husserlian notion of intentionality into the notion of sense.

A text on Heidegger, written in 1940,[32] deals in particular with the theme of death in *Being and Time*. Lévinas admits that Heidegger, while describing all the dimensions of time, emphasizes the future, and that he considers philosophy to be the opportunity for a living human being to transcend his life. In both cases it seems that Heidegger, like the most important philosophers of the past, recognizes human freedom. However – Lévinas remarks – as Heidegger does not think of being as eternity, as does idealistic philosophy, although they share the concept of being, Heidegger's concept of death annuls the actual possibility of man being free. In spite of the possibilities of choice and having a project, which are typical of man, according to Heidegger's analysis, man cannot escape from his mortal destiny because being is no more than pure contingency. Precisely because Heidegger premises the question of the being of an entity to the question of being as an entity – in contrast with earlier philosophy – he comes to negate eternity: he no longer reflects on the possibility of an eternal Entity which could be distinct from the world as existing in time. Therefore, the *Dasein* exists in a world which has no longer an end or a ground. When Heidegger's philosophy considers death – Lévinas concludes – it does not determine the being of human *Dasein*, but only the being of that *Dasein* which has a particular attitude towards the world because of its particular situation:

> In this manner Heidegger's ontology offers its most tragic accents and becomes the witness of an age and a world which it will perhaps be possible to supersede tomorrow.[33]

In the years 1947 and 1948 Lévinas takes other important steps with regard to the elaboration of his peculiar philosophical orientation. In 1947 *From Existence to Existent* appears;[34] in 1948 *Time and the Other*.[35] In both writings the theme of the Other is discussed: the author analyzes Eros and connects it to Plato's notion of the Good as transcending being. Nevertheless, in order to meet the Other – so Lévinas argues in these texts – the "ego" must previously be an "existent," that is to say a point of resistance, a nucleus enclosed in itself before being: in this being, absolutely contingent, having no sense, horrible – the being of nature or of society as an impersonal or anonymous force – "existence" is inserted, and it annuls itself in its openness to such a being. Therefore the author in describing the subject as an "hypostasis" offers phenomenological analyses of weariness, laziness, fatigue, the body's position in a certain place or moment, attention and vigilance in insomnia as the different ways in which the magic of pure being, without any "ego," is broken. Lévinas defines this pure being as the *il y a*. But the being of the *il y a* is not only the being of the world which submerges the "ego," but also the being of the infinite consciousness which denies the real exteriority of the world. The world without "existent" subjects and particular things – that world which is affirmed by the philosophers of "existence" – has a similarity with the consciousness without world of the idealistic philosophers. Beyond the being which takes on these two forms, there is however the Other: time presupposes the Other – the time of fecundity, but also of justice and redemption, because in these two texts of Lévinas, Ethos arises from Eros. The dimension of the Other than being is therefore connected not only with Plato, but also with the Prophets' messianism and their idea of a transcendent God.[36]

When in 1949 the author once again wrote on Husserl and Heidegger,[37] grounded in the results of the writings of 1947 and 1948, he criticized both because they were philosophers of being. Moreover, Lévinas now thinks that Husserl – who, in spite of his fidelity to the idealistic notion of the freedom of consciousness, does not recognize, as Plato and Descartes did, a clear distinction between idea and world, infinite and finite, thinking and existing – has opened the path to Heideggerian philosophy.

Finally, Heidegger sees a continuity between *Dasein* and being. But Lévinas also considers Plato's and Descartes' idealism insufficient as a defence of freedom or the spirit of the "I." In fact, this defence – as Lévinas now maintains – requires the bringing out of the creatureliness, or sexuality, of the human being in its love towards the Other.

Thus Lévinas, who in his first philosophical steps had followed the paths of Husserl and Heidegger, gradually separates more and more from them. However, he keeps phenomenological analysis as a philosophical instrument, particularly as Heidegger had shaped it in his determination of affectivity in human beings.[38]

6.2 The Other as expression in *Totality and Infinity*

It is remarkably interesting that as one passes from reading Lévinas' philosophical writings of 1947 and 1948 to reading *Totality and Infinity*[39] one can find the same fundamental themes and exigencies.

In fact, in this book as in those writings there is the criticism of the notion of being which Lévinas considers prevalent in Western philosophy, affirmed as it is by its most important currents: in idealism, which identifies being either with an objective eternity (simply reflected by the "I" as if this were no more than a mirror), or with an "I" perceived sometimes as a position, an absolute identity, sometimes as directed to the conquest of the world as a "non-I" (therefore, in all these cases, an "I" which annuls the actual plurality of other "egos" and takes on the form of a universal or general "I"); in materialism, which identifies being with the world of nature or society determining the "I," and so voids the "I" of any independence; in the doctrine of existence, which sees the "I" solely as that being open to being and disposed to receive it according to its own specific forms. In this book of Lévinas, the term which unifies these different forms of being in Western philosophy – objective truth, universal "I," substance, social organization or structure and the being of entities before these are determined as entities – is "totality." Being is totality because it does not give room to the "ego" as single and unique, the "ego" which refuses to recognize its absolute power (a power only grounded on force even in the case of an ideal relation between being and the "I," because ethics is in fact excluded from this kind of relation). Being as totality identifies with that being where there are not any empirical "egos," with the impersonal and the anonymous, with that *il y a* where nothing has a sense or – what is exactly the same – everything assumes ever new and changing senses because there are no longer any criteria of truth or falsity, justice and injustice. Then, in *Totality and Infinity*, as in the texts published in 1947 and 1948, Lévinas emphasizes on one side the necessity that the "I" separates from being, finding its own space and place in order to resist every external assault which threatens to destroy its consistency; on the other, the fact that the relationship between the "I" – in this way formed – and the Other is first of all an erotic and afterwards an ethical relationship. In *Totality and Infinity* Lévinas gives the term of "enjoyment" (*jouissance*) to that dimension in which a human being appears as an "I," through its distinction from being precisely in immediate contact with being, and the term of "economy" to the field of production and exchange on the ground of this connection between the "I" and being (but economy, as the author explains, also presupposes other elements). He gives the term of "feminine" (without linking it to the feminine sex, rather as a human characteristic) to the way of being of the Other who is the partner in an erotic relationship: this Other, although sometimes present only in an ideal sense, permits the "I" to recollect himself or herself in the "home" (*demeure*). And he gives the term of "face" (*visage*) to the form of being of the other human being with whom the "I" keeps an ethical relationship.

Finally, there is also in *Totality and Infinity* – as in both the above mentioned texts of 1947 and 1948 – the concept of a close connection between the erotic or ethical relationship and the Platonic idea of the Good beyond being on one side, and on the other the idea of God defended by the Prophets. In this book Lévinas gives the name "Infinite" no less to the first idea than to the second one: but he explains that the Infinite is more than an idea in the sense that it does not belong only to the theoretical attitude. Therefore in *Totality and Infinity*, as in the previous writings, the author expounds a thinking which defends (a) the "ego" as a person, (b) human sociality grounded on erotic or ethical affectivity, and (c) Transcendence in a philosophical and religious sense, against any philosophy centered on the concept of being.

Thus, one could say that there is a deep continuity between Lévinas' philosophical positions in the 1940s and the 1960s. Certainly, the analysis of the different aspects of the "I" – from the "I" as "existent" to the "I" in relationship with the Other – is more diffuse and complex, the terminology more effective, the determination of the links between the different points of his philosophical proposal more detailed, the polemical references more extended and explicit in the later than in the earlier Lévinas. Nevertheless, there is no radical difference between the first and the second period of the evolution of his thought.

A theme, however, emerges from *Totality and Infinity* which was not underlined in the essays published immediately after the end of the Second World War: this theme is what Lévinas calls "expression." Expression (the "face" or the "noumenon," as Lévinas also defines what that expression indicates) has a connection with language and opposes what is purely "phenomenal." Therefore the Other who enters into a relationship with the "I" is described, in this book, as we shall see, under the general term of "expression": it can be the Other as the person who is loved (but in this case, it is not only "expression," as we shall see shortly); or the Other as the widow, the stranger, the orphan, that is to say the person towards whom one has ethical obligations; or the Other as Transcendence. And therefore, moreover, the true identity of the "I" forms through erotic love, or goodness, or "longing" (*désir*) for the Infinite.

In the part of *Totality and Infinity* whose title is *Interiority and Economy*, Lévinas analyzes the aspect of that human being who separates from being, that is to say from nature or society which menace it, threatening to submerge it as an individual. This human being simply reacts by enjoying things, nature, the world. There is an original naiveté of life which consists in the enjoyment of what is around us. Certainly, in this enjoyment there is a fruition of things which permits the "I" to survive: aliments, air and light allow the "I" to exist by transforming what is different from the "I" into an integral part of its body. There is a spontaneous and non-reflexive egoism in this immediate and innocent appropriation of the world which the "I" realizes. Nevertheless, in his analysis of "enjoyment" Lévinas does not insist so much on instinct, according to which a human being is driven to conquer all things for the satisfaction of its needs, as on the free capacity of enjoying and tasting, savoring and enjoying. "Life" – so he writes – "is affectivity and sentiment."[40] What characterizes human beings is exactly their separation from instinct, which occurs when somebody enjoys things which are completely useless as a means of physical subsistence: "To enjoy (*jouir*) without utility, as pure loss, gratis, without another aim, as pure waste – this is what is human."[41] "The inversion of the instincts of nourishment which have completely lost their biological ends, is the sign of man's disinterest itself."[42]

Lévinas establishes an identity between sensibility, "enjoyment," and the egoism of the "I": the "I" becomes an interiority and an individual just in the moment in which its fruition or enjoyment of things opposes the totality of nature or environment. What is an absurdity from the logical point of view – the fact that the "I," which is close and secret, forms precisely through its first contact with exteriority – is a reality from the point of view of philosophical analysis of the human being. This elementary level of life of the "I," which certainly is not separated from other levels (the erotic or the ethical, love or justice) in social reality, nevertheless is not only the result of an abstraction: it also indicates a real aspect of the "I" which Lévinas defines as the happiness of existing or living. Now, precisely from this dimension of "enjoyment," through which the solitude of the "I" forms, that is, its "atheistic separation" from the world, indispensable for establishing the relation with the Other – because the terms of the "I" and the "Other" are always different and independent within their relation itself – the field of economy arises, that is to say work, utilization of instruments, production of objects, possession, commerce. Thinking arises from the economic dimension, and also representation, that is to say the constitution of objectivity. Certainly, economy and representing also have, as their grounds, the erotic (gathering in the *demeure*, which is essential to economy and representation, in fact presupposes the feminine) and even ethics; nevertheless, they could not arise if this purely sensible "I" did not have an elementary and original contact with natural or non-natural elements. Therefore, sensibility as "enjoyment" – previous to other forms of sensibility, such as the erotic form or the ethical one, which are also founded on "enjoyment" because they have the separate "I" as their condition – is the basis of human activity and human reason as the faculty of knowledge.

But – thus Lévinas continues his description of "interiority" and "economy" – "enjoyment" has the aspect of insecurity and precariousness in human life: the "I" which lives in an immediate contact with things, in a kind of paganism without gods and temples, can in every moment succumb to the power of what was before enjoyed unreflectively. Hence the necessity of the gathering of the "I" in the *demeure*, at home: this could not happen if there were not first the relationship of the "I" with a protective, sweet presence – neither intrusive nor indifferent – that is to say the Other as the feminine.

Now, Lévinas further observes, the Other as the feminine – which enters into relationship with the "I" as immediately sensitive – has an ambiguous dimension: certainly, in this case, the Other enters the world of the egoistic subject which enjoys things and reduces what is different from itself to itself; but it also escapes from the "ego" because it always remains beyond the "ego" – different from the world, in this way embraced. So the Other, when it identifies with the feminine, is what belongs to the world and – at the same time – is beyond the world: thus, according to its first aspect, the Other is a "phenomenal" reality; according to its second aspect, the Other is a "noumenon," that is to say the Other does not appear, but expresses itself and expresses. The Other, as the feminine, is expression, that is, face, and – at the same time – is what is perceived and represented as a "phenomenon." Therefore, as expression, the Other is language. But, because it is not only an expression, the Other is silence too. It is a pure meaning without any sign, and it is also a sign. It has the dimension of height and superiority in its relationship with the "I" and – contemporaneously – the dimension of equality and reciprocity.

Thus, the relationship with this Other permits the constitution of the "ego" in its *demeure*: the "ego" abandons the field of elements, or the elementary, in order to become an "ego" at home in being. Economy certainly begins in immediate contact with enjoyable things, but nevertheless takes on determinate figures only when being at home takes on form. The "I" which lives and acts in concrete economic connections – as the "I" which meets the Other in an ethical relationship within the economic field – is the subject which already has experience of the Other in Eros. This experience is absolutely necessary to its formation and rooting in the world.

The part of *Totality and Infinity* entitled *Beyond the Face* is dedicated particularly to the "I"–"Thou" relationship through erotic love. Lévinas adds the terms of image, entity, visibility, and intimacy without words to the terms of face, expression, and language to characterize the Other in this case. Eros is the equivoque itself, the dimension of ambiguity: here together are enjoyment and respect of the Other, identity and difference, light and mystery, to encounter and to separate, immanence and transcendence, profane and holy, allusion and frankness. Eros between lovers opens the future through fecundity: time originates here. And the relationship between father and son has the same structure as the relationship between lovers because the one and the different are not separable. "Being" – Lévinas writes – "reveals itself (*se produit*) as multiple and divided into itself and into the Other. That is its ultimate structure. Being is society and, through society, time."[43] The time of fecundity, which is continuous–discontinuous, is the basis of Messianic time, which is the infinite time of ethics.

If the erotic relationship – according to *Totality and Infinity* – is the original one in the human being, divided between its belonging to the world and its reference to a beyond the world, it is not, however, the most important. Rather, the book is mainly oriented towards ethics: in the part entitled "The Face and Exteriority" the author describes how the ethical link is established on a plane where the face of the Other is pure expression, the sphere of language substitutes the sphere of the world, transcendence is immediately Infinite, and the word as a teaching arises from the Other, superior to the "I." Ethics is not the field of vision, looking, representation, light, but the field of the word, goodness, pure meaning, peace. Thus the ethical – unlike the field of Eros, intermediate between ontology and ethics – completely abandons the ontological although it presupposes the erotic, because the "I" as independent and separate forms precisely in this sphere. In fact, Lévinas writes: "Preexisting the disclosure (*dévoilement*) of being in general taken as the basis of knowledge and as the meaning of being is the relation with the existent that expresses itself; preexisting the plane of ontology is the ethical plane."[44]

Therefore, ethics is the true plane of authenticity: here the "I," instead of having vision, knowledge, or contemplation of the truth, is its "witness." In this plane, language is not exchange of verbal signs, but originally "word of honor," that is, promise of truth and sincerity, which solely allows the exchange itself. "The verbal sign" – Lévinas writes – "takes place where somebody signifies something to somebody else. It already presupposes an authentication of the signifying."[45] At the end, reason, evidence, the signifying signs, the objectivity of the world, words which have content, originate in the ethical relation. "It is not the mediation of the sign which makes for signification, but it is the signification (whose original event is the face to face) which makes the function of the sign possible."[46] "The thing becomes theme. To make a thing a theme is to offer the world to the other through the word."[47] Objectivity presupposes an ethical relationship between the "I" and the Other.

Thus, society, humanity, justice, universal reason, are already immanent in the face to face because the third, which asks for measure and equilibrium, to ponder and reflect, is already involved in the "I"-Other. The world of signs having signification arises only from this root. Lévinas does not mean to go far from rationalism when he looks for the source of reason in ethics as the first and original experience: "The absolute experience is reason itself."[48] If devoid of ethics, history, economy (because this implies – beyond the "I" in immediate contact with things and beyond the dimension of being at home – language and justice), politics, and historiography as well, would be given up to being, that is to say to non-sense and violence. Of course, all these fields are necessary because what is first and original must be defended by economic and political institutions, sciences and culture; nevertheless, these fields do not have their foundations within themselves, but in that "I"-Other encounter which presupposes goodness or hospitality. This moral affection is not a pathological feeling, that is to say an empirical characteristic of human beings, or a consequence of something external acting on them in a cause–effect relation, but spirit itself in humankind.

Therefore, the "I" is free when it is responsible for the Other, or hears a moral commandment which comes from the Other as face or expression, and as superior to the "I." The Other is the way in which the Infinite itself – non-imaginable, or non-representable, or non-phenomenizable – enters into human reality. The ethical – in this precise sense – occurs before the objectivity of those moral laws which govern the life of history and States. The ethical is rather the firm ground of these laws. So Lévinas writes: "I am necessary to justice as responsible, beyond every limit fixed by an objective law."[49] So the "I," which already assumes identity in sensibility as "enjoyment" and in erotic relationship, is finally truly a subject, a soul, a single and unique person, only through the ethical relationship with the Other.

In the introductory part of *Totality and Infinity*, entitled *The Same and the Other*, and in the concluding remarks the author explains the sense of his philosophical position through a polemic against the philosophy of being. He observes how for Western thought, as ontology, what is true is what corresponds exactly to being: and this is identified either with nature or history – the conflictual relations between States, the fight of everybody against everybody else, the contrast between individuals who find a formal and uncertain agreement only empirically or pragmatically – or with a supersensible being, sometimes beyond concrete reality (as in metaphysical pre-Kantian systems), sometimes within nature and history itself (as in Hegel's system). In all these cases, the individual is prisoner of a fatal force, be it history or politics or an ideal abstract world with its own laws, a force that is indifferent with regard to the destiny of the individuals. The rebellion of the individual against this force seems pathetic – tragic and comic at the same time – to every philosophy of being because it expresses either a subjective feeling, devoid of any sense faced with the necessity of events, or what is not true, a contingency that is only apparent faced by the necessity of the idea.

Certainly, Lévinas does not deny that Western culture, generally speaking, recognizes a deep longing for ethics in human beings: this culture knows that man is sometimes disloyal to ethics; still, it defends this aspect of humanity. But Lévinas thinks that this longing was subordinated to the wish of building a theory which exalts either the being of nature or history, or an ideal being; or – another possibility – this longing was identified with a subjective faith. Thus, now it is necessary that the concepts of pure expressivity, language and face oppose the concept of being. Through these concepts philosophy considers not so much those who speak, as those who prepare themselves to speak. Only in this way, according to Lévinas, is it possible to reach the field of ethics, Infinity, the Other, beyond being: "Peace" – so he writes – "occurs (*se produit*) as this attitude to the word."[50]

Now, Plato as philosopher of the Good, and the Prophets – thus Lévinas maintains in the introductory part of *Totality and Infinity* – indicate this thinking beyond being as a non-subjective, universal one: and therefore, this thinking is not faith, but knowledge, although this knowledge is directed to evidence which is not an image, a phenomenon or an appearance. The idea of the Infinite – which originally is not an idea at all, but captures the human being and immediately brings him into a region different from being in the world – inspires such thinking. Lévinas gives the name of "desire" to the relationship which links the "ego" to the Infinite, or to the face as expression, or to the noumenon, that is to say to what is beyond the senses or reason as oriented towards material or ideal being. The Infinite is the other human being, but also the Transcendent: "Otherness is the otherness of the Other (*Autrui*) and the otherness of the Highest."[51] Humanity in human beings identifies with the metaphysical desire of the Infinite.

Thus Lévinas identifies the sphere of language with ethics, and ethics with revelation or religion, that is to say entering into a relationship with the Infinite. Hence the possibility of an ontology – a theory of politics, a philosophy of history, a natural science, every knowledge of the world – which does not lose humanity in human beings (as was the case, according to the author, in past ontologies). I am independent from being in my "atheism," but still finite. Language itself identifies with goodness as an answer to the commandment which comes to me from the Infinite. And only this answer could permit me to escape from my finitude. Moreover, only from this face to face, where the spoken word and the speaking persons coincide – because here there are no objective impersonal contents which embrace both subjects and, therefore, threaten to destroy them – where there are not yet forms or signs, can a meaningful discourse arise, that is to say a discourse which allows a common world to be determined. The face to face dimension is one of frankness or absolute sincerity: hence the field of science as ontology, that is to say the field of transparency, light, and clear evidence. If that dimension is not considered, this field loses its clearness and univocity. "The beginning (*commencement*) of knowledge" – thus Lévinas writes – "is not possible if the sortilege (*ensorcellement*) and the permanent equivoque of a world, in which every appearance is a possible dissimulation and the beginning escapes, are not broken."[52] The phenomenal becomes a pure appearance, a magic world if it is detached from the *noumenon*.

Certainly, to arrive at the relationship between the "I" and the Other involves – Lévinas admits – abandoning formal logic as the fundamental rule of discourse. In fact, this logic is completely useless for analyzing the connection between the "I" – at the same time independent and dependent – and the Infinite. Only the category of creation – man created by a God who let him live as a being separated from him – permits us to describe such a connection. The thinker himself who tries to describe such a relation – in a book and with respect for the forms of articulate language – finally entrusts his work to the living word and to living human relations: he invites a commentary and a commentary on the commentary because he knows that only in this way can his work acquire a meaning. The spoken word precedes the written word.

Thus in *Totality and Infinity* Lévinas partly continues his investigation on the anteriority of the Other with regard to being – the investigation which he had begun, as we have seen, at the time of his separation from Heidegger and Husserl and from the philosophies of the "I" as a position or identity; and partly hones and develops his analyses and concepts.

But the philosophy which Lévinas defends in *Totality and Infinity* is not devoid of obscurities and unresolved problems. These come out if one pays attention precisely to that primacy of ethics before ontology which he wants to maintain. In fact, in this book, is not the face as expression – although time and again separated from the phenomenal – still connected with appearance because expression after all implies a sign, that is to say something which is in the world, although allusive of a beyond the world? Is the face connected only with goodness or also with looking or representing? Is not the erotic, as an intermediate sphere between being and beyond being, made a presupposition of ethics by Lévinas himself? Moreover, is not the erotic as well as ethics founded on an "ego" enclosed within itself, which after all reproduces the ontological "ego" as *conatus essendi*, notwithstanding its separation from being?

And, although Lévinas insists on the distance between the "I" and the Other, human finitude and Infinity, is there not a risk that "desire" of the Infinite – because of its difference from theory or contemplation of the Infinite – will turn into a non-rational or quasi-mystical connection? Is not the book itself, in which the author reveals his thinking, the proof of the impossibility of philosophy going back beyond philosophy? Is philosophy really able to reach an original dimension which consists in a face to face completely devoid of all objectivity? On the other side: if, instead of considering only ethics as a basis for ontology, erotic life is presupposed by ethics itself, then is it not necessary to introduce into ethics some elements which bring it closer to the ontological? Perhaps, in this last case, could philosophy re-acquire its rights with regard to ethics? Is it truly possible, then, to introduce ethics into philosophy when ethics is interpreted as immediate contact between finite and Infinite? If the teaching of the Jewish sources is identified as the sign of this immediacy, does not this teaching contradict philosophical thinking whose roots are Greek? Do not these traditions – the Jewish and the Greek – turn out to be absolutely ununifiable? Is not Plato the philosopher who not only affirms the Good beyond being, but also considers it necessary to ascend gradually from the world towards the pure intelligible?

Totality and Infinity brought about passionate discussions in France[53] and beyond.[54] But Lévinas, in order to reply to the perplexities and objections concerning his book, rather than taking one step back – either in returning to the anteriority of ontology to ethics, or in keeping the ambiguity of ontology and ethics in the "I"-Other relationship as it occurs in the erotic tie – preferred to take one step forward. In fact, as we shall see, in his following writings he was to make his philosophical proposal more radical and extreme.

He could not have taken this step forward if he had not dedicated himself to intensive study of and deep meditation on Jewish sources, particularly the Bible and the Talmud, especially from the 1950s. The reading of Biblical and Talmudic texts was to engage him until the end of his life. From there, as we will remark, he took the concepts, the terminology, the expressions – so troubling and disconcerting – which are characteristic of the orientation he followed after 1961. This last philosophical orientation was to prove audacious and without comparison in past and present philosophy.

6.3   The interpretation of Jewish sources as philosophical analysis

The discovery of the Other as a philosophical theme, which Lévinas expounds in *From Existence to Existent* and *Time and the Other* – a theme that he does not think was really discussed in the history of Western philosophy because of the continuing primacy of the problem of being over the problem of piety or justice – brings Lévinas to a philosophical interest in Judaism, especially from the 1950s until his last writings.[55]

In fact, according to the author, the concept of the Other is almost completely forgotten in that thought whose beginnings are located in Greece, while this concept remains an essential topic for that thought which the Jewish sources express.

The Transcendent is what inspires these sources – not only in the sense that they evoke and describe it, albeit in the consciousness of its Infinity, therefore beyond human beings' capacity to grasp it completely, but also in the sense that they were written under its impulse. The Other, which the authors of these sources make the most important object of their reflection and writings, is also the Other with whom they have close–distant relations through their affectivity.

Lévinas emphasizes in all his contributions on Judaism or religious Jewish literature how Jewish tradition exalts just that Other which almost disappears in Western philosophical tradition. Christianity, according to Lévinas, was influenced by this tradition in a decisive manner because it had separated from Judaism from its very beginning: in fact, when in the Gospels the Redeemer is presented as the man–God, this contradicts Jewish consciousness of the immediacy of the contact between finite and Infinite; it is true, however, that Jewish roots continue to live in Christian works and institutions.[56] Western philosophical tradition prefers the glorification of truth, given to man or accessible to him, to the glorification of the Other. The glory of the Other coincides with its remaining beyond representation. If the Other is completely open to the light of truth (or to a faith conceived as the organon which allows comprehension or embrace of the Totality, exactly as representative reason does, notwithstanding the apparent conflict between faith and reason), then the Other loses its meaning for man. In fact, in this case, the Other is identified either with the eternal in history, or with being which is beyond history.

Nevertheless, in his writings on Judaism, Lévinas not only ponders the concept of Transcendence within the Jewish sources, and recalls how these sources were written, according to Jewish tradition itself – themes which arise, as we have seen, from his criticism of the philosophy of being. He also emphasizes, through a precise reading of the sources of Judaism, first how they contain some important concepts about the human being, which originate from the theme of the Other – concepts not known by Western philosophy at all; and second, how these sources have a peculiar structure with regard to the connection between the spoken word and the written word, a living inter-human relation and a work. In fact, this structure is grounded on a criterion different from the one typical of Western culture – that culture whose dominant principle is either abstract and impersonal spirit or the empirical subject. These concepts as well as this structure acquire a remarkable meaning for philosophy, according to the ideas Lévinas defends in his Jewish writings.

Now, it is precisely these concepts and this structure, present in the Jewish sources, which Lévinas makes evident in his writings on Judaism from the 1950s onwards: they are considered – as we shall see – as examples and models for the philosophical thinking in his philosophical writings published after *Totality and Infinity*. Philosophy should introduce these concepts within itself, or should have this structure as its ground, in order to really emerge from ontology as first philosophy.

Thus, one could say with regard to the relation between Judaism and philosophy in Lévinas' Jewish texts that on one side philosophical thinking – with its problems, concepts, and instruments – inspires a philosophical reading of Judaism; and that, on the other side, Judaism gives him fresh ideas for a thought where philosophy itself acquires a new field of research and a new perspective. After 1961 this second aspect emerged more strongly than the first. It is possible to take into consideration some of these texts of Lévinas from this double point of view.

In the essay *Ethics and Spirit*, published in 1952,[57] where the concept of religion as connection between man and God is examined, Lévinas first of all underlines how the sense of Jewish religion is certainly ethics – but lived and thought as a dimension beyond being. Only in this dimension does man become an entity which has spirit or soul. The exegesis of Jewish sources should always be carried out paying attention to this requirement. In fact, while Greek civilization is oriented by being – which is represented, thought, embraced – Jewish civilization is oriented by what is beyond being at the very beginning. "Jewish people – so Lévinas writes – have thought for many centuries that all the situations recognized as religious by humankind, find their spiritual meaning, that is to say their truth for adults, in ethical relations. Therefore, they have thought ethics with the greatest energy."[58] The term "spirit" indicates in Jewish religious literature that ethical spirit which opposes violence. But the history of thinking whose beginnings were in Europe remains connected to violence. In fact, the ideal being of the first philosophers corresponds to that cosmos which is the first object of their reflection – that is to say, the ideal being is governed by universal rules beyond individuals. In this essay Lévinas proposes to establish a close link between spirit – in a Jewish sense, as the spirit of justice – reason, ethics, and language: the Other, as both the beyond and the other human being, is the partner of an encounter before the word forms, and oriented towards the word. This is the origin of Jewish religious literature; from here arises the theory and knowledge of the world. Second, however, in this contribution: Lévinas deems that there is a deep antithesis between Judaism and Hellenism with regard to their notion of subjectivity. It seems, at this point, that Lévinas refuses to identify spirit, in the Jewish sense, with language or reason (no matter how this term can be understood). In fact, while the expression characterizing Greek civilization is "know yourself," that is the human faculty of self-knowing, of self-identifying through the return to the inner "self," the expression characterizing Jewish civilization is "do not kill," that is the vision of man as a person who can hear a divine commandment. In this case, absolute autonomy opposes absolute heteronomy. In Judaism, therefore, the human subject is not a subject who expresses something or expresses himself; rather it is a subject who hears the commandment to let the Other live. Thus, on one side in the Jewish sources the author finds the aspiration to what is beyond being: he comes to this idea – which introduces deep changes in philosophical tradition – from the philosophical questions he asks in reading these sources. On the other side, however, he emphasizes the distance between Judaism and Greek philosophy – the mother of all the philosophies – with regard to the concept of the "I": he opposes the "I" as subject and the "I" as accusative.

The article *A Religion of Adults*, published in 1957[59] – just like the essay of 1952 – brings out two themes: first, how it is possible to give a different sense to particular terms which characterize the philosophical tradition, such as entity, reason and autonomy, through analyzing the Jewish sources; the second – at this moment still almost in a minor key – how there is a hard contrast between the philosophical idea of man and the Jewish one. In fact, in this article, by referring to the Biblical sources, there is a description of ethics as the field of the spirit given by God to man as an independent being (this is the atheistic moment of the subject without which the subject could not form in full freedom); and, at the same time, there is the remark that, according to Rashi – the most authoritative Jewish commentator of the Bible in the Middle Ages – the first chapter of Genesis teaches that only God is the owner of the land, and therefore man does not have the immediate right to conquer or enjoy it. In this text Lévinas also remarks how Abraham becomes free, according to the traditional Jewish exegesis, only when he completely separates from his native land: he becomes an exile in a choice which absolutely denies his independence as a being rooted in the world, and implies absolute respect for the divine commandment. Therefore Abraham – Lévinas observes – qualifies himself as an errant's son and an errant himself. This depreciation of the world because of its fixity and immobility, this negation of the land as the primary dimension where human beings live is so important in Judaism from the very beginning that the tablets of the Law themselves are kept in an ark which is transportable in the desert: in their presence Moses can hear the voice of God – as Exodus recounts. Before houses, temples, and cultivated and irrigated lands there is the infinite space of ethics where only faces appear – but not as belonging to the world, therefore as phenomena. In fact, faces do not need any previous affirmation of the reality of nature in order to live in human existence; only faces as noumena allow human beings to have access to a divine presence, to be in contact with divine activity. Therefore, if it is true that the Bible and its commentaries can be read with the help of philosophical notions – as world, independence and entity – it is also true that the Bible and its commentaries have their own notions. And it is not possible to express these last notions through terms which belong to the history of philosophy.

In a short note introducing commentaries – composed in the 1960s – to Talmudic texts on Messianism,[60] Lévinas makes a distinction between different forms of Talmudic interpretation. Beyond the reading of the simple believer or the reading of the mystic, there is philosophical reading. This again separates into two types: either the reader can find in Talmudic texts concepts which he or she can express in a traditional philosophical language, or he or she can find in them a specific kind of thought that is not otherwise expressible. Lévinas who certainly does not reject the first approach to the Talmud for the philosopher – because he himself, as we have seen, evaluates the Jewish sources from a philosophical perspective and with the help of ordinary philosophical terminology – now chooses the second approach. So he writes in this note while explaining how the meaning of Talmudic texts can also emerge from this second reading:

> We start [...] from the idea that this meaning is not only expressible in philosophical language, but refers to philosophical problems. The thinking of the doctors of the Talmud proceeds from a reflection radical enough to satisfy also the demands of philosophy. This rational meaning was the object of our research.[61]

The texts which he intends to introduce – so Lévinas continues – are simply directed to an understanding of what is human. They clarify some human paths which are not recognized by Greek philosophy, such as culpability faced by an exigent God, the suffering of the just for the individual or collective redemption, human freedom in relation to divine forgiveness, prayer and the individual acting in history. These paths in Judaism have a peculiar character – different from that maintained by Christianity or other religious faiths. Now, all these aspects which show the life of the soul in its connection with an invisible God, have a deep meaning for philosophical investigation. They offer this investigation experiences which is not only worthwhile to ponder, but are also central to human life.

Also in some other essays on Judaism published in the 1950s and 1960s,[62] Lévinas points out some peculiar concepts which it is possible to deduce from Jewish sources, and have value and importance for a philosophical analysis of the human being: patience, as antidote against premature Messianism; suffering of the just in doing justice because it involves a violence against the unjust; not only welcoming the Other, but also responsibility and expiation for the Other; guilt of simply existing, irrespective of wrongdoing; freedom as an absolute obligation, before one as an independent being occupies a part of the land; identity as singleness of the chosen in responsibility for the Other.... Through the study of the old Jewish texts, especially the Bible together with the Talmudic commentaries, which brings us to the "intimate breathing of the human soul" and its "secret contradictions," a new wisdom emerges for the world – a world which has until now preferred either knowledge grounded on an egoistic "self" or an impersonal, and therefore nonsensical, objectivity.

A text dated 1972[63] – in a period in which Lévinas, as we shall see, used the specific concepts of the Jewish religious tradition in a philosophical sense in his philosophical writings – explains the link between the Bible and the subsequent Biblical commentaries and discussions, in Jewish readings of the books of the Bible. What is "told" (dit) – that is to say the written word – necessary in order to keep memory alive for future generations, must nevertheless come back to the act of telling (dire), to the spoken word, from which the "told" once arose. In fact, the "told" finds its meaning every time again only in the "telling." The different interpretations of the Bible only emerge in time and history, through intensive studies, in the schools, communities and circles of believers: the authors address their written commentaries on the Bible to readers who are members of the people. In this sense, continuity is stronger than the necessary and inevitable discontinuity. This Jewish reading of the Bible does not exclude the use of instruments offered by philology or historiography, as found in Biblical criticism. But there is a remarkable difference between those who find their own experience in the Bible and hold onto this way of reading in relating to the results of Biblical criticism, and those who consider the Bible only as the object of a scientific investigation. The ultimate sense of the Jewish Bible is ethics: this expresses not so much a connection between freedom and law, as freedom through commandments received in the interiority of the human being.

Lévinas published collections of commentaries on Talmudic texts between 1968 and 1988.[64] In the introduction to the first of these books, which collects commentaries on texts concerning difficult moral problems – such as the forgiveness of a serious crime, the violence of the State and its relation with private ethics, limited or unlimited goodwill towards everybody – he emphasizes the universal character of the Talmudic doctors' thinking. Certainly, in this case, we do not face philosophical arguments, nor it is possible to present the meditation on pages of the Talmud, although universally oriented, as philosophy. In fact, philosophy consists in analysis directly oriented to the phenomena of human life. But this meditation can show us the way in which these same phenomena are noticed and interpreted in rabbinical discussions. "If the Talmud is not philosophy" – Lévinas writes – "its traits are an eminent source of those experiences which sustain philosophies."[65] Anyway, to read the Talmudic treatises in this way involves looking for universal problems and truth in them. These treatises give the philosopher rich material for reflection: meaningful human events which the philosopher finds in life, are considered in the discussions in the Talmud; the phenomenological analysis of the philosopher who works with his peculiar methods and instruments, can be completed by the analysis of the philosopher who takes his material from Talmudic texts. In this last case, the philosopher keeps the reference to its object, the page of the Talmud itself, in his way of expounding, proceeding, asking, and answering.

Thus, only after his discovery of Jewish thought as directed to some specific human experiences – not fully recognized by the Greek philosophers and their heirs – Lévinas would make his philosophical proposal more rigorous and consistent while keeping his aim, the priority of the problem of ethics with regard to the problem of being. His activity as exegete and commentator on Jewish sources, first of all an effect of his philosophical research, exercises a decisive influence on his activity as philosopher with regard to his fundamental orientation and terminology. He would continued, however, the path he had already chosen in the 1930s.

But Lévinas' activity of studying and teaching Jewish texts not only has a meaning for the development of his philosophical thought (and therefore for philosophy), but also for the Jewish world. Lévinas offers the results of this activity as attempts at an encounter between Jewish tradition and Jewish modernity, Judaism and Hellenism, Jewish culture and non-Jewish culture, which he considers absolutely necessary: only in this way will Judaism neither lose its own identity, nor deny its relation with what is not identical with itself in refusing all contact.[66] His objective is the defence of a living Judaism, neither enclosed in itself, nor far away from its traditional sources.[67]

6.4 The Other in the "self" in *Otherwise than Being* and in the last essays

Thus, the book *Otherwise than Being or Beyond Essence*[68] is the point of confluence of two currents of thinking: Lévinas' meditation on the possibility of a philosophy which really could bring us beyond ontology, after the publication of *Totality and Infinity*; and Levinas' reflection on the Jewish Bible and Jewish religious literature, especially the Talmud, as meaningful texts for a philosophy which intends to renovate itself.

At the beginning of this book, after two dedications – the first one, in French, "to the memory of the closest beings" among those who were the victims of "anti-semitism," or "hate for the other man;" the other, in Hebrew, to the members of his family, called by their own names, almost in a *Kaddish* which transforms the following pages into a continuation of prayer – there are some quotations; and these already show the radical form now given to ethics by Lévinas. The quotations are from Ezekiel, 3: 20, and 9: 4–6, Rashi's commentary to this last verse, and two of the *Pensées* de Pascal – passages where ethics is interpreted as an absolute lack of egoism, unrest in the most profound recesses of the soul for the actions of the Other, negation of one's occupation of a physical place and space in the world, the only element on which it is possible to establish the common good, and the only way to sanctify God, that is to keep the Name which calls human beings to moral obligations. The first part of the book focuses the "argument" – the principal theme – which is simply "disinterest" (*désintéressement*) exactly in the meaning one commonly gives to this term. Certainly, being seems the only horizon in which we introduce our feeling, thinking, acting, and speaking, because we are actually involved in being, live in being, are "interested," engaged in order to affirm our *conatus* to existence. When we think a beyond being – Lévinas remarks – this beyond acquires a similarity, correspondence or analogy with being, as happens in the sciences, religions, or philosophies which recognize only the objectivity of their doctrine, knowledge, and thought. Nevertheless, the very miracle of "patience" in being – the renunciation of the "allergic intolerance" which first makes everybody distrustful or suspicious with regard to every Other, and finally becomes dramatic in the fight of everybody against all the Others – shows that being is not the characteristic and inevitable sphere of human beings. There is a peace which is only the result of balance, commerce, calculation, mediation, and politics, and there is a peace which presupposes an aspect of the human being different from the affirmation and protection of egoistic needs and exigencies. There is a being which closes up in itself (as matter, but also as memory or history), after every apparent rupture produced within being by an active or passive subject which tries to defend itself against totality or impersonality – because the subject has not got a real identity in being, is only a part of being, a revelation or manifestation of being; but there is also a discontinuity in time because there are real differences between subjects. However – so Lévinas explains – the question is not to find another dimension, such as non-being, which oppose being because it has all the characters that this lacks, for example contingency, movement, and pluralism. In fact, there is no real opposition between these two poles – being and non-being. Rather, the question is to describe the otherwise than being.

Now, according to Lévinas, the otherwise than being is what there is before the word, the *Logos*, the "told" (*dit*), the verbal signs or systems of communication: here, the human being appears not as "spirit," but as "breathless spirit" (*esprit essoufflé*). The "telling" (*dire*), before the "told" establishes itself, is not "signification," but "signifying the signification" (*signifiance de la signification*); and the terms "substitution," "hostage," and "expiation," in order to define the "I," which in this way is considered suffering, unrestful, non-enclosed in itself and non-identical with itself, take the place of those which define the "I" as an existent in being (as in enjoying the world, or in Eros, economy, discourse, expression). The otherwise than being is the "grave" against the "play" of being: here, the terms "grave" and "play" have an absolutely literal sense, because "grave" is what is incumbent upon the "I," and "play" is the absolutely free movement of the "I" which can continue to decide its own relations and duties in full autonomy. Lévinas also describes the otherwise than being with the terms of "unsayable," "anarchic," "pre-original": when *Logos* tries to indicate it, *Logos* can only allude to it, because it is beyond any "telling" of the "told," a pure "telling," beyond the origin or "arché," something non-representable or non-determinable. Certainly, the passage from otherwise than being to being is inevitable because *Logos*, thinking and knowledge necessarily arise from this "an-arché." But these elements would lose their sense if they were free of every reference to this prior dimension; although they cannot express it at all, they can evoke it. In fact, spoken words belong to the field of being even when they are used to describe the beyond being. Thus, language which intends to present the otherwise than being becomes necessarily ambiguous or enigmatic: this language emphasizes – up to extreme limits – those terms which define the ethical "self" in being, such as freedom, obligation, and duty, precisely in order to allude to an anterior ethic, older and more exigent and rigorous. The "expiation" or "substitution" for the Other is the emphasis on goodness or hospitality with regard to the Other. The otherwise than being is what cannot be inserted in the eternal present of the "I" as a universal consciousness, a pure interiority, in the Totality of being as matter or impersonal substance, in the lack of real temporal differences. In this sense the otherwise than being is time itself. The logical contradiction which appears when thinking goes back to that beyond which denies thinking itself, is resolved when this contradiction expands in time. "The subject," Lévinas writes, "is the knot (*noeud*) and the loosening of the knot (*dénouement*) – the knot or the loosening of the knot – of essence and of other than essence."[69]

Therefore, the place (or non-place) in which Lévinas finds the otherwise than being is the fact – very simple, but extraordinary – of disinterest, that is to say responsibility or taking care of the Other as an "investiture" of the subject. The subject's freedom, in this case, is neither autonomy, nor heteronomy: prior to them there is freedom as suffering for the Other. The Good with which the subject is here in touch is the invisible or non-imaginable. The term "love" is chosen by Lévinas to characterize this call which comes from the Good and is immediately perceived by a loving subject: but this love – which Lévinas thinks about according to the Jewish religious texts – is devoid of any sentimentalism and pathos and is a sober and severe love. This requires that the "I" completely renounces its egoism: "In spite of me (*malgré moi*) for (*pour*) an Other" – so Lévinas puts it – "that is the signification *par excellence*."[70]

Now, the Infinite while remaining external to the present event of the "One for the Other" and leaving a "trace" (*trace*) of its passage – "trace" which "shines" in the "face" of the Other – indicates the otherwise than being. Certainly, the words which try to describe the Infinite are connected with phenomena, but what they evoke are not phenomenal at all. In this case too, we are faced with the ambiguity of a language which "denies itself" (*se dédit*) just in the moment in which "tells" (*dit*) issues in a "told" (*dit*): "The trace" – Lévinas writes – "is and is not in the face as the equivocal of the telling, and so it modulates the very modality of the Transcendent."[71] "He-ness" (*illéité*) – the divine Name, but only indirectly pointed out, as a third person, different from any other "he" (*ille*) – is the form in which the Infinite enters into the "intrigue" of the responsibility for the Other as "expiation." Thus, the subject becomes a "self" – a particular "self," the "chosen," and the "unique" – in the moment in which it is obliged in love, before it can catch the content of the obligation. Lévinas also qualifies this "self" as "sensitive," "vulnerable," "susceptible": the subject does not submit to "persecution" voluntarily, but – before it lives in being – is open to the Other in pure "abnegation." The element which brings us from the otherwise than being to being, is the "third man": hence the necessity of reasoning, mediating, pondering, so that obligations with regard to the Other and the Third can find a balance. Therefore politics, history, and culture – fields of being – have their beginning in ethics, considered in its "absolute difference"[72] from being.

In the part of *Otherwise than Being* entitled "The Exposition" the author explains better the concepts sketched in the first part where he presents only his theme.

In these pages Lévinas asks first if language, before it communicates contents, is not an urgent call for help. The Other is not immediately a partner in a conversation; rather, the Other is the "closest" – neither as a definite human being, nor as an object of consciousness, but as a simple "exteriority" which obliges the "self." Certainly, philosophy mostly pays attention to being because it intends to reach the truth which shines as an image in front of thought: being, as the object of thought, is philosophy's characteristic dimension. "Philosophy" – Lévinas writes – "is the discovery that being and the essence of being is truth and philosophy."[73] But there is also a philosophical thinking which tries to express its own condition (or non-condition, because this is only evokable, not knowable). The attempt involves this philosophical thinking abandoning the field of formal logic – that logic which so perfectly corresponds to ontology and theology.

Then the author analyzes sensibility. Certainly, as the philosophers have well known from ancient times onwards, there is a sensibility which is connected with imagination and, through imagination, with knowledge. But, there is also a sensibility which consists in unrest for the Other; this sensibility is immediate, independent from images and concepts, and coincides with "the miracle of ethics before light."[74] Phenomenological analysis which is usually directed to the phenomenal – to the being of entities in such a way that these two elements, being and entities, cannot separate – here confronts a deep difficulty. In fact, this analysis shows sensibility in ethics giving up the tie between sensibility and ontology. However, this analysis cannot renounce the task of discovering – in human reality just as it appears to us – an aspect of human beings which escapes any manifestation. "Proximity" – so the author expresses this point – "occurs from one soul to another soul beyond any manifestation of phenomena."[75] This aspect forms humanity in man, the "psychic" (*psychique*) in his being.

In ethics – Lévinas adds – sensibility indicates the concreteness of the subject and its suffering for the Other in obligation; but the subject itself is not an entity, rather it is before every entity, because even innocent "enjoyment" of the "self" living immediately in the world is broken by this sensibility. The subject, in reference to this kind of sensibility – identifying with extreme delicacy in contact with "exteriority" – is "animated body" or "embodied identity." Lévinas observes that sensibility as "enjoyment," as well as sensibility as the first step in the process of knowledge, before imagination and intellect, have their ground in sensibility as "the Other in the self," as if the world was given as an object to enjoy and to know only because previously there is "the one for the Other" of "substitution."

The "anarchic" is what is alluded to by sensibility as "animated body" or "maternity" (beyond the biological dimension). Although the "anarchic" is not accessible to theoretical reason, it is not darkness. On the contrary, every sense originates in signification: "Signification as witness or martyrdom – intelligibility before light."[76] The contact between the one and the Other – the Other within myself up to my exhaustion – is not a holy or numinous contact, but is that human event which alone gives a sense to language, symbols, science, and actions in the world. Therefore, as Lévinas notes, ethics is absolutely different from the erotic: ethics is "sincerity" or "uprightness," the place where the "glory" of the Infinite enters and manifests itself (though beyond all manifestation). Ethics is now indicated as that "intrigue" where the "I" is "hypostasis," body animated by the soul or "psyche," not so much an "ego," that is a subject aspiring to identity with itself, as a "myself" (an accusative form without its prior nominative!), a "finite freedom," an "interiority without secrets," a "witness of the glory of the Infinite." The "witness" given to the "glory" of the Infinite occurs before knowledge, arts or symbolic activities.

Many pages of *Otherwise than Being* – in the part on the "exposition" of the "argument" – are dedicated to the passage from ethics to politics, history, and culture. Justice, the economy, the State, reciprocal duties and rights, historiography, arts, sciences, technology..., all the dimensions of being take their impulse and rationality from the hidden root (which however is not planted in any soil) of the otherwise than being. This is the "non-problematic," what is absolutely sure and nondestroyable, faced with the "problems" formed by these fields. Therefore, precisely what will never be properly defined permits the development of language, meanings, all the different fields of human activity. But, the fact that it is impossible to give a precise definition of the otherwise than being produces its similarity with the dangerous *il y a*, that is the dimension of impersonality or fragmentation of meaning in being. In fact, in ethics sense is not separable from nonsense because the "self" cannot comprehend or grasp it completely: in the darkness of the night – as Lévinas poetically says – an intermittent light (or, better, only a bolt of light) shines. For this reason, notwithstanding sense, the suffering of the "self" as "expiation" remains nonsensical. Hence, the impossibility of a philosophical theodicy.

The last paragraph of the second part of *Otherwise than Being*, entitled "Scepticism and reason" returns to the problem of the relation between the immediacy of ethics – pure reason beyond theoretical reason – and the mediation necessary to philosophical discourse. Lévinas is well aware of the fact that he introduces in this book an allusive, ambiguous, enigmatic language, which is neither philosophical nor mystical.

He is well aware of the fact that in his book there is an "abuse of language" because the terms he uses have a different sense from what they have in everyday life (a "trace" which is not a "sign"!). But, according to Lévinas, scepticism's continuous coexistence with philosophy in the history of philosophical thought just shows how the defence of reason as the organon of knowledge has always been united with the suspicion that reason could not be autonomous, self-grounded, self-justified. Beyond reason, in the diachrony of time, according to Lévinas, the condition (or the non-condition) of reason itself and its activity in the world reveals itself as different from all phenomena. It is to this Infinite that the Prophets, and those poets who follow the Prophets, allude. Therefore, ethics involves criticism of every system and closure of knowledge and the return of the "told," which necessarily develops from the "telling," to the "telling" itself.

The final part of the work, entitled "With other words" (*Autrement dit*), is a moving call to rediscover the otherwise than being, and thus to escape the usual philosophical alternative between being and non-being, "spirit" and "life," sublimation – or negation – of death and resignation to death, essence and existence, freedom beyond the world and subordination to fatality of the world, universalism and individualism. There is in human beings – so Lévinas concludes – a "nobility" which does not imply any naiveté: the law and petty aspects of mankind are not ignored, but simply not taken into consideration by the "noble" person. This extreme lucidity, "ignorance with open eyes," expresses the rejection of humanity's abandoning itself to its participation in being. In this case, "astonishment," which is the beginning of philosophizing, is what the thinker feels not so much confronted by being as by human sensibility in the form of "disinterest." This sensibility witnesses the truth of Infinity, different and prior with regard to philosophical truth. In the last lines, Lévinas recalls the disjunction, characteristic of the Jewish reading of the Bible and Jewish prayer, between the way in which the name of God is written and the way in which it is pronounced, in order to allude to the beyond consciousness. The Infinite, which coincides with this beyond, indicates the ethical moment itself in human experience.

Thus in *Otherwise than Being*, unlike in *Totality and Infinity*, Lévinas offers an ethics which drastically renounces any ontological basis, and which uses ontological language only in an allusive manner: this language "denies what it tells" even while it "tells" the intrigue of the "one for the Other."

Certainly, this book too – like *Totality and Infinity* – could raise questions that would make its general orientation problematic. For example: is there truly a human sensibility – which actually is not so much sensibility as the "spirit" or "soul" – prior to sensibility as "enjoyment" or perception of things in the world? Is the philosopher's need to use terms that do not correspond exactly with what he or she wants to say, only a consequence of a difficulty with language, which is always linked with the phenomena of the world? Or does this necessity imply a limit in human beings, their inability to live in the otherwise than being, if considered in its purity and absolute difference from being? If in the world ethic takes on the aspect of justice – and no longer that of "substitution" or "expiation" – because in every "one for the Other" there is already and always the "third man," alluded to by the Infinite as "he-ness" (*illéité*), does one not need to ponder precisely this ethic rather than the ethic of immediate contact in love between the "self" and the Other? Moreover, if time, or diachrony, enters the pure ethics of the otherwise than being, is not this fact a proof of the connection of this beyond with the being of nature or history? Can philosophy, as expression of the *Logos*, tolerate prophetic or poetic language within itself? Can anything be intelligible before *Logos*? Or, perhaps, does every element prior to *Logos* inevitably become non-*Logos*, that is to say myth or an unjustified and therefore subjective, faith? But, on the other side: should not history and politics necessarily refer to a beyond, radically different from them, if they really intend to avoid the risk of being only fields of violence and conflict? Is not *Logos* or theoretical reason, as the faculty of knowledge of objects, unable to establish a true contact with the Other as the "closest" person? Does not Judaism itself live in the otherwise than being when it maintains itself only through "spirit," only through the renunciation of every instrument of force?

In his last essays, published between 1974 and 1991, Lévinas would deal on one side with the connection of ethics with justice, politics, culture, on the other with currents and authors present in contemporary philosophy and literature.[77] Thus, in his intensive encounters with the Other, Lévinas manifested himself as a man of dialogue and peace – not only in his thought, but also in his life.

7

A FINAL REMARK

Human rights, the truth of witnessing, a philosopher's duty

In his copy of his book *Remarks on the Feeling of the Beautiful and Sublime* Kant wrote a series of notes. One of them says:

> I am a researcher by inclination. I feel all the thirst for knowledge and avid inquietude for progress in it, and satisfaction after every conquest. There was a time when I believed (*glaubte*) that only this could represent the honour of humanity, and I despised the plebs who do not know anything. Rousseau has shown me the right way. This illusory superiority disappears, I learn to honour human beings, and I should find myself less useful than the common worker if I did not believe (*glaubete*) that this consideration can give a value to all the others: to let human rights emerge.[1]

This note has particularly caught the interpreters' attention. It has been seen as a sign of Rousseau's strong influence on Kant. Rousseau is the philosopher who criticizes metaphysical knowledge as the necessary basis for ethics, and defends every man's moral consciousness as an immediate fact. According to some interpreters,[2] Rousseau inspires not only Kantian ethics, but also Kantian criticism of the faculties of reason: Kant takes from Rousseau's work not only the idea of the independence of morality from knowledge of the supersensible, but also the program of a philosophy which immediately presupposes man's moral dignity, and then on this assumption builds the analysis of other fields of experience. This analysis has the task of explaining how these fields are grounded in ethics with regard to both the form of their principles and their ultimate justification: the whole of civilization – science, work, technology, the arts, the economy, law, and politics – acquires a value because it is a manifestation of moral freedom, and should more and more put into effect the human disposition to respect the moral law.

But perhaps this note has a meaning which is still deeper than has been supposed until now. One could ask if this deeper meaning shows a new aspect of Kant's philosophy.

This meaning could consist in giving anteriority – with regard to ontology and theology – to an ethics grounded on faith (*Glauben*). In this case, faith no longer refers to reason as an autonomous force in man, therefore expressed by reasoning and arguing, as if every individual were able to identify simply with a universal consciousness; instead, faith refers to a moral truth to be supported by every individual through his feelings, thoughts and actions – by every individual as a witness. In this case, God is not only an object of knowledge; we can think Him, as the legislator of a moral community, only if and after we have an immediate perception of his presence when we act in society according to moral commandments. God as an object for meditation is only an image; God as the legislator of a moral code always remains beyond images, even when we speak about him and try to know him. The only way God has to make himself knowable to man is in the commandment of "You must" in the different circumstances of life. In this case, onto-theology does not close in on itself – this happens only when it is grounded on an independent reason, indifferent towards concrete reality; nor does the dissolution of onto-theology produce a complete fragmentation of being, relativism or moral scepticism. Onto-theology, if grounded in ethics, permits the knowledge of being without the transformation of being into a totalitarian system and, at the same time, without the loss of the unity of knowledge. Kant could be a representative, or a precursor, of this kind of philosophy. In fact, is it not remarkable that Kant calls moral consciousness "God's voice" in man – as he does in the chapter on the feeling of respect in the *Critique of Practical Reason*?[3] That he never disconnects the idea of the moral law, typical of man as a finite rational being, from the idea of a transcendent God – as he does in his moral writings?[4] That Kant sees Job as a hero who is close to God for his "uprightness" or "sincerity" even when Job considers him, as creator, responsible for the evil in the world – as he does in his essay on theodicy?[5] In this interpretation of Kantian philosophy the concept of the primacy of ethics would have a deeper meaning than that given to this concept in a Neo-Kantian reception: in this case, ethics would no longer mean the field where the moral law as a factum of practical reason is the center, but the field where the individual – considered in his or her integrity of affections, feelings and reason – receives the moral commandments (we do not exactly know how), and where the sense of these commandments does not annul the obscurity, and therefore the non-sense of the world. From the point of view of this ethics human history and culture would be a proof of, but also an accusation against, God's justice and benevolence.

The Jewish philosophers, whose doctrines we have recalled in this book, have in their writings sometimes sketched precisely this interpretation of Kant.[6] Like him, they have defended human rights by means of a philosophy founded on faith in morality: if the old Cohen recalls compassion as the main force in human heart, and Rosenzweig and Buber focus on love, Strauss points out fidelity and Lévinas humility as that quality which first of all forms the subject. For all of them – beyond their different languages and styles – human rights could be maintained only by means of an immediate recognition by humanity of a non-egoistic attitude in human beings, before one analyzes economy, politics, science, arts, and culture. Therefore, all of them trusted the goodness of human nature – the good which enters into human reality – notwithstanding man's radical limits. A human being has rights, that is to say some titles which no human power can cancel, only because he or she is a moral being – a being who is able to be obliged and to oblige him or herself with regard to another human being. Like Kant, all these philosophers are Enlighteners or rationalists; but their Enlightenment or rationalism has roots in their recognition of the moral data in everyday life – for example when a human being encounters another human being and they give each other a word of greeting or blessing.

NOTES

1 PREMISES

1 B. Groethuysen, *Philosophische Anthropologie*, München: Oldenbourg, 1928. Cf. about the life and work of this writer, K. Grosse Kracht, *Zwischen Berlin und Paris, B. Groethuysen (1880–1946)*, Tübingen: Niemeyer, 2002.

2 Groethuysen, *Philosophische Anthropologie*, p. 7.

3 K. Löwith, *Von Hegel zu Nietzsche. Der revolutionäre Bruch im Denken des neunzehnten Jahrhunderts*, Zürich-Wien: Europa Verlag, 1941 (Eng. trans. by D. E. Green, Garden City, KS: Doubleday, 1967). On this author cf. O. Franceschelli, *K. Löwith. Le sfide della modernità tra Dio e il nulla*, Roma: Donzelli, 1997.

4 Löwith, *Von Hegel zu Nietzsche*, p. 58.

5 M. Foucault, *Les mots et les choses: une archéologie des sciences humaines*, Paris: PUF, 1966. Cf. on Foucault's work, *M. Foucault. A Bibliography*, ed. by J. Nordquist, Santa Cruz, CA: Reference and Research Services, 1986.

6 Foucault, *Les mots et les choses*, p. 375.

7 Ibid., p. 398.

8 Cf. among the Italian researchers who analyze philosophical events behind the present humanist crisis, A. Caracciolo, *Pensiero contemporaneo e nichilismo*, Napoli: Morano, 1976; M. M. Olivetti, *Filosofia della religione*, in *La Filosofia*, ed. by P. Rossi, Torino: Utet, 1995, I, pp. 137–220. Cf. in other milieus, H.-J. Gawoll, *Nihilismus und Metaphysik: entwicklungsgeschichtliche Untersuchung vom deutschen Idealismus bis zu Heidegger*, Stuttgart-Bad Cannstatt: Frommann-Holzboog, 1989; P. E. Devine, *Relativism, Nihilism and God*, Notre Dame (Ind.): University of Notre Dame Press, 1989; *Evil Spirits, Nihilism and the Fate of Modernity*, ed. by G. Barnham and Ch. Blake, Manchester: Manchester University Press, 2000.

9 F. Antonicelli, who first edited Levi's work in 1947 for the De Silva publishing house, chose the title, taking it from the verse of Levi's poem: cf. P. Levi, *Opere*, Torino: Einaudi, 1997, I, p. LXXXIII.

10 Levi, *Se questo è un uomo*, in Levi, *Opere*, I, p. 20; Eng. trans. by S. Wolff, New York: Orion Press, 1959, pp. 32–3.

11 Ibid., p. 23; Eng. trans., p. 35.

12 Ibid., p. 28; Eng. trans., pp. 39–40.

13 Ibid., p. 64; Eng. trans., p. 42.

14 Ibid., p. 36; Eng. trans., p. 77.

15 Ibid., p. 86; Eng. trans., p. 96.

16 Ibid., pp. 54–5; Eng. trans., p. 66.

17 On the witness – as an objective and precise report of facts which should have been hidden – in Levi's thought, cf. D. Del Giudice, Introduzione, in Levi, *Opere*, I, pp. XIV–XXIV;

P. Levi as Witness, Proceedings of a Symposium held at Princeton University, 1989, ed. by P. Frassica, Fiesole (Firenze): Casalini, 1990. Cf. also *Archivio di filosofia*, 1972, N. 1–2: "La testimonianza"; N. 3: "Informazione e testimonianza."

18 Levi, *Opere*, p. 109; Eng. trans., p. 119. Dante's verses sound in Italian: "Considerate la vostra semenza:/ Fatti non foste a viver come bruti, /Ma per seguir virtute e conoscenza." Cf. about Levi's attitude towards Dante, B. Sodi Risa, *A Dante of Our Time: Primo Levi and Auschwitz*, New York: Lang, 1990.

19 Levi, *Opere*, pp. 109–110; Eng. trans. (slightly modified in the text), pp. 119–20.

20 Ibid., p. 145; Eng. trans., pp. 155–6.

21 Ibid., p. 130; Eng. trans., pp. 139–40.

22 Ibid., Eng. trans. (slightly modified in the text), p. 140.

23 E. Wyschogrod (*Concentration Camps and the End of the Life World*, in *Echoes from the Holocaust. Philosophical Reflections on a Dark Time*, ed. by A. Rosenberg and G. Myers, Philadelphia, PA: Temple University Press, 1988, pp. 327–40) refers precisely to *If This is a Man* when she describes how ethics was not demolished even in those places, although extremely rare. Cf. also, on ethics in Levi's work, *Reason and Light: Essays on P. Levi*, ed. by S. Tarrow, Ithaca, NY: Ithaca University Press, 1990.

24 R. Goetschel ("Y a-t-il une Philosophie Juive?," *Revue de Métaphysique et de Morale*, 1985, N. 3, pp. 311–27) rightly observes that after the Hellenistic and Middle Ages, a third movement in Jewish philosophy arises in the nineteenth and twentieth centuries, especially in German speaking areas. But, because of the different forms taken by Jewish existence during the epoch of emancipation, Jewish philosophy has many different expressions and a loose frame in these centuries. In the present book, I only examine those authors who are the most important representatives of a Jewish thought which – as will be seen – maintain the encounter between Jewish sources and philosophy as a means of defending ethics. Therefore, this research does not deal with other remarkable Jewish thinkers who are either mostly oriented by philosophical tradition – for example, Hans Jonas, Hannah Arendt, Gershom Scholem, Walter Benjamin, Jacques Derrida – or mostly inspired by Jewish sources – for example, André Neher or Abraham Heschel – or abruptly move from Judaism to philosophy – for example, Mordechai Kaplan, Richard L. Rubenstein, Emil L. Fackenheim. For an orientation in Jewish philosophy – problems, currents, figures – from ancient times up to now, cf. Z. Levy, *Yafeth and Shem. On the Relationship between Jewish and General Philosophy*, New York: Lang, 1987; *La Storia della Filosofia Ebraica – The History of Jewish Philosophy*, ed. by I. Kajon, Padova: Cedam, 1993; *History of Jewish Philosophy*, ed. by D. H. Franck and O. Leaman, London and New York: Routledge, 1997; G. Veltri, *"Judische Philosophie." Eine Philosophisch-Bibliographische Skizze*, in *Wissenschaft vom Judentum. Annäherungen nach dem Holocaust*, ed. by M. Brenner and S. Rohrbacher, Göttingen: Vandenhoeck-Ruprecht, 1999, pp. 134–63.

2 HERMANN COHEN (1842–1918)

1 Cohen, born in Coswig (Anhalt) in 1842, was a member of a observant Jewish family. He attended a German gymnasium in Dessau between 1853 and 1857, and in that year entered the rabbinical seminary of Breslau; he left this school in 1863 because of the discussion between Zacharias Frankel and Samson Raphael Hirsch about the written and oral Torah. About this discussion, and the reasons behind Cohen's interruption of his rabbinical education, cf. J. Melber, *H. Cohen's Philosophy of Judaism*, I, New York: J. David, 1968, pp. 194 ff.; I. Kajon, *H. Cohen. Filosofia ed ebraismo*, in *Dio nella filosofia del '900*, ed. by R. Penzo and R. Gibellini, Brescia: Queriniana, 1993, pp. 41–52.

2 H. Cohen, "Die platonische Ideenlehre psychologisch entwickelt," in *Zeitschrift für Völkerpsychologie und Sprachwissenschaft*, 1866; "Mythologische Vorstellungen von Gott und Seele psychologisch entwickelt," ibid., 1868; "Die dichterische Phantasie und der

Mechanismus des Bewusstseins," ibid., 1869. These three essays have been reprinted in H. Cohen, *Schriften zur Philosophie und Zeitgeschichte*, ed. by A. Görland and E. Cassirer, Berlin: Akademie Verlag, 1927, I, pp. 30–87; 88–140; 141–228 (the following quotations in the text refer to this edition). Cf. about the *Völkerpsychologie* H. Dussort, *L'école de Marbourg*, Paris: PUF, 1963, pp. 70 ff.; and, in particular, about Steinthal, the contributions in *Haim H. Steinthal. Linguist and Philosopher of the Nineteenth Century*, ed. by H. Wiedebach and A. Winkelmann, Leiden: Brill, 2002. A bibliography of the writings published by Cohen is in H. Holzhey, *Cohen und Natorp, I: Ursprung und Einheit. Die Geschichte der "Marburger Schule" als Auseinandersetzung um die Logik des Denkens*, Basel-Stuttgart: Schwabe, 1986, pp. 335–80.

3 Cohen, "Mythologische Vorstellungen von Gott und Seele psychologisch entwickelt," p. 140.

4 Cohen, "Die dichterische Phantasie und der Mechanismus des Bewusstseins," p. 195.

5 Cohen, "Heinrich Heine und das Judentum," in *Die Gegenwart. Berliner Wochenschrift für jüdische Angelegenheiten*, 1867 (this text was published anonymously); repr. in Cohen, *Jüdische Schriften*, ed. by B. Strauss, *Einleitung* of F. Rosenzweig, Berlin: Schwetschke & Son, 1924, II, pp. 2–44 (the quotations in the text refer to this edition). (For the Rosenzweig-Cohen relation cf. Chapter 3 of this book.)

6 H. Cohen, "Der Sabbat in seiner kulturgeschichtlichen Bedeutung," lecture held in Berlin in 1869, published in 1880 in *Der Zeitgeist*; repr. in *Jüdische Schriften*, II, pp. 45–72.

7 Cohen, "Heinrich Heine und das Judentum," p. 23.

8 Ibid., p. 8.

9 Cohen, "Der Sabbat in seiner kulturgeschichtlichen Bedeutung," p. 55.

10 Dussort, *L'école de Marbourg*, pp. 70 ff., has remarked the contrast between psychology and philosophy in Cohen's first writings, while G. Gigliotti (*"Avventure e disavventure del trascendentale." Studio su Cohen e Natorp*, Napoli: Guida, 1989, pp. 9 ff.) emphasizes the continuity between the psychological and philosophical methods in Cohen's thought.

11 The idea that Jewish monotheism, as a celebration of spirit beyond nature, is the source of the modern concept of freedom, proposed by Cohen in his first Jewish pieces, is explained by H. Liebeschütz (*Von Georg Simmel zu Franz Rosenzweig. Studien zum jüdischen Denken im deutschen Kulturbereich*, Tübingen: Mohr [Siebeck], 1970, pp. 7 ff.) in the light of the situation of German Jews in the age of emancipation: they intended by this means to build a bridge between their Jewish legacy and their participation in non-Jewish culture.

12 H. Cohen, "Zur Controverse zwischen Trendelenburg und Kuno Fischer," in *Zeitschrift für Völkerpsychologie und Sprachwissenschaft*, 1871; repr. in *Schriften*, I, pp. 229–75. On this discussion, in the German philosophical culture of the second half of the nineteenth century, cf. R. Malter, "Main Currents in the German Interpretation of the Critique of Pure Reason since the Beginnings of Neo-Kantianism," *Journal of the History of Ideas*, 42, 1981, pp. 531–51; K. Ch. Köhnke, *Entstehung und Aufstieg des Neukantianismus*, Frankfurt a. M.: Suhrkamp, 1986.

13 H. Cohen, *Kants Theorie der Erfahrung*, Berlin: Dümmler, 1871. In 1885 Cohen published a second edition of this book, which was modified and enlarged, and in 1918 a third edition (on them cf. note 28 and § 2.5 in Chapter 2). This book is now reprinted in H. Cohen, *Werke*, ed. by Hermann-Cohen-Archiv Zürich, Hildesheim and New York: Olms, 1987, I, volumes 1–3 (volume 1 reproduces the third edition; volume 2 gives the variants between the third and the second edition; volume 3 reproduces the first edition).

14 Among those who appreciated *Kants Theorie der Erfahrung* there is Fr. A. Lange, professor of philosophy from 1872 in the University of Marburg, where Cohen received, in summer 1873, the *venia legendi* for his presentation of research on Kant's precritical writings (*Die systematische Begriffe in Kants vorkritischen Schriften nach ihrem Verhältnis zum kritischen Idealismus*, Habilitationsschrift, Berlin, 1873; repr. in *Schriften*, I, pp. 276–335). In the first edition of *Kants Theorie der Erfahrung* (pp. 206 ff.) Cohen criticizes Lange's interpretation of the Kantian *Deduktion* of the categories in *Geschichte des Materialismus und Kritik seiner*

Bedeutung in der Gegenwart, Iserlohn: Gütersloh, 1866, pp. 249 ff., 269 ff.; Lange partially changed his point of view on Kant in the second edition of this work, published in 1873. Between 1871 and 1873 there is a correspondence between Cohen and Lange: cf. H. Cohen, *Briefe*, ed. by Bertha and Bruno Strauss, Berlin: Schocken, 1939; Fr. A. Lange, *Ueber Politik und Philosophie. Briefe und Leitartikel 1862–1875*, ed. by G. Eckert, Duisburg: W. Braun Verlag, 1968, pp. 360–79. On Lange, as teacher, journalist, member of the German Social Democratic party, cf. *Fr. A. Lange. Leben und Werk*, ed. by J. H. Knoll and J. H. Schoeps, Duisburg: W. Braun Verlag, 1975; and Th. E. Willey, *Back to Kant: The Revival of Kantianism in German Social and Historical Thought 1860–1914*, Detroit, MI: Wayne State University Press, 1978, pp. 83–101. But *Kants Theorie der Erfahrung* did not receive a positive evaluation at the University of Berlin, where after 1871 Cohen tried in vain to get the *venia legendi*. After Lange's death, in 1875, Cohen became professor of philosophy in 1876 in Marburg and later the leader of a school: cf. on this school, M. Ferrari, *Introduzione al neocriticismo*, Roma-Bari: Laterza, 1997; E. Dufour, *H. Cohen: Introduction au néokantisme de Marbourg*, Paris: Cerf, 2001.

15 Cohen, *Kants Theorie der Erfahrung*, 1st ed., p. III.
16 Ibid., p. VI.
17 Ibid., p. 10.
18 Ibid., pp. 35–6.
19 Ibid., p. 54.
20 Ibid., p. 57.
21 Ibid., p. 59.
22 Ibid., p. 145.
23 Ibid., p. 270.
24 The Neo-Kantianism defended in Marburg differed from that of Freiburg and Heidelberg at the time, whose main representatives were W. Windelband and H. Rickert, due to the decisive and constructive role given to reason as superior to the receptivity of the senses: about these different styles of Neo-Kantianism and their consequences, cf. I. Kajon, "Il dialogo tra Ernst Cassirer e Jonas Cohn (1903–1918)," in *Rivista di storia della filosofia*, 2001, N. 1, pp. 91–112.
25 H. Cohen, *Kants Begründung der Ethik*, Berlin: Dümmler, 1877. The second edition, modified and enlarged, appeared in Berlin in 1910 with the title *Kants Begründung der Ethik nebst ihren Anwendungen auf Recht, Religion und Geschichte*, B. Cassirer Verlag, repr. in *Werke*, II. On this second ed. cf. note 40 in § 2.4 of this chapter.
26 Cohen, *Kants Begründung der Ethik*, 1st ed., p. 88.
27 Cohen, *Platons Ideenlehre und die Mathematik*, Marburg: Elwert, 1879 (repr. in *Schriften*, I, pp. 336–66); *Das Prinzip der Infinitesimal-Methode und seine Geschichte. Ein Kapitel zur Grundlegung der Erkenntniskritik*, Berlin: Dümmler 1883 (repr. in *Werke*, V, Part 1).
28 In the second edition of *Kants Theorie der Erfahrung*, Cohen (a) explains that his philosophical analysis of experience refers to mathematical natural sciences, (b) again presents Kant's theory of ideas, now considered the climax of the *Kritik der reinen Vernunft* (and this consideration implies a revision of the transcendental *Deduktion* and of the doctrine of the synthetic a priori principles), and (c) inserts Kantian thought within the history of scientific and philosophical thought. Cohen now considers as the fundamental concept of Kantianism the "transcendental method" which presupposes – as he explicitly says – the "faith" (*Glauben*) in pure scientific reason as the base of the system of philosophy.
29 Cohen, *Kants Begründung der Aesthetik*, Berlin: Dümmler, 1889.
30 Ibid., pp. 94–5. E. Cassirer, in "Hermann Cohen und die Erneuerung der kantischen Philosophie," in *Kant-Studien*, 17, 1912, N. 3, pp. 252–73, quotes this passage as a proof of the truth of his interpretation of Cohen: he thinks that Cohenian Neo-Kantianism, after it has accomplished the analysis of the different objective forms of the culture, looks at the subject as the source of these forms.

31 H. Cohen, *Biographisches Vorwort und Einleitung mit kritischem Nachtrag* to Fr. A. Lange, *Geschichte des Materialismus*, Leipzig, 1896, 5th ed. (The *Einleitung* had in 1902 and 1908 a second edition; in 1914 a third edition, repr. in *Werke*, V, part 2.)

32 H. Cohen, *System der Philosophie*, (1) Teil, *Logik der reinen Erkenntnis*, Berlin: B. Cassirer, 1902 (2nd revised ed., 1914; repr. in *Werke*, VI); (2) Teil, *Ethik des reinen Willens*, Berlin: B. Cassirer, 1904 (2nd revised ed., 1907; repr. in *Werke*, VII); (3) Teil, *Aesthetik des reinen Gefühls*, 2 volumes, Berlin: B. Cassirer, 1912 (repr. in *Werke*, VIII–IX).

33 Cohen, *Logik*, 2nd ed., p. 495.

34 Ibid., p. 588. Cf. about Cohen's logic, H. Holzhey, *Cohen und Natorp*, I: *Ursprung und Einheit*; G. Edel, *Von der Vernunftkritik zur Erkenntnislogik. Die Entwicklung der theoretischen Philosophie H. Cohens*, München–Freiburg: Alber, 1988; P. Fiorato, *Geschichtliche Ewigkeit. Ursprung und Zeitlichkeit in der Philosophie Cohens*, Würzburg: Königshausen & Neumann, 1993. The *Logik* has the task of making possible the full idealization of the material element of knowledge by the means of the infinitesimal method. However, as we will see later, this request does not cancel in the *Logik* the thesis of the permanence of an indeterminacy – in itself not knowable and such as to permit a progressive determination – beyond thinking.

35 Cohen, *Logik*, 2nd ed., p. 612.

36 The nexus juridical science–ethics in the *Ethik* already raised perplexity among its first readers, as is proven by the different receptions of R. Stammler, E. Cassirer, P. Natorp, H. Kelsen: cf. on this topic, S. Schwarzschild's *Introduction* to the *Ethik*, in *Werke*, VII; E. Winter, *Ethik und Rechtswissenschaft. Eine historisch-systematische Untersuchung zur Ethik-Konzeption des Marburger Neukantianismus im Werke H. Cohens*, Berlin: Duncker & Humblot, 1980; A. Poma, *La filosofia critica di Hermann Cohen*, Milano: Mursia, 1988, in particular ch. VI; G. Gigliotti, *Dalle facoltà alle forme. Introduzione al concetto di volontà in Cohen*, Premise to the Italian edition of the *Ethik*, Napoli: Edizioni Scientifiche Italiane, 1994, in particular pp. LI ff. There is in Cohen's thought, besides the identification of ethics with the logic of juridical science (a prelude to juridical positivism), a demand to maintain the difference between positive law and ethics – implying an acceptance of natural law: although ethics, through juridical science, has a connection with logic, it is also independent from it and, therefore, from every science. On this theme cf. note 37 of this chapter.

37 The ambiguity in the *Ethik*, with regard to the relation between juridical science and ethics, makes it difficult to understand Cohen's attitude to Hegel: in this work Cohen does not criticize Hegel for identifying the "actual" with the "rational," but because he has identified the "rational" with the "actual." But does not actualizing the rational imply exactly the non-identity between facts and reason? Cohen himself – as we have noticed (cf. note 34 of this chapter) – like Kant continues to maintain the difference between what is ideal and what is non-ideal in his *Logik*. On Cohen's reception of Hegel, cf. H. Levy, *Die Hegel-Renaissance in der deutschen Philosophie mit besonderer Berücksichtigung des Neukantianismus*, Charlottenburg, 1927.

38 The *Jüdische Schriften*, which collect Cohen's texts on Jewish topics, have a systematic order: I, "Ethische und religiöse Grundfragen"; II, "Zur jüdischen Zeitgeschichte"; III, "Zur jüdischen Religionsphilosophie und ihrer Geschichte." (In volume II there are Cohen's articles about Zionism which he wrote against Buber's position: cf. Chapter 4 of this book.) In *Werke*, these texts together with non-Jewish essays and articles are given in chronological order in volumes XII–XVII. In 1997 volume XVI (*Kleinere Schriften*, V, 1913–15) was published. Cf. also *Reason and Hope. Selections from the Jewish Writings of H. Cohen*, trans. by E. Jospe, New York: Norton, 1971.

39 The problem of the individual, within Cohen's *Ethik*, was raised by W. Herrmann, professor of Protestant theology at Marburg University, in his review published in *Die Christliche Welt*, 21, 1907, cols 51–9, 222–8 (repr. in W. Herrmann, *Schriften zur Grundlegung der Theologie*, ed. by P. Fischer-Appelt, München: Alber, 1967, II, pp. 88 ff.). Some addenda to

the second edition of the *Ethik* (pp. 351, 501–2) intend to reply to Herrmann's doubts: Cohen confirms his point of view, critical of the concept of the individual as an empirical existence. About the discussion Cohen–Herrmann and the addenda to the second edition, which mostly refer to the nexus between experience and idea, cf. I. Kajon, *Ebraismo e sistema di filosofia in Hermann Cohen*, Padova: Cedam, 1989, p. 54.

40 The second edition of *Kant's Begründung der Ethik* (1910) includes a new part – with regard to the edition of 1877 – referring to Kant's teachings on law, religion and history: Cohen tries to prove that Kant himself, after he had connected theoretical and practical philosophy with the idea of freedom, had considered ethics as the center of humanistic sciences and particularly identified law as the fundamental science. But Cohen also remarks Kant's limits in this research, as he had done in his *Ethik*, pp. 26–8, 269 ff., 277.

41 H. Cohen, *Ein Bekenntnis in der Judenfrage*, Berlin, 1880; repr. in *Jüdische Schriften*, II, pp. 79–94. (This essay by Cohen was included in the collection *Der Berliner Antisemitismusstreit*, ed. by W. Boehlich, Frankfurt a. M.: Insel Verlag, 1965.) On the debate between Cohen and H. von Treitschke, then an influential professor of history at the University of Berlin – later considered by Cohen as the event which was the cause of his return to an active Judaism – cf. A. Poma, "La risposta di H. Cohen all'antigiudaismo," in "Atti del 2. Convegno dell'Associazione Italiana per lo Studio del Giudaismo," Idice (Bologna), 4–9 novembre 1981, ed. by F. Parente and D. Piattelli, Roma: Carucci Editore, 1983, pp. 59 ff.

42 H. Cohen, "Der Messiasidee" (1892), repr. in *Jüdische Schriften*, I, pp. 105–24.

43 Cohen, "Liebe und Gerechtigkeit in den Begriffen Gott und Mensch" (1900), repr. in *Jüdische Schriften*, III, pp. 43–97; "Charakteristik der Ethik Maimunis" (1908), ibid., pp. 221–89 (Eng. trans.: *Ethics of Maimonides*, trans. with commentary by A. Sh. Bruckstein, Foreword by R. Gibbs, Madison, WI: University of Wisconsin Press, 2004); "Die Einheit des Herzen bei Bachja" (1910), ibid., pp. 213–20.

44 Cohen, "Die Versöhnungsidee" (1890–92), repr. in *Jüdische Schriften*, I, pp. 125–39.

45 Cohen, "Autonomie und Freiheit" (1900), repr. in *Jüdische Schriften*, III, pp. 36–42.

46 Cohen, *Logik*, pp. 84 ff. Cf. note 34, § 2.3 of this chapter.

47 Cohen, *Ethik*, pp. 408 ff., 425 ff., 446 ff. Cf. notes 36 and 37, § 2.3 of this chapter.

48 Cohen, *Aesthetik*, I, pp. 186–7; II, pp. 35, 259 ff.

49 Cohen, "Religion und Sittlichkeit. Eine Betrachtung zur Grundlegung der Religionsphilosophie" (1907), repr. in *Jüdische Schriften*, III, pp. 98–168; "Religiöse Postulate" (1907), ibid., I, pp. 1–17.

50 Cohen, *Der Begriff der Religion im System der Philosophie*, Giessen: Töpelmann, 1915; repr. in *Werke*, X. The lectures which form this book were attended by F. Rosenzweig, at the time a "Ba'al Teshuva" (cf. Chapter 3 of this book).

51 H. Troeltsch in his review of *Der Begriff der Religion im System der Philosophie*, published in *Theologische Literaturzeitung* (1918, 4–5, cols 57–62), observed that in this book it was very difficult for Cohen to make compatible philosophy and life, his idealism with his animated description of religious experience.

52 Cohen, *Der Begriff der Religion*, p. 131.

53 Ibid., p. 136.

54 Cohen, *Religion der Vernunft aus den Quellen des Judentums*, Leipzig, 1919; 2nd ed. Frankfurt a. M., 1929, repr. Köln: Melzer, 1959 (quotations in the text refer to this repr.). Cf. *Religion of Reason out of the Sources of Judaism*, Eng. trans. by S. Kaplan, *Introductory Essay* by L. Strauss, New York: F. Ungar Publ. Co., 1972. (On this *Introductory Essay* cf. Chapter 5 of this book.)

55 Ibid., p. 11.

56 Ibid., p. 83.

57 Ibid., p. 101.

58 Ibid., p. 138.

59 Ibid., pp. 169–70.

60 Ibid., pp. 68 ff.

61 Ibid., pp. 276 ff., 314 ff., 344 ff.

62 Cohen, *Kants Theorie der Erfahrung*, 3rd ed.

63 Cohen, *Deutschtum und Judentum mit grundlegenden Betrachtungen über Staat und Internationalismus* (1915; 1916, 2nd ed.), repr. in *Jüdische Schriften*, II, pp. 237–301.

64 Psychology, as the last part of the "System of philosophy," was the theme of a series of lectures held by Cohen at Marburg University in the summer semester 1916: cf. on these lectures, H. Holzhey, "Das Hermann-Cohen-Archiv in Zürich," in *Zeitschrift für philosophische Forschung*, 31, 1977, pp. 444 ff. For other news about Cohen's research on psychology in the last period of his life, cf. I. Kajon, *Ebraismo e sistema di filosofia in Hermann Cohen*, pp. 176 ff.

65 H. Cohen, "Spinoza über Staat und Religion, Judentum und Christentum" (1915), repr. in *Jüdische Schriften*, III, pp. 290–372. For the influence which this essay had on the genesis of Leo Strauss' thought cf. Chapter 5 of this book.

66 H. Cohen, "Das soziale Ideal bei Platon und den Propheten," repr. in *Jüdische Schriften*, I, pp. 306–30. This lecture – as the note which presents the text informs us – was held in Vienna on October 19, 1916, at the "Soziologische Gesellschaft," and then in Berlin in January 7, 1918, at the "Lehranstalt für die Wissenschaft des Judentums."

3 FRANZ ROSENZWEIG (1886–1929)

1 Cf. F. Rosenzweig, *Der Mensch und sein Werk. Gesammelte Schriften*, Haag-Dordrecht: Nijhoff, 1976–84, I, *Briefe und Tagebücher*, 2 volumes. (In volume 1 there are letters and diaries written between 1900 and 1918; in volume 2 those written between 1918 and 1929.) The diary entries or letters which we will quote in this chapter by date, are all taken from this book. Part of Rosenzweig's handwritten material is still unpublished. For different editions of his writings, critical literature on him and trends of research on his thought, cf. *F. Rosenzweig. A Primary and Secondary Bibliography*, ed. by L. Anckaert and B. Casper, Leuven: Bibliothek van de Faculteit der Godgeleerdheid van de KU, 1990 (1995, 2nd ed.); F. P. Ciglia, "Scrutando la 'Stella'. Storia e preistoria della ricezione di F. Rosenzweig," first part, *Cultura e Scuola*, 1993, N. 127, pp. 42–60; second part, *Cultura e Scuola*, 1994, N. 129, pp. 134–61. Rosenzweig, born in Kassel, Germany, in 1886, came from a Jewish family which although integrated into the non-Jewish *milieu*, was not completely detached from religious tradition. Although he had an intellectual education much more directed towards literature, sciences and philosophy than Jewish sources, he kept some elements of the tradition, such as participating in the religious service in synagogue (with an observant uncle), reading the Bible and studying the Hebrew language. After attending the German gymnasium in Kassel, he studied medicine between summer 1905 and autumn 1907 at the Universities of Göttingen, München and Freiburg; then, between winter 1907 and summer 1912, modern history at the Universities of Berlin and Freiburg. After he had obtained his doctoral degree in modern history with a dissertation on Hegel's political thought – to which we will return later – he continued his studies in law in Leipzig. After a conversation with Eugen Rosenstock and Rudolf Ehrenberg, on July 13, 1913, he thought – for reasons which we will later explain – of converting to Christianity. In October 1913 he decided to remain a Jew: but, at this time, he followed a particular form of Judaism concentrated only on Messianic hope and praying. Only after autumn 1913, as we shall see, did his Judaism become richer, more elaborated and more reflexive: after this date, Rosenzweig included different aspects of human life within Judaism as a complex reality. For a still useful introduction to Rosenzweig's work edited by a pupil of his: cf. *F. Rosenzweig. His Life and Thought*, presented by N. N. Glatzer, New York: Schocken, 1953 (1961, 2nd ed.).

2 The expression "king of the world" appears, in the letter quoted in the text, under the prayer formula, *melech ho-aulom*, according to the Hebrew pronunciation used by Ashkenazi Jews: God is here named in an intimate and familiar way.

3 Rosenzweig quotes in this note W. Windelband's *Lehrbuch der Geschichte der Philosophie* (1891), Tübingen: Mohr, 1903, 3rd ed. This philosopher had thrown light on how Goethe and Kant defend a subjectivity which looks at the objective value of science and art: in fact, both are followers of the Platonic doctrine of the ideal as form or order of the sensible. Cf. in this work of Windelband, pp. 103 ff., 434 ff., 460 ff.

4 Rosenzweig attended a seminar on Kant's first *Critique*, held by J. Cohn in autumn 1906, as he tells his parents in a letter of November 4, 1906 from Freiburg. This philosopher, a pupil of W. Windelband and H. Rickert, but also a reader of H. Cohen (cf. J. Cohn, *Selbstdarstellung*, in *Die Philosophie der Gegenwart in Selbstdarstellungen*, 1921, ed. by R. Schmidt, Leipzig, 1923, 2nd ed., pp. 61–81), in *Führende Denker. Geschichtliche Einleitung in die Philosophie*, Leipzig: Teubner, 1907 (this book is composed of a series of lectures that Cohn held in Freiburg in December 1906) considered Kant to be a philosopher who had introduced mathematics and mathematical natural sciences as grounding philosophical analysis. This thesis was also later maintained by Cohn in *Voraussetzungen über die Grundfragen der Logik*, Leipzig: Engelmann, 1908. For other information on Cohn, cf. I. Kajon, "Il dialogo tra Ernst Cassirer e Jonas Cohn (1903–1918)."

5 In his letter of November 13, 1909 to his mother from Freiburg, Rosenzweig gives a very positive evaluation of Meinecke's *Weltbürgertum und Nationalstaat* (1907). In this book (now in Meinecke, *Werke*, München, 1962, V) Hegel appears, along with Ranke and Bismarck, defending the meeting between universal reason and the particularity of a historical fact. Hegel is nevertheless criticized for his metaphysical orientation and ideas. Although Meinecke influenced Rosenzweig in his Hegelian interpretation, he had already arrived at Hegel in the spring 1908 – as we have seen – by refusing Kantian rationalism and individualism.

6 Rosenzweig was to write the first part of his dissertation between 1911 and 1912; the second part between 1913 and 1914; the footnotes to the second part in 1919–20. This work was published in Munich and Berlin in 1920 with the title *Hegel und der Staat*, 2 volumes (repr. Aalen: Scientia Verlag, 1962). On the writing of this work, cf. Rosenzweig's letters to G. Oppenheim of September 28, 1911, and to H. Ehrenberg of May 29, 1917. When the dissertation appeared, with a *Preface* and a *Conclusive Remark*, written in 1920, Rosenzweig openly criticized Hegel; however, he kept – as we will see in the following note – the original intention of Hegel's philosophy, whose aim is the connection between life and thinking.

7 On *Hegel und der Staat* and its place within the *Hegel-Renaissance* of the first decade of the twentieth century, cf. G. Petitdemange, "Hegel et Rosenzweig, la différence se faisant," in *F. Rosenzweig*, textes rassemblés par O. Mongin, J. Rolland, A. Derczanski, in *Les Cahiers de la Nuit surveillée*, Paris, 1982, 1, pp. 157–70; P. Mendes-Flohr, "F. Rosenzweig and the German Philosophical Tradition," in *The Philosophy of F. Rosenzweig*, ed. by P. Mendes-Flohr, Hannover and London: University Press of New England, 1988, pp. 1–19; O. Pöggeler, "Between Enlightenment and Hegel," ibid., pp. 107–23. Rosenzweig's idea that Hegel's philosophy, as a synthesis of Enlightenment rationalism and historical or empirical thinking, represents the culmination and, at the same time, the crisis of European philosophical tradition, will inspire K. Löwith, *Von Hegel zu Nietzsche*, and E. L. Fackenheim, *The Religious Dimension in Hegel's Thought*, Bloomington, IN: Indiana University Press, 1968. E. Weil (*Hegel et l'Etat*, Paris: PUF, 1950), on the contrary, criticizes Rosenzweig's interpretation of Hegelian political thought: he thinks that this thought should not be closely connected with European history – as Rosenzweig does – because it has a universal meaning beyond its genesis and historical context.

8 Along with the cultural and intellectual reasons which drove Rosenzweig to give up his conversion to Christianity – as the text tries to explain – there were affective, emotional reasons: Glatzer, in *F. Rosenzweig: His Life and Thought*, pp. XVI ff., 25 ff.; and in "F. Rosenzweig: The Story of a Conversion," *Judaism*, 1, 1952, N. 1, pp. 69–79, tells that Rosenzweig attended the religious service at "Yom Kippur," the day of atonement, the most important recurrence in the Jewish liturgical year, in a little orthodox synagogue in

Berlin, and that he was very much impressed by the fervor of the praying. Later, as we will see, he underlined the existential root of all thinking.

9 F. Rosenzweig, *Deutschtum und Judentum*, in *Ges. Schriften*, III, pp. 169 ff. This text, written between the end of 1915 and the beginning of 1916, was published only after Rosenzweig's death (he did not want to publish it in order to avoid bitterness with Cohen, as Rosenzweig himself says in his letters of September 20, 1917 to his parents, and of the same date to G. Oppenheim). The text criticizes Cohen's essay *Deutschtum und Judentum*. On the last period of Cohen's life, when the encounter with Rosenzweig happened, cf. Chapter 2, §§ 2.4 and 2.5 of this book. There was not only cooperation and intellectual exchange between Cohen and Rosenzweig, but also a deep affective relationship: we will return later to their dialogue (cf. Cohen's letters to Rosenzweig's parents of April 12, 1917, September 19, 1917, February 5, 1918, in Cohen, *Briefe*).

10 F. Rosenzweig, "Atheistische Theologie" (1914), in *Ges. Schriften*, III, pp. 687 ff. As can be deduced from its content, this text refers to the lectures Buber had given between 1908 and 1910 at the Zionist circle in Prague "Bar Kochba," published in 1911 with the title *Drei Reden über das Judentum*, as well as to the lectures he had given between 1912 and 1914 ("Der Geist des Orients und das Judentum," "Jüdische Religiosität," "Der Mythos der Juden"), published in 1916 with the title *Vom Geist des Judentums*. (On these lectures of Buber, cf. Chapter 4, § 4.1, of the present book.) Rosenzweig's text should have appeared in the second volume of the annual publication *Vom Judentum*, edited by the "Bar Kochba" circle themselves: this volume was never published. But this essay of Rosenzweig, criticizing Buber, at the time considered the spiritual leader of this circle, was already rejected by Leo Hermann, editor of the volume, because, according to him, it referred not so much to the theme, as to a reflection on the theme. (In his letter to the parents of July 7, 1917, Rosenzweig, recalling this event, accuses himself, jokingly, of *Chuzpe*, which in Yiddish means "insolence.")

11 Particularly interesting are Rosenzweig's letters to his parents of June 7, July 9, August 17, September 28, October 4, November 4, of the year 1916 and January 6, January 11, October 1, of the year 1917, in which he discusses the problems of pacifism, the future order of the European States, the relation between Western and Eastern Jews; and letters to his parents of November 3, 1916 and March 10, 1917, in which he evaluates the Cohen–Buber debate on Zionism during 1916 (about this debate, cf. this book, Chapter 4, § 4.1). With regard to this controversy Rosenzweig takes a position which is equally distant from both authors. During 1917 Rosenzweig wrote some historical–political essays, now published in *Ges. Schriften*, III, pp. 241 ff. (cf. on them, P. Mendes-Flohr, "F. Rosenzweig and the Crisis of Historicism," in *The Philosophy of F. Rosenzweig*, pp. 138–61).

12 The correspondence of 1916 between Rosenzweig and Rosenstock was already published as an appendix in F. Rosenzweig, *Briefe*, Berlin: Schocken, 1935; afterwards, in Eng. trans., with the title *Judaism despite Christianity. The Letters on Christianity and Judaism between E. Rosenstock-Huessy and F. Rosenzweig*, ed. by E. Rosenstock-Huessy, Tuscaloosa, AL: University of Alabama Press, 1969; repr., New York: Schocken, 1971. This correspondence is now in Rosenzweig, *Ges. Schriften*, I.1. The main subject of the letters is not only the relation between Judaism and Christianity, but also – as we explain in the text – the problem of the relation between revelation and philosophical systems. The correspondence between Rosenzweig, Rosenstock, and Margrit Rosenstock-Huessy in the years 1917–22 has also been published recently: F. Rosenzweig, *Die "Gritli" – Briefe*, ed. by I. Rühle und R. Mayer, Tübingen: Mohr, 2002. For the relations between these three persons, cf. H. Rosenstock-Huessy, "Franz-Margrit-Eugen," in *Der Philosoph F. Rosenzweig (1886–1929)*, ed. by W. Schmied-Kowarzik, Freiburg-München: Alber, 1988, I, pp. 105–7; and H. M. Stahmer, "The Letters of F. Rosenzweig to Margrit Rosenstock-Huessy: 'Franz', 'Gritli', 'Eugen', and the 'Star of Redemption'," ibid., pp. 109–37.

13 F. Rosenzweig, "'Urzelle' des *Stern der Erlösung*, Brief an R. Ehrenberg vom 18.11.1917," in *Ges. Schriften*, III, pp. 125 ff. After the writing of this letter, the author developed his

project by reading Cohen's *Religion der Vernunft aus den Quellen des Judentums*, which Cohen himself gave him in manuscript during their encounter in Berlin, February 1918. On March 9, 1918 Rosenzweig wrote a letter to Cohen where he expresses his deep appreciation of this work. After Cohen's death, in April 1918, Rosenzweig wrote some texts on him, where he emphasizes the new ideas which Cohen's *Religion der Vernunft* had introduced into Cohen's philosophy and the history of philosophy as well: "Ein Gedenkblatt" (1918), in *Ges. Schriften*, III, pp. 239–40; "H. Cohens Nachlasswerk" (1921), ibid., pp. 229 ff.; *Einleitung* a H. Cohen, *Jüdische Schriften*. Rosenzweig wrote *Der Stern der Erlösung* in the period August 22, 1918–February 16, 1919, as he mentions to R. Ehrenberg in his letters of September 4, 1918, and July 24, 1919.

14 Rosenzweig, in *Das neue Denken. Einige nachträgliche Bemerkungen zum "Stern der Erlösung"* (1925), in *Ges. Schriften*, III, pp. 139–75 (Eng. trans.: *The New Thinking*, ed. by B. E. Galli and A. Udoff, Syracuse, NY: Syracuse University Press, 1999), invites the reader of the book to concentrate his attention on the theme of revelation as the "heart of the whole."

15 Rosenzweig, *Der Stern der Erlösung*, in *Ges. Schriften*, II, p. 202 (Eng. trans.: *The Star of Redemption*, trans. from the 2nd ed. by W. H. Hallo, New York: Holt, Rinehart and Winston, 1971).

16 Cf. Rosenzweig, letter of June 24, 1919 to H. Ehrenberg, in *Ges. Schriften*, I.2.

17 Rosenzweig, *Das neue Denken*, pp. 141 ff. E. Lévinas ("Entre deux mondes. Biographie spirituelle de F. Rosenzweig," 1963, repr. in Rosenzweig, *Difficile liberté*, Paris: Albin Michel, 1976, pp. 235–60; "Une pensée juive moderne," in *Revue de Théologie et de Philosophie*, 1965, 15, pp. 200–21) and S. Mosès (*Système et Révélation. La philosophie de F. Rosenzweig*, Paris: Seuil, 1982; Eng. trans., Detroit, MI: Wayne State University Press, 1992) have underlined Rosenzweig's importance for the history of philosophy as the builder of a non-closed system of philosophy, grounded on the connection between the Self and the Other. The Lévinas–Rosenzweig relationship will be discussed in Chapter 6 of this work.

18 F. Rosenzweig, "'Zeit ist's' (Ps. 119:126). Gedanken über das jüdische Bildungsproblem des Augenblicks," *Verlag der neuen jüdischen Monatshefte*, Berlin, 1917, now in *Ges. Schriften*, III, pp. 461 ff. This text is the Jewish *pendant* of Rosenzweig's essay "Volksschule und Reichsschule," written in October 1916 (*Ges. Schriften*, III, pp. 371 ff.). This essay was directed to Rosenzweig's cousin Victor Ehrenberg who also had written a programme for German schools (on this essay, cf. Rosenzweig's letters to his parents of November and December 1916). "Zeit ist's," which Rosenzweig conceives as an invitation to action (cf. his letters to his parents of March and April 1917, September 5, 1917, and November 5, 1917; and to H. Ehrenberg of May 5, 1917), is instead directed to Cohen, whose counsel and support Rosenzweig had looked for in this matter (cf. his letter to Cohen of March 23, 1917).

19 H. Cohen ("Zur Begründung einer Akademie für die Wissenschaft des Judentums," *Neue jüdische Monatshefte*, 2, March 10, 1918, now in *Jüdische Schriften*, II, pp. 210–17) in particular supported the proposal of "Zeit ist's" to establish a Jewish scientific institute in order to develop Jewish culture and also to educate teachers. In February 1918, in Berlin, Rosenzweig will act with Cohen for the realization of this part of his programme (cf. Rosenzweig's letter to Cohen of February 23, 1918; his *Vorwort* to the 2nd ed., 1918, of "Zeit ist's"; his *Einleitung* to H. Cohen, *Jüdische Schriften*, I, pp. XXXVI ff.). In fact, an "Akademie für die Wissenschaft des Judentums" will be founded in Berlin in May 1919, but only as a research institute: on this episode in Rosenzweig's life, in which he as a liberal and religious Jew opposed the liberal and modern current within the German Judaism of his age, cf. Ch. Hoffmann, "Jüdisches Lernen oder judaistische Spezialwissenschaft? Die Konzeptionen F. Rosenzweigs und E. Täublers zur Gründung der 'Akademie der Wissenschaft des Judentums' (mit drei unveröffentlichten Briefen Rosenzweigs)," *Zeitschrift für Religions- und Geistesgeschichte*, 45, 1993, pp. 18–32. Leo Strauss was active in this "Akademie" from 1925 and also cooperated with the "Lehrhaus," founded by Rosenzweig

in Frankfurt in 1920. "Zeit ist's," although received by the Zionists with sympathy (cf. Rosenzweig's letters to J. Prager of September 30, 1917, and October 23, 1917), was however criticized by H. S. Bergmann (*Der Jude*, 3, 1918–19, pp. 42–3), for being grounded more on Jewish tradition, abstractly considered, than on the feelings and needs of the living people. (About the journal *Der Jude*, which Buber founded in 1916, as expression of Zionist ideas and aims, cf. Chapter 4 of this book.)

20 F. Rosenzweig, "Die Wissenschaft und das Leben" (1918), in *Ges. Schriften*, III, pp. 483–9.

21 A. Harnack's *Das Wesen des Christentums*, published in Berlin at the end of the nineteenth century, inspired Leo Baeck's *Das Wesen des Judentums*, Frankfurt a. M., 1921, 2nd ed. Rosenzweig, who – as we shall see – arrives at a new position on the relation between essence and existence, critically reviewed this book in "Apologetisches Denken" (1923), *Ges. Schriften*, III, pp. 677 ff. On the Baeck–Rosenzweig dialogue, cf. A. H. Friedlander, "Leo Baeck and F. Rosenzweig," in *Der Philosoph F. Rosenzweig*, I, pp. 239–50.

22 Rosenzweig, "Die Wissenschaft und das Leben," p. 489.

23 Rosenzweig, "Bildung und kein Ende" (1920), in *Ges. Schriften*, III, pp. 491 ff.; "Neues Lernen" (1920), ibid., pp. 505 ff. On Rosenzweig, as director of the "Lehrhaus," and on the organization, method and meaning of this institution, cf. N. N. Glatzer, "Das Frankfurter Lehrhaus," in *Der Philosoph F. Rosenzweig*, I, pp. 303–26; F. Rosenbaum, "Lehrhaus Then and Now," ibid., pp. 325–60; W. Licharz, "Mit F. Rosenzweig im Lehrhaus," ibid., pp. 391–95.

24 Rosenzweig, "Bildung und kein Ende," p. 492.

25 Ibid., p. 494.

26 Rosenzweig, "Das Wesen des Judentums" (1919), *Ges. Schriften*, III, pp. 521 ff.

27 Ibid., p. 526.

28 Rosenzweig, "Geist und Epochen der jüdischen Geschichte" (1919), in *Ges. Schriften*, III, pp. 527 ff.

29 Ibid., p. 538.

30 Rosenzweig, "Jüdische Geschichte im Rahmen der Weltgeschichte" (1920), in *Ges. Schriften*, III, pp. 539 ff.

31 Rosenzweig, "Der jüdische Mensch" (1920), *Ges. Schriften*, III, pp. 553 ff.

32 Rosenzweig, "Das neue Denken," p. 159.

33 *Sechzig Hymnen und Gedichte des Jehuda Halevi. Deutsch. Mit einem Nachwort und mit Anmerkungen*, Konstanz, 1924; second enlarged edition, Berlin, 1927; repr. *Ges. Schriften*, IV, part 1, under the title *Jehuda Halevi. Fünfundneunzig Hymnen und Gedichte. Deutsch und Hebräisch. Mit einem Vorwort und mit Anmerkungen*, ed. by R. Rosenzweig (we will quote from this edition). About Rosenzweig's relation with Yehuda Ha-Levi, cf. N. M. Samuelson, "Halevi and Rosenzweig on Miracles," in *Approaches to Judaism in Medieval Times*, ed. by D. R. Blumenthal, Chicago, IL: Chicago University Press, 1984, pp. 157–73; E. Starobinski-Safran, "Rosenzweig interprète de Juda Halevi," in *La pensée de F. Rosenzweig*, ed. by A. Münster, Paris: Cerf, 1994, pp. 199–216; B. E. Galli, *F. Rosenzweig and Yehuda Halevy. Translating, Translations and Translators*, Montreal: McGill-Queen's University Press, 1995; I. Kajon, *Profezia e filosofia nel "Kuzari" e nella "Stella della redenzione." L'influenza di Yehudah Ha-Lewi su F. Rosenzweig*, Padova: Cedam, 1996. It is noticeable that, after the publication of *Der Stern der Erlösung*, in 1921, Rosenzweig did not go on expressing his philosophical ideas in systematic writings, but in lessons or in his commentaries to the poems of the poet–philosopher Yehuda Ha-Levi, poems he had translated. In his lessons Rosenzweig identifies his philosophy either with the thought of everyday life (cf. "Glauben und Wissen," 1920, in *Ges. Schriften*, III, pp. 579 ff.; and the texts "Die Wissenschaft von Gott, Die Wissenschaft vom Menschen, Die Wissenschaft von der Welt," 1921–22, ibid., pp. 619 ff.), or with a "Jewish thinking," that is, a thinking oriented by categories different from those of the philosophy inspired by the Greeks (cf. "Anleitung zum jüdischen Denken," 1921, ibid., pp. 597 ff.). The dialogue forms of

these texts corresponds well to the spirit of the anti-idealistic philosophy which he maintains. *Das Büchlein von gesunden und kranken Menschenverstand*, written in 1921 in order to
introduce the new thinking, was perhaps not published by Rosenzweig because of its
monologue and didactic form: this essay appeared only after his death (first ed., by N. N.
Glatzer, Düsseldorf: Melzer, 1963). (But the commentaries to Yehuda Ha-Levi's poems are
not only a description of Rosenzweig's philosophy; they also tell many beautiful and
moving stories about H. Cohen, deal with problems of Jewish life in modernity and discuss
subtle points of Hebrew philology and Biblical criticism.)

34 Rosenzweig, *Jehuda Halevi*, p. 3.

35 Ibid., p. 17.

36 Ibid., p. 28. This is the poem: "Recently thoughts belonging to You awakened me/ and let
me look upon the round dance of Your grace./ They taught me illuminatingly how Your
creation, the soul,/ intertwined with me – a miracle, never to be silent!/ And did not my
believing heart see You, as if it had/ been permitted to be a witness at Sinai?/ My vision
sought You. Into me entered/ Your brilliance, to descend into my clouds./ Then my reflections roused me from the bed,/ to bow down, Lord, before Your magnificence" (trans. by
Galli, *F. Rosenzweig and Yehuda Halevy*, p. 20).

37 Rosenzweig, *Jehuda Halevi*, ibid., p. 28.

38 Ibid., p. 29.

39 Ibid., pp. 112–3. We reproduce the first verses of this poem: "We strive to arrange the
song to show His radiance,/ The very One Who has given to us this soul here./ The loftier
the thoughts the further His flight/ While I must creep along the earth, He can move
world high/ And yet: in the limits of the spirit – the heart finds Him,/ Because pearls of
light sank from the throne canopy,/ Those who are now in the realm of the ray, desire for
Him seizes them,/ The very One Who has given to us this soul here" (trans. by Galli,
F. Rosenzweig and Yehuda Halevy, p. 82).

40 Rosenzweig, *Jehuda Halevi*, p. 114.

41 Ibid., p. 168. This is the poem: "Draw out Your arm, Your strong right hand,/ to help Your
remnant of the flock in battle!/ For doesn't Your arm have the strength to save?/ Time and
chance touch You like those made from dust./ And yet, lights of heaven, they circle round
You/ and stand slaves of Your mouth, of Your word./ Your word, the flocks on high await
it tranquilly,/ starlight bears witness to Your treasure's authenticity./ Its brightness is kin-
dled by Your splendour,/ its ray by the garland of Your network of stars" (trans. by Galli,
F. Rosenzweig and Yehuda Halevy, p. 114).

42 Rosenzweig, *Jehuda Halevi*, p. 168.

43 Ibid., p. 248. "Your heart – if it wants that my will be done,/ leave me, so that I may see
the countenance of my Lord./ For I shall not find rest for these two feet/ until, where He
dwells, I procure my dwelling./ My step, do not hold it back from setting out,/ for I have
a presentiment that my sorrow will meet me beforehand./ My prayer: a place under the
gleaming wings and/ that, where my fathers rest, I may go to rest!" (trans. by Galli,
F. Rosenzweig and Yehuda Halevy, p. 162).

44 Rosenzweig, *Jehuda Halevi*, p. 249.

45 Yehuda Ha-Levi, *Kuzari*, part I, 95.

46 The first books, from Genesis to Isaiah, the joint work of Rosenzweig and Buber, were
published in Berlin between 1925 and 1929. The translation was completed by Buber only
in the sixties: *Die Schrift*, verdeutscht von M. Buber in Verbindung mit F. Rosenzweig,
durchges. Ausg., 4 volumes, *Die fünf Bücher der Weisung* (1954), *Bücher der Geschichte*
(1955), *Bücher der Kundung* (1958), *Die Schriftwerke* (1962), Köln-Olten, 1962; repr.
Stuttgart: Deutsche Bibelgesellschaft, 1992. Some essays of Rosenzweig and Buber on the
Bible and on some problems in translating the Bible are in F. Rosenzweig – M. Buber, *Die
Schrift und ihre Verdeutschung*, Berlin: Schocken, 1936. (Eng. trans.: *Scripture and Translation*,
Bloomington, IN: Indiana University Press, 1994.) Some documents on the method which

Rosenzweig and Buber applied in their translation have been published in F. Rosenzweig, *Ges. Schriften*, IV, part 2, with the title "Arbeitspapiere zur Verdeutschung der Schrift." On Rosenzweig's and Buber's German version of the Bible, cf. R. Klaus, *"Zeit ist's." Die Bibelübersetzung von F. Rosenzweig und M. Buber im Kontext*, Stuttgart: Kohlhammer, 1993; W. Licharz, *Neu auf die Bibel hören: die Bibel-Verdeutschung von Buber-Rosenzweig heute*, Gerlingen: Bleicher Verlag, 1996; H. Ch. Askani, *Das Problem der Uebersetzung – dargestellt an F. Rosenzweig: Die Methoden und Prinzipien der Rosenzweig'schen und Buber-Rosenzweig'schen Uebersetzungen*, Tübingen: Mohr, 1997. The relation between Buber and Rosenzweig, in spite of their differences over intersubjectivity, law and Zionism (as we shall see in Chapter 4), was characterized by deep respect and friendship: their correspondence in the years 1922–29 is a witness to these feelings (cf. F. Rosenzweig, *Briefe und Tagebücher*, in *Ges. Schriften*, I.2; and M. Buber, *Briefwechsel aus sieben Jahrzehnten*, ed. by G. Schaeder, Heidelberg: Schneider, 1973–75, II: 1918–38). Buber was active in the "Lehrhaus" from 1922; and Rosenzweig contributed to the journal *Der Jude*, of which Buber was the director in the period 1916–24. Buber promoted the collection of 46 contributions given to Rosenzweig for his fortieth birthday in 1926: this collection has been reprinted, with an English translation, to commemorate Rosenzweig's hundredth birthday by the "Leo Baeck Institute" of New York: *F. Rosenzweig zum 25. Dez. 1926. Glückwünsche zum 40. Geburtstag*, ed. by M. Goldner, New York, 1987. And Rosenzweig promoted the collection of essays which was published in Berlin February 1928, for Buber's fiftieth birthday, in the journal *Kunstwart*, 5. L. Strauss and E. Lévinas both consider Buber and Rosenzweig to be thinkers of Jewish modernity, who nevertheless defend Jewish religious tradition, as we shall see in Chapters 5 and 6.

47 Rosenzweig, "Vom Geist der hebräischen Sprache" (1921), in *Ges. Schriften*, III, pp. 719 ff.
48 Rosenzweig, *Briefe und Tagebücher*, in *Ges. Schriften*, I.2.
49 Rosenzweig, "Die Bibelkritik" (1921), in *Ges. Schriften*, III, pp. 747 ff.
50 Rosenzweig, "Neuhebräisch?" (1926), ibid., pp. 723 ff.
51 Rosenzweig, "Die Schrift und Luther" (1926), ibid., pp. 749 ff.
52 Rosenzweig, "Unmittelbare Einwirkung der hebräischen Bibel auf Goethes Sprache" (1927), ibid., pp. 773 ff.
53 Rosenzweig, "Die Schrift und das Wort" (1925), ibid., pp. 777 ff.
54 Rosenzweig was informed about Kafka through Buber, who from the beginning of 1900 was in friendly relationship with Max Brod, a member of the Prague Zionist circle "Bar Kochba," and editor of Kafka's unpublished work.
55 In his letter to J. Rosenheim of April 21, 1927, Rosenzweig quotes on one side S. R. Hirsch as an Orthodox translator of the Bible, and on the other, as representatives of the liberal position, the authors who are influenced by Biblical criticism and by scientific research on the genesis and structure of the Biblical books. Rosenzweig thinks that it is possible to follow both using his point of view – grounded on the truth of revelation, but open to reflection. Certainly, the centre is revelation; but revelation without culture, philosophy, Christianity – which rise up from revelation through thinking – will be incomplete. About this theme, implying the defence of a Judaism open to the non-Jewish world, and at the same time with its own strong identity, and the primacy of *Judentum* with regard to *Deutschtum*, but without the refusal of dialogue of *Judentum* with *Deutschtum*, cf. Rosenzweig's letters to H. Sommer, January 16, 1918, to H. Ehrenberg, May 9, 1918, to E. Hahn, January 13 and 17, 1920, to R. Hallo, January 14, 1920 and the end of January 1923, to G. Oppenheim, July 1923.
56 Rosenzweig shows his similarity with Yehuda Ha-Levi (*Kuzari*, part IV, 3) also in this interpretation of the words "Eye asher eye" as "I am who will be with you, when called by you."
57 F. Rosenzweig, "Zur Encyclopaedia Judaica" (1928–29), in *Ges. Schriften*, III, p. 731.
58 Rosenzweig, "Der Ewige" (1929), ibid., pp. 817 ff. On Rosenzweig's interpretation of Moses Mendelssohn, cf. P. Mendes-Flohr, *German Jews. A Dual Identity*, New Haven,

CT and London: Yale University Press, 1999, pp. 75–7; I. Kajon, "'Due uomini in uno': Dio e intersoggettività in Moses Mendelssohn," in *Intersubjectivité et théologie philosophique*, textes réunis par M. M. Olivetti, Padova: Cedam, 2001, pp. 577 ff.

59 F. Rosenzweig, "Das Formgeheimnis der biblischen Erzählungen" (1928), in *Ges. Schriften*, III, pp. 817 ff.

60 On the *Lebensphilosophie*-philosophy, existence-essence conflict in German culture during the first decades of the twentieth century, cf. Chapter 1, § 1.1.

61 F. Rosenzweig, *Weltgeschichtliche Bedeutung der Bibel* (1929), in *Ges. Schriften*, III, pp. 837 ff.

4 MARTIN BUBER (1878–1965)

1 Cf. on Buber's life and thought, M. Friedman, *M. Buber's Life and Work, I: The Early Years 1878–1923; II: The Middle Years 1923–1945; III: The Later Years 1945–1965*, New York: E. P. Dutton, 1981–83; *M. Buber. A Bibliography of His Writings, 1897–1978*, ed. by M. Cohn and R. Buber, Jerusalem: Magnes Press, 1980. (About English translations of his works and English reception cf. *M. Buber and his Critics: An Annotated Bibliography of Writings in English through 1978*, ed. by W. Moonan, New York: Garland, 1981.) P. Mendes Flohr and P. Schäfer now lead the project of publication of Buber's complete work, at the "Gütersloher Verlagshaus," Gütersloh, Germany, in 21 volumes: up to the present time the first volume has been published under the title *Frühe Kulturkritische und philosophische Schriften (1891–1924)*, ed. by M. Treml in 2001. Buber was born in Vienna in 1878; because of the divorce of his parents, he lived in Lvov with his grandfather until his fourteenth year. His grandfather was a scholar of Rabbinic literature; during this time he could experience eastern European Judaism, and particularly that of the Hasidim – the followers of the Jewish movement begun with the Baal Shem Tov at the end of the eighteenth century. He studied German literature, philosophy and psychology in Vienna, Leipzig, Zürich and Berlin, where he was a pupil of W. Dilthey and G. Simmel. In 1898 Buber joins Zionism, which was already alive in the last decades of the nineteenth century (cf. Leo Pinsker, *Autoemancipation! Mahnruf an seine Stammesgenossen von einem russischen Juden*, Berlin, 1882), but had become a political movement only with Th. Herzl at the Basel Congress, 1897. (Herzl's programmatic book, *Der Judenstaat. Versuch einer modernen Lösung der jüdischen Frage*, also appeared in 1897.) As we shall see in this paragraph, while Buber appreciated Herzl's political Zionism, it is also true that he criticized him from the point of view of the Zionist ideas maintained by Achad Ha-am (Asher Ginzberg): this writer, whose essays are collected in *Al Parashat Derahim (at the Cross of the Paths)*, 2 volumes, Jerusalem, 1949, supported Zionism only as a spiritual or cultural movement. (Cf. as a preliminary introduction to Zionism, the writings collected in *Zionism*, Jerusalem: Keter Publ. House, 1973.) Between the beginning of the twentieth century and the end of the first world war, Buber was able to express the feelings and ideas of the greater part of the German speaking Jewish youth of his times. Buber recalls his first years of life and youth in *Autobiographische Fragmente*, in *M. Buber*, ed. by P. A. Schilpp and M. Friedman, Stuttgart: Kohlhammer, 1963, pp. 1–34 (Eng. ed.: *The Philosophy of M. Buber*, ed. by P. A. Schilpp and M. Friedman, La Salle, IL: Open Court, 1967).

2 M. Buber, *Die jüdische Bewegung. Gesammelte Aufsätze und Ansprachen 1900–1915*, Berlin, 1916. Many of these texts were published in "Die Welt," the organ of the Zionist movement, of which Buber was the chief redactor. (Cf. *The first Buber: Youthful Zionist Writings of M. Buber*, ed. and trans. by G. G. Schmidt, Syracuse, NY: Syracuse University Press, 1999.)

3 The journal *Der Jude*, that Buber directed between 1916 and 1924, unified German speaking Jewish intellectuals in the fields of philosophy, history, politics, Biblical and Rabbinical exegesis and literature: contributors were G. Scholem and Leo Strauss, J. Klatzkin and F. Rosenzweig, F. Kafka and M. Brod, O. Baum and M. Susman, G. Landauer and H. N. Bialik, H. S. Bergmann and E. Simon, H. Kohn and A. Zweig. On these figures

cf. M. Löwy, *Le Judaisme Libertaire en Europe Centrale. Une Étude d'Affinité Élective*, Paris, 1988. In the first issue of *Der Jude*, published in April 1916, in his article entitled "Losung" (pp. 1–3), Buber invited the Jews to concentrate on themselves and find the energy needed to fight the mental confusion produced by the war: this is the only way they could assume the aspect of a people living side by side with other peoples, and moreover offer to other peoples their own religious legacy as an element of unity and cooperation. In the issue of April 1917, which introduced the second year's series of *Der Jude*, Buber's contribution "Unser Nationalismus" (pp. 1 ff.) invited every Jew to be active within the people, and the Jewish people to extract what had human and universal meaning from their own life: a new Jewish culture and solidarity could only arise from life. (In 1926 three issues of *Der Jude*, dedicated to "Antisemitismus und jüdische Volkstum," "Judentum und Christentum," "Judentum und Deutschtum," were published. In 1928 the last issue, edited by R. Weltsch, appeared: it collected essays on Buber and was dedicated to him for his fiftieth birthday. About *Der Jude* and its role in the German Jewish culture of this time, cf. A. A. Cohen, *Introduction* to *The Jew. Essays from M. Buber's Journal "Der Jude" 1916–1928*, trans. by J. Neugroschel, Tuscaloosa, AL: University of Alabama Press, 1980.)

4 The Cohen–Buber conflict about Zionism took place when German Jews, accused by a part of public opinion of being neutral in the war, discussed the question of nationalism or loyalty to the German fatherland. To Cohen's article, "Zionismus und Religion. Ein Wort an meine Kommilitonen jüdischen Glaubens," published in the journal of the German Jews students' society "Kartell-Convent" at the beginning of 1916, Buber replied with the contribution, published in the August 1916 issue of *Der Jude*, "Begriffe und Wirklichkeit. Brief an Herrn Geh. Regierungsrat Prof. Dr H. Cohen." Cohen replies to this article with "Antwort auf das Offene Schreiben des Herrn Dr M. Buber an H. Cohen," published in the issue July–August 1916 of "Kartell-Convent"; and Buber replies once more with "Der Staat und die Menschheit. Bemerkungen zu H. Cohens 'Antwort'," in the October 1916 issue of *Der Jude*. (Buber collected these writings of his in *Völker, Staaten und Zion. Ein Brief an H. Cohen und Bemerkungen zu seiner "Antwort,"* Berlin-Wien, 1917. Cohen's texts are in *Jüdische Schriften*, II, pp. 319 ff., 328 ff.) However, between Autumn 1916 and Autumn 1917, Cohen himself must defend the Jewish community against criticism from those German nationalists who did not recognize any peculiarity of the Jews within the German nation and State: these nationalists were not only authors influenced by the biologism and vitalism of the beginning of the twentieth century, but also Neo-Kantians like B. Bauch or P. Natorp. Cohen, in spite of his defense of the legitimacy of Jewish particularism, was a supporter of the primacy of the German people from the point of view of their scientific and philosophical culture: he gave this culture a universal or cosmopolitan meaning, and so tried to convince his coreligionists to support Germany during the war. Cf. on Cohen's position regarding the problem *Deutschtum-Judentum* in 1916–17, I. Kajon, *Ebraismo e sistema di filosofia in H. Cohen*, pp. 131 ff.

5 The historical context, in which the discussion between Cohen and Buber on Zionism took place, has been described by P. E. Rosenblüth, "Zionismus – Ideal und Verwirklichung bei M. Buber" (1968), in *M. Buber 1878–1978*, ed. by W. Zink, Bonn, 1978, pp. 73–80; and by H. Wiedebach, *Die Bedeutung der Nationalität für H. Cohen*, Hildesheim: Olms, 1997. This discussion is the topic of some of Rosenzweig's letters to his parents in 1916 and 1917: cf. in particular, the letters of September 23, 1916; September 28, 1916; March 10, 1917, in *Ges. Schriften*, I.1. Cf. also this book, Chapter 3, § 3.2.

6 M. Buber, *Drei Reden über das Judentum*, Frankfurt a. M., 1911 (Eng. trans.: *At the Turning: Three Addresses on Judaism*, New York: Farrar, 1952); *Vom Geist des Judentums*, Leipzig, 1916. These collections will be reprinted – with the addendum of two essays published in 1919 (see note 9 of this chapter) – under the title *Reden über das Judentum*, Frankfurt a. M., 1923 (Berlin 1932, 2nd ed.) (Eng. trans.: *On Judaism*, ed. by N. N. Glatzer, New York: Schocken, 1967). The *Preface* to this book will offer – as we will see – a different point of

view from that defended in the essays collected. (Quotations in the text of this chapter refer to the 2nd German ed.) The lectures, later collected by Buber, were held at the "Bar Kochba" Circle, Prague – the first lectures between 1908 and 1911, and the second ones in 1913 and 1914. Members of the Circle were H. S. Bergmann, M. Brod, Robert and Felix Weltsch, Hans Kohn, F. Kafka. (Kafka writes about Buber's presence in Prague in his letters of January 16 and 19, 1913 to Felice Bauer: cf. Kafka, *Briefe an Felice*, Frankfurt a. M.: Suhrkamp, 1967.) Buber's correspondence with these figures is important in under-standing the Jewish situation at that time: cf. Buber, *Briefwechsel*, II: *1918–1938*.

7 Buber, *Reden über das Judentum*, p. 6.

8 Ibid., p. 15.

9 M. Buber, *Der Heilige Weg*, Frankfurt a. M., 1919; *Cheruth. Eine Rede über Jugend und Religion*, Wien-Berlin, 1919: both essays are included in *Reden über das Judentum* (cf. note 6). About Buber's heavy influence on the Judaism of his times through his lectures on Jewish topics, cf. P. Mendes Flohr, "Fin-de-Siècle Orientalism, the Ostjuden and the Aesthetics of Jewish Self-Affirmation," in *Studies in Contemporary Jewry*, ed. by J. Frankel, Bloomington, IN: Indiana University Press, 1984.

10 M. Buber, *Die Geschichten des Rabbi Nachman*, Frankfurt a. M., 1906 (repr. in Buber, *Werke*, München-Heidelberg: Kösel-Schneider, 1962, III: *Schriften zum Chassidismus*); *Die Legende des Baal-Schem*, Frankfurt a. M.,1908 (Eng. trans.: *The Legend of the Baal-Shem*, New York: Schocken, 1955; 2nd ed., 1969); *Sieben Geschichten vom Baalschem*, Jüdischer National Kalender 5678, Wien, 1917.

11 M. Buber, *Ekstatische Konfessionen*, Jena, 1909 (Eng. trans.: *Ecstatic Confessions*, ed. by P. Mendes Flohr, San Francisco, CA: Harper & Row, 1985); *Reden und Gleichnisse des Tschuang-Tse*, Leipzig, 1910; *Chinesische Geister- und Liebesgeschichten*, Frankfurt a. M., 1911.

12 Buber, *Daniel. Gespräche von der Verwirklichung*, Leipzig, 1913.

13 M. Buber, *Ich und Du*, Leipzig, 1923; repr. in Buber, *Werke*, I: *Schriften zur Philosophie*, pp. 79 ff. (quotations in the text from this ed.). Eng. trans.: *I and Thou*, New York: Scribner, 1970. About the genesis of this writing, and the project it was a part of, cf. M. Buber, "Zur Geschichte des dialogischen Prinzips" (1953), in Buber, *Nachwort zu Schriften über das dialogische Prinzip*, Heidelberg: Schneider, 1954 (repr. in *Werke*, I).

14 About the way in which *Ich und Du*, in the definitive redaction, had its origin in the series of lectures held by Buber at the "Lehrhaus" of Frankfurt in 1922, entitled "Religion als Gegenwart," cf. R. Horwitz, *Buber's Way to "I and Thou." An Historical Analysis and the First Publication of M. Buber's Lectures "Religion als Gegenwart,"* Heidelberg: Schneider, 1978. R. Horwitz formulates the hypothesis of the influence of Rosenzweig's *Stern der Erlösung* – read by Buber between December 1921 and January 1922 – on the writing of *Ich und Du*; she thinks, however, that this influence is less than that of F. Ebner's *Das Wort und die geistigen Realitäten. Pneumatologische Fragmente*, Innsbruck, 1921. (About the Buber-Rosenzweig-Ebner relation cf. B. Casper, *Das dialogische Denken. Eine Untersuchung der religionsphilosophischen Bedeutung F. Rosenzweigs, F. Ebners und M. Bubers*, Freiburg i. B.: Herder, 1967.) On the contrary, M. Friedman, *M. Buber's Life and Work*, I, Part IX, denies the influence of Rosenzweig or Ebner on the writing of *Ich und Du*: he demonstrates how this text arises from Buber's previous research. On the passage from the first to the second moment in Buber's intellectual evolution, cf. also P. Mendes Flohr, *Von der Mystik zum Dialog. M. Bubers geistige Entwicklung bis hin zu "Ich und Du,"* Berlin: Jüdischer Verlag, 1979 (Eng. trans.: *From Mysticism to Dialogue: M. Buber's Transformation of German Social Thought*, Detroit, MI: Wayne State University Press, 1989).

15 M. Buber, *Ich und Du*, p. 81.

16 Ibid., p. 101.

17 Ibid., p. 103.

18 Ibid., p. 154.

19 Ibid., pp. 121, 131 ff., 158 ff.

20 Buber, *Vorrede* to *Reden über das Judentum*, p. XVIII. Cf. the note 6, § 4.1 of this chapter.

21 Buber, *Ich und Du*, p. 95; *Vorrede*, pp. XV ff.

22 Buber, *Ich und Du*, pp. 155 ff.; *Vorrede*, pp. X ff.

23 Buber, *Ich und Du*, pp. 106 ff.

24 Rosenzweig's letter of September 1922 to Buber (cf. Rosenzweig, *Briefe und Tagebücher, Ges. Schriften*, I.2) is a response to Buber's delivery of the proofs of *Ich und Du* to him for his suggestions: Rosenzweig criticizes Buber because in *Ich und Du* he has not sufficiently clarified the themes of the link between revelation, creation and redemption, of language, of the transformation of the "eternal Thou" into an object of thinking, although this "eternal Thou" partially remains beyond thinking – themes that Rosenzwig had just developed in *Der Stern der Erlösung* (cf. Chapter 3, § 3.2 of this book). (Later Rosenzweig, moved to reproach Buber for subjectivism and romanticism because of his main theses in *Ich und Du*, defended – in 1924 – the *Halacha* or rules and customs in Jewish life against Buber's antinomianism or anarchism; and he affirmed a non-Zionist attitude – in 1928 – against Buber's emphasis on the active side of Judaism: cf. F. Rosenzweig, "Bauleute. Ueber das Gesetz," in *Der Jude*, 1924, repr. in *Ges. Schriften*, III, pp. 699 ff., Eng. trans.: *On Jewish Learning*, ed. by N. N. Glatzer, New York, 1965, repr. Madison, WI: University of Wisconsin Press, 2002; the correspondence in June and July 1924 between Rosenzweig and Buber about the law, in Rosenzweig, *Briefe und Tagebücher*, I.2; and Rosenzweig's contribution, entitled "Brief eines Nichtzionisten an einen Antizionisten," in *Der Jude* 1928, issue dedicated to Buber. In the forties and fifties however, as we shall see, Buber will change his ideas about the law and the activity–passivity link in Judaism.) B. Casper, in "F. Rosenzweigs Kritik am Bubers 'Ich und Du,'" *Philosophisches Jahrbuch*, 86, 1979, agrees with Rosenzweig's criticism of *Ich und Du*. Casper's assessment is not accepted by M. Friedman (*M. Buber's Life and Work*, I, Part IX) because this interpreter thinks that Rosenzweig's theses are indeed present in *Ich und Du*, if in an "existential" rather than "theological" form. By contrast, E. Lévinas ("Façon de parler," 1980, in Lévinas, *De Dieu qui vient à l'idée*, 1982, Paris: Vrin, 1986, 2nd ed., pp. 266–70) accepts Casper's evaluation because he emphasizes how onto-theo-logy – and this means to think Being, creation and redemption, articulate language, consciousness and knowledge – necessarily completes ethics, revelation, "I" and the "Other," even if the first has not a primacy any more. In Chapter 6 we shall return to Lévinas' evaluation of Buber's dialogic philosophy.

25 On Rosenzweig's and Buber's German translation of the Hebrew Bible and bibliographical references about this translation, cf. Chapter 3, § 3.5.

26 M. Buber, "Die Sprache der Botschaft" (1926); "Leitwortstil in der Erzählung des Pentateuchs" (1927); "Das Leitwort und der Formtypus der Rede" (1935); "Zur Verdeutschung der Preisungen" (1935); "Ein Hinweis für Bibelkurse" (1936). These essays, together with other writings of Buber and Rosenzweig on the Bible, are collected in Buber–Rosenzweig, *Die Schrift und ihre Verdeutschung*; they are also reprinted in Buber, *Werke*, II: *Schriften zur Bibel*. Eng. trans.: Buber, *On the Bible: Eighteen Studies*, ed. by N. N. Glatzer, New York: Schocken, 1968; Buber–Rosenzweig, *Scripture and Translation*, trans. by L. Rosenwald with E. Fox, Bloomington, IN: Indiana University Press, 1994.

27 M. Buber and F. Rosenzweig think that the criteria of their translation of the Bible do not clash with either the attitude maintained by the orthodox rabbi S. R. Hirsch in his translation and commentary, or the attitude, inspired by the historical and philological sciences, maintained by liberal Jews: cf. Chapter 3, § 3.5.

28 M. Buber, "Der Mensch von heute und die jüdische Bibel" (1926); "Biblischer Humanismus" (1933); repr. in *Werke*, II.

29 Buber, "Nachahmung Gottes" (1926); repr. in *Werke*, II.

30 Buber, "Was soll mit den zehn Geboten geschehen?" (1929); repr. in *Werke*, II.

31 Buber, "Biblisches Führertum" (1933); "Geschehende Geschichte" (1933); "Die Erwählung Israels" (1938); "Abraham, der Seher" (1939); "Falsche Propheten" (1940); "Die Götter der Völker und Gott" (1941); repr. in *Werke*, II.

32 Buber, "Die Götter der Völker und Gott," in *Werke*, II, p. 1079.
33 Buber, *Königtum Gottes* (1932), Eng. trans.: *Kingship of God*, London, 1967, 3rd ed.; *Der Gesalbte* (text written in the thirties, unfinished, partially published in 1938 and 1950); *Der Glaube der Propheten* (1942), Eng. trans.: *The Prophetic Faith*, New York: McMillan, 1949; *Moses* (1945), Eng. trans.: *Moses: The Revelation and the Covenant*, New York, 1958. (This last book was published first in Hebrew, then in German and other European languages: Buber had emigrated to Palestine in 1938, after he had taught Judaism and philosophy of religion in the University of Frankfurt, until 1933, and worked as organizer and teacher in the field of education for Jewish institutions.) These writings are collected in *Werke*, II. Buber himself talks about continuity and discontinuity between them. In the *Preface* to the first edition of *Königtum Gottes* Buber explains that he wanted to write a large work dedicated to a description of Biblical faith through commentary on the Jewish Bible, and to publish it with the title *Der biblische Glaube*. Because of the huge extension of the work, he abandoned this project and concentrated his research on the origin of Messianism in Israel. This theme should be expounded in three volumes: "The first volume" – so Buber writes – "will show at the beginning of Israel the representation, inspired by faith, (*Glaubensvorstellung*) of a kingship of God's people as actual–historical; the second will describe how with regard to this kingship the sacred character of Israel's king as JHWH's 'anointed' operates; the third will have the task of clarifying how both conceptions change in the passage from history to eschatology, from the age of the kings on" (*Werke*, II, p. 490). Eschatology – so the author continues in this *Preface* – is the result of a historical deception and identifies the memory of the past with Messianism and hope in a future Messianism. In this way Messianic faith is interlaced with "myth": "Myth is as much the spontaneous and legitimate language of the faith which waits as of the faith which reminds. But it is not the substance of faith" (ibid., p. 490). On the contrary, Messianic faith as center of Jewish faith is a living faith in the perfect kingship of God, actual and present in history. Buber assigned to *Königtum Gottes* the task of making clear how God was the real leader of the people who believed in Him, in some periods of the history of Israel, through an analysis of the Pentateuch, Joshua, Judges. The following book, dealing with the figure of God's "anointed," was to consider Samuel. The third book, dealing with the transformation of Israel's faith, was dedicated to the Prophets. But, after a partial writing of *Der Gesalbte*, Buber did not realize his project any further. In a note in the first page of *Königtum Gottes*, in *Werke*, II, published in 1962, Buber returns to his idea of Jewish faith in the thirties: he says that the title of the trilogy – of which the presented book is the first part – should be "Das Kommende. Untersuchungen zur Entstehungsgeschichte des messianischen Glaubens," and that the second volume *Der Gesalbte* could not appear due to the closing of Schocken Publishers in Berlin which had the job of printing it. In the *Preface* to *Der Glaube der Propheten* the author explains that the book arose in 1939–40 as a contribution to a collective work entitled "Religions of the world," and edited in Holland. Thus, this book has no continuity with the original project, and rather satisfies the need to offer a synthesis of the Jewish faith. This book was followed by *Moses*. Now, listening to these statements of Buber shows that the trilogy was not accomplished because of external events – antisemitism, or cooperation in an enterprise where Jewish participation was necessary. But it is also possible to formulate another hypothesis, on the ground of a careful analysis of Buber's books on the Bible. Buber's rejection of the original program of describing Biblical faith – from history to Prophetism – and of the emphasis on faith in God's presence within the Jewish people as well, seems to reflect a change in Buber's conception of the faith of the Prophets: in fact, in 1939–40 this faith seems to be identified with trust not only in God as the creator and redeemer beyond history (as in the original project), but also in God as living in history. If this concept of Prophetic faith substitutes the original one – that is to say, Prophetic faith as connected to "myth" that expresses a longing for the past and future   then the Jewish people's life in history and the Jewish people's life in

memories and hopes do not oppose, but complete each other: moreover, it seems that the second kind of life precedes the first one. The defence – expressed by Buber in *Moses*, chapters "Israel in Aegypten" and "Baal" – of the "nomadic" character of the Jewish people, before they acquire their "sedentary" character, seems inspired by this attitude: the author lets the people's relationship with God precede their existence in the world and history, ethics preceding politics. However, it is true that Buber did not see any rupture between his works on the Bible of the thirties and those of the forties. Therefore he established a link between the "kingship of God" and the "Prophetic faith." About the theme of unmediated contact between man and God in Buber's writings of the forties and fifties, see later, and §§ 4.4 and 4.5 of Chapter 4.

34 On Buber's interpretation of the Bible, cf. N. N. Glatzer, "Buber als Interpret der Bibel," in *M. Buber*, ed. by P. A. Schilpp und M. Friedman, pp. 346–61; J. Muilenberg, "Buber als Bibel-Interpret," ibid., pp. 364–83.

35 M. Buber, *Der Glaube der Propheten*, in *Werken*, II, pp. 448 ff.

36 *Moses* is a tale of Moses' life and relations with the Egyptian court, Jethro and Jethro's family, his sister and brother, his people – with their doubts, certainties, desperations and hopes – and tells how Moses reacted to different situations. Here particularly an extraordinary variety of figures and attitudes appears.

37 M. Buber, "Ueber das Erzieherische" (1926), contribution to a conference dedicated to "Die Entfaltung der schöpferischen Kräfte im Kinde"; "Bildung und Weltanschauung" (1935); "Ueber Charaktererziehung" (1939), repr. in *Werke*, I. About Buber's philosophy of education cf. B. Wittschier, *Das Zwischen als dialogischer Logos: die Bedeutung der Anthropologie M. Bubers für die Pädagogik*, Frankfurt a. M.: Lang, 1980.

38 Buber, "Ueber Charaktererziehung," in *Werke*, II, p. 824.

39 Buber, "Zwiesprache" (1930), repr. in *Werke*, I.

40 Buber, "Die Frage an den Einzelnen" (1936), ibid.

41 Buber, "Die Forderung des Geistes und die geschichtliche Wirklichkeit" (1938), ibid.

42 Buber, *Das Problem des Menschen* (1943), ibid.

43 Buber, "Zwiesprache," in *Werke*, I, p. 209.

44 Buber, "Die Frage an den Einzelnen," in *Werke*, I, p. 225.

45 Buber mentions Spengler's *Der Untergang des Abendlandes* (1918), Schmitt's *Der Begriff des Politischen* (1935–36), Gogarten's *Politische Ethik. Versuch einer Grundlegung* (1932).

46 M. Buber, "Die Forderung des Geistes und die geschichtliche Wirklichkeit," in *Werke*, I, p. 1068.

47 In "Die Forderung des Geistes und die geschichtliche Wirklichkeit" Buber – as one can deduce from the content – is inspired by two important writings: H. Cohen's "Das soziale Ideal bei Platon und den Propheten"; E. Husserl's *Die Krisis der europäischen Wissenschaften und die transzendentale Phänomenologie* (1935–36). About the influence of this Husserlian work on Buber, see below this paragraph.

48 Buber particularly refers to M. Scheler's work *Die Stellung des Menschen im Kosmos*, published in 1928.

49 Heidegger's text criticized by Buber is *Sein und Zeit* (1927). Buber precedes Lévinas in establishing a link between the analysis of human existence in this Heideggerian work and a specific historical situation: cf. Chapter 6 of this book about Lévinas' evaluation of Heidegger.

50 M. Buber, *Des Rabbi Israel Ben Elieser genannt Baal-Schem Tow das ist Meister vom guten Namen Unterweisung im Umgang mit Gott aus den Brüchstücken gefügt* (1927), repr. in *Werke*, III. *Gog und Magog. Eine Chronik* (1943), ibid.; Eng. trans. entitled *For the Sake of Heaven*, New York: Atheneum, 1959.

51 M. Buber, *Bilder von Gut und Böse* (1952), repr. in *Werke*, I. This writing – as Buber says in his *Preface* – develops ideas which were expounded in a lecture held in 1936 in Pontigny (France) during a meeting on the question of evil. During this meeting Buber discussed

his point of view with Léon Brunschvicg, Ernesto Buonaiuti, Nikolai Berdjaew. The text of this lecture was published by D. Bourel: M. Buber, "Le mal est-il une force indépendante?," *Archives de Philosophie*, 51, 1988, pp. 529–45. About Buber's position with regard to the problem of theodicy within contemporary Jewish philosophy, cf. I. Kajon, *Fede ebraica e ateismo dopo Auschwitz*, Perugia: Benucci, 1993.

52 Buber, *Recht und Unrecht. Deutung einiger Psalmen* (1950), repr. in *Werke*, II.

53 Buber, *Elija. Ein Mysterienspiel* (1963), repr. in *Werke*, II.

54 Buber, "Urdistanz und Beziehung" (1950); "Elemente des Zwischenmenschlichen" (1954); "Der Mensch und sein Gebild" (1955); "Das Wort, das gesprochen wird" (1960); "Dem Gemeinschaftlichen folgen" (1956), repr. in *Werke*, I.

55 Buber, *Pfade in Utopie* (1950), in *Werke*, I; Eng. trans.: *Paths in Utopia*, trans. by R. C. Hull, New York: McMillan, 1950. "Zwischen Gesellschaft und Staat" (1950), in *Werke*, I. "Geltung und Grenze des politischen Prinzips" (1953), ibid.

56 Buber, *Eclipse of God. Studies in the Relation between Religion and Philosophy*, New York: Harper, 1952. (The lectures were held at American universities in November and December 1951.) The German version of this book (1953) is in *Werke*, I.

57 Buber, *Zwei Glaubensweisen* (1950), repr. in *Werke*, I. Eng. trans.: *Two Types of Faith*, London and New York: Routledge, 1951.

58 M. Buber, "Schuld und Schuldgefühle" (1957), repr. in *Werke*, I.

59 Buber, *Der Weg des Menschen nach der chassidischen Lehre* (1948), in *Werke*, III; *Die Erzählungen der Chassidim* (1949), ibid. (Eng. version: *Tales of the Hasidim*, New York, 1947); "Die chassidische Botschaft" (1952), ibid.; "Christus, Chassidismus, Gnosis" (1954), ibid.; *Der Chassidismus und der abendländische Mensch* (1956), ibid. (Eng. trans.: *Hasidism and Modern Man*, trans. by M. Friedman, New York: Harper & Row, 1966); "Zur Darstellung des Chassidismus" (1963), ibid.; "Noch einiges zur Darstellung des Chassidismus" (1963), ibid.; "Abfolge der Zaddikim" (1963), ibid.

60 While resolving the question of theodicy through the primacy of morality – grounded on "faith" or "trust" in an Absolute which is certainly identified with the moral ideal, but is enigmatic as well – over ontology, Buber precedes Lévinas, as we shall see in Chapter 6. Rosenzweig too – as we have seen – in *Der Stern der Erlösung* maintains the anteriority of revelation, that is to say the encounter between man and God, with regard to knowledge of the world: faith leads reason in researching finality in events; reason, however, is not able to comprehend the totality of being. In maintaining this thesis about the relation between moral conscience and theoretical reason, Rosenzweig, Buber, and Lévinas draw on Kant. In fact, after his criticism of speculative reason, Kant considered practical reason as the only instrument which could give a final order to the world. In Chapter 7 we shall try to show the link between Kant and the Jewish philosophers of the twentieth century who emphasize the moral life in man.

61 In "Urdistanz und Beziehung" (1950), Buber remarks that man keeps reality at a distance before he enters into the "relation" with the "Thou." Some interpreters have noticed a change in Buber's philosophical anthropology because, in this case, "relation" is no more the primary element in human life, as he had asserted in his previous texts (cf. for example, N. Rotenstreich, "Gründe und Grenzen von M. Bubers dialogischem Denken," in *M. Buber*, ed. by P. A. Schilpp und M. Friedman, pp. 97 ff.). However, the "original distance" is not an action or event in being, as the "relation" is; it is only the condition of possibility of the "relation." Certainly, the "original distance" could become very real – but only when some obstacle does not allow the immediate link between the "I" and the "Thou," previous to their determination as different subjectivities. In other texts, written in the same period, Buber remains faithful to his idea of sociality as the primary character of man. But it is also true that the terms he now uses to qualify his philosophical anthropology are not always clear or univocal.

62 M. Buber, "Geltung und Grenzen des politischen Prinzips," in *Werke*, I, p. 1107.

63 In the contemporary age there are – so Buber maintains in his contribution "Schuld und Schuldgefühle" – two writers who were deeply aware of the importance of guilt in human life: Dostoevsky and Kafka. They know that every human being who ignores the very concept of commandment or duty runs the risk of losing his identity. Buber mentions Kafka also in *Zwei Glaubensweisen*; and in his correspondence with M. Brod (cf. Buber's *Briefwechsel*). On the relation between Buber and Kafka cf. I. Kajon, *Introduzione* a Kafka, *Cinque storie di animali*. Through Buber, Rosenzweig received Kafka's novel *The Castle*, which reminded him – as he himself said – of the Biblical world: cf. Chapter 3, § 3.5.

64 Buber's interpretation of Hasidism was criticized by G. Scholem and his pupils in the sixties: Buber's writings "Zur Darstellung des Chassidismus" and "Noch einiges zur Darstellung des Chassidismus" (see note 59) reply to Scholem's and Rivka Schatz Uffenheimer's criticism: Buber makes a distinction between the evaluation of Hasidism dependent on the attitude of the researcher, and an investigation accomplished by means of historical and philological instruments, and he recognizes both as legitimate. Cf. G. Scholem, "M. Buber's Interpretation of Hasidism" (1971), in *The Jewish expression*, ed. by J. Goldin, New Haven, CT: Yale University Press, 1976, pp. 397–418. About the connection between Buber's interpretation of Hasidism and Buber's philosophy of education, cf. K. E. Nipkow, *M. Bubers philosophische pädagogische Anschauungen auf dem Hintergrund des Chassidismus*, in *M. Buber*, ed. by F. D. Lucas, Berlin, 1995, pp. 77–103.

65 M. Buber, "Antwort," in *M. Buber*, ed. by P. A. Schilpp and M. Friedman; partially repr. under the title "Aus einer philosophischen Rechenschaft," in *Werke*, I, pp. 1112 ff.

5 LEO STRAUSS (1899–1973)

1 Cf. L. Strauss, *Die Religionskritik Spinozas als Grundlage seiner Bibelwissenschaft. Untersuchungen zu Spinozas theologisch-politischem Traktat*, Berlin: Akademie Verlag, 1930. Strauss, born in Kirchhain (Hessen) in 1899, came from an orthodox Jewish family, and in his youth followed the non-religious and nationalistic current of Zionism led by V. Jabotinsky. He studied philosophy, history and mathematics, in Marburg, Frankfurt, Berlin, and Freiburg. During his studies he met Husserl and Heidegger (for Strauss' relation with these philosophers, see § 5.2, note 16 in § 5.3, § 5.4, and notes 43 and 44 in § 5.5). In 1921 he obtained his doctor's degree in philosophy with a thesis presented with E. Cassirer at the University of Hamburg, entitled *Das Erkenntnisproblem in der philosophischen Lehre F. H. Jacobis*. Between 1923 and 1925 he taught at the "Lehrhaus" in Frankfurt; and, between 1925 and 1932, he was a researcher at the "Akademie für die Wissenschaft des Judentums" (on these two institutions, cf. Chapter 3, § 3.3 of this book). (On Strauss' relations with Cassirer and Rosenzweig, director of the "Lehrhaus," see later.) Between 1929 and 1932 he contributed to the edition of Moses Mendelssohn's complete works, begun in 1929 by the "Akademie" for the celebration of the two hundredth anniversary of Mendelssohn's birth (this *Jubiläumsausgabe*, interrupted in 1938, was continued in the sixties): in volume II, published in Berlin in 1931, Strauss introduces Mendelssohn's writings *Pope, ein Metaphysiker, Sendschreiben an den Herrn Magister Lessing in Leipzig, Kommentar zu den "Termini der Logik" des Mose ben Maimon, Abhandlung über die Evidenz*; in volume III, published in Berlin in 1932, the writings *Phädon, Abhandlung von der Unkörperlichkeit der menschlichen Seele, Ueber einen Schriften Aufsatz des Herrn de Luc, Die Seele*. The articles, published by Strauss in *Der Jude* (on this journal cf. Chapter 4, § 4.1), have the titles: "Das Heilige," 1923, VII, pp. 240–2; "Der Zionismus bei Nordau," 1923, VII, pp. 657–60; "Paul de Lagarde," 1924, VIII, pp. 8–15. (Cf. L. Strauss, *The Early Writings, 1921–1932*, trans. and ed. by M. Zank, Albany, NY: State University of New York Press, 2002.) A bibliography of Strauss' writings is in Strauss, *Studies in Platonic Political Philosophy*, ed. by Th. L. Pangle, Chicago, IL and London: University of Chicago Press, 1983, pp. 249–58. Strauss' *Gesammelte Schriften*, in 6 volumes, are in the course of publication, ed. by H. Meier at Metzler publisher house,

Stuttgart: 3 volumes have so far appeared; in 1996, volume I (covering the book on Spinoza and some other writings on Spinoza written in the twenties and thirties); in 1997, volume II (which collects the writings on medieval Jewish and Islamic philosophy composed in the thirties, other texts from his youth, and the doctoral dissertation); in 2001, volume III (which concerns some texts on Hobbes and political philosophy written in the thirties, and Strauss' correspondence with G. Krüger, J. Klein, K. Löwith, G. Scholem between 1928 and 1973). An English edition of Strauss' writings on Judaism, in 5 volumes, is in the course of publication with the title *The Jewish Writings of Leo Strauss* (Albany, NY: State University of New York Press): in 1997 volume V appeared, which collects the writings published after 1945, entitled L. Strauss, *Jewish Philosophy and the Crisis of Modernity. Essays and Lectures in Modern Jewish Thought*, ed. by K. Hart Green.

2 L. Strauss, *Preface* to *Spinoza's Critique of Religion*, trans. by E. M. Sinclair, New York: Schocken, 1965.

3 K. Hart Green (*Jew and Philosopher. The Return to Maimonides in the Jewish Thought of Leo Strauss*, Albany, NY: State University of New York Press, 1993, p. 148, note 6) draws attention to the correspondence between Strauss and G. Scholem in November and December 1962 about the *Preface* to *Spinoza's Critique of Religion*. Scholem remarks in his letter of November 28, 1962, that Strauss does not mention in this text some stages of his intellectual evolution; Strauss replies on December 6, 1962, that this is true, but only "in a sense": although in the end it is only with short indications and hints, the *Preface* actually describes Strauss' entire path. On the role that the history of philosophy has in Strauss' work, cf. N. 3 of the *Revue de Métaphysique et de Morale*, 1989, dedicated to "Leo Strauss historien de la philosophie": Strauss was never only a philologist or historian, but also a philosopher when he analyzed sources with the greatest attention and care.

4 Strauss, *Preface*, p. 1.

5 Ibid., p. 2.

6 Ibid., p. 3.

7 Ibid., p. 7.

8 Ibid., pp. 18 ff. Cohen's essay, which Strauss refers to, when he writes that Cohen inspired him in his evaluation of Spinoza, is "Spinozas über Staat und Religion, Judentum und Christentum" (1915), in *Jüdische Schriften*, III, pp. 290–372. (On Cohen's attitude to Spinoza, cf. Chapter 2, §§ 2.1 and 2.5.) Strauss had already identified Cohen's theses on Spinoza as a point of reference for his research on Spinoza in two articles published in the twenties: "Cohens Analyse der Bibel-Wissenschaft Spinozas," in *Der Jude*, 1924, VIII, pp. 295–314; and "Zur Bibelwissenschaft Spinozas und seiner Vorläufer," in *Korrespondenzblatt des Vereins zur Gründung und Erhaltung einer Akademie für die Wissenschaft des Judentums*, 1926, VII, pp. 1–22. Certainly, in these articles Strauss criticizes Cohen's essay on Spinoza: he thinks that Cohen does not have enough information about the historical context in which the *Tractatus theologico-politicus* arises; and therefore that he cannot understand Spinoza's sympathy for the non-dogmatic Christianity of his times, nor the influence of Jewish sources on Spinoza's idea of Judaism. Strauss recognizes in Cohen, however, the great merit of having judged Spinoza from a Jewish point of view; and he asks whether what is of Jewish interest cannot be identified with the object of interest of universal culture, because Spinoza's criticism of revelation problematizes not only Judaism but every revelation. In "Das Testament Spinozas," in *Bayerische Israelitische Gemeindezeitung*, 8, 1932, 21, pp. 322–6, Strauss had seen Cohen's interpretation of Spinoza as a sign of the crisis of modernity: in the course of Spinoza's Jewish and European reception this interpretation represented the last phase, after the phase of "damnation," between the end of the seventeenth century and the first half of the eighteenth century, the phase of "saving," of which Moses Mendelssohn had been the most famous representative, the phase of "sanctification" (Heinrich Heine and Moses Hess) and the phase of "neutrality" (Manuel Joel and Jacob Freudenthal). Cohen's interpretation opposed that of Zionism which was positive about the

figure of Spinoza and his nationalistic ideas for the Jewish people. In "Das Testament Spinozas" Strauss praises Spinoza's independence, subtlety, and prudence, which make the reduction of his thought to a single and univocal direction difficult. Strauss – see § 5.4 of this chapter (particularly note 37) – also wrote later about this philosopher, and in a different manner from that defended in the texts he wrote on him in the twenties or thirties.

9 Strauss, *Preface*, p. 1.

10 Strauss, "Anmerkungen zu Carl Schmitt, 'Der Begriff des Politischen'" in *Archiv für Sozialwissenschaft und Sozialpolitik*, 67, 1932, N. 6, pp. 732–49; repr. in *Ges. Schriften*, III (Eng. trans.: "Comments on 'Der Begriff des Politischen' by Carl Schmitt," in Strauss, *Spinoza's Critique of Religion*, pp. 329–51). Schmitt's essay, which Strauss reviews, had been published in 1927 in *Archiv für Sozialwissenschaft und Sozialpolitik* (58, pp. 1–33). The essay was reprinted with some changes in 1932 together with another text, having already appeared in 1929 in *Europäische Revue*: cf. *Der Begriff des Politischen. Mit einer Rede über das Zeitalter der Neutralisierungen und Entpolitisierungen*, ed. by C. Schmitt, München-Leipzig, 1932. Strauss reviews this edition. (In 1933 Schmitt's essay appeared in a new edition where some changes are due specifically to Strauss' criticism, although he is never quoted. On the difference between the 1932 and the 1933 eds, cf. K. Löwith, "Politischer Dezisionismus," in *Revue internationale de la théorie du droit – Internationale Zeitschrift für Theorie des Rechts*, 1935, pp. 101–23; repr. in Löwith, *Sämtliche Schriften*, Stuttgart: Metzler, 1984, VIII. On Buber's criticism of Schmitt's essay, cf. Chapter 4, § 4.4 of this book.) The relations between Strauss and Schmitt, limited to the years 1932–33, were in part cordial, partly dramatic (in 1933 Schmitt took up with national socialism, from which he withdrew in 1935): H. Meier describes them in *Carl Schmitt, Leo Strauss und der Begriff des Politischen. Zu einem Dialog unter Abwesenden*, Stuttgart: Metzler, 1928. Three letters of Strauss to Schmitt dated March 13, 1932, September 4, 1932, and July 10, 1933, are also published in this book as an appendix. The last one is sent from Paris, where the author was able to emigrate with a Rockfeller fellowship, obtained with Schmitt's help. But Schmitt did not reply to this letter.

11 L. Strauss, *The Political Philosophy of Hobbes. Its Basis and Its Genesis*, trans. from the German manuscript by E. M. Sinclair, Foreword by E. Baker, Oxford, 1936 (repr. Chicago, IL: University of Chicago Press, 1952). The author was at that time in England where he stayed until 1938. The German version of the book, published in Berlin in 1965, is reproduced in *Ges. Schriften*, III.

12 Strauss, *The Political Philosophy of Hobbes*, 1. ed., pp. XII–XIII.

13 Ibid., p. 138.

14 S. Munk, the translator of the *Guide of the Perplexed* from Judeo-Arabic to French (Paris, 1856, 3 volumes), for example, introduces Maimonides in his *Preface* as the "founder of rational theology": in the history of western philosophy he was the pioneer of thought that intends to reconcile the contents of revelation and the arguments of reason. The thesis that Maimonides is the beginner of a philosophical trend which will find its full realization in Hegel's system, is also maintained by Rosenzweig in his diary entries of July 11 and 18, 1914, in *Briefe und Tagebücher*, in *Ges. Schriften*, I.1. Hence the emphasis on the Aristotelianism of the *Guide of the Perplexed* by these authors.

15 Various scholars in the "Wissenschaft des Judentums" had dedicated their investigations to Judaism and Islam in medieval Spain: S. D. Luzzatto, H. Hirschfeld, A. Geiger, M. Steinschneider, S. Schechter, and D. Kaufmann, between the second half of the nineteenth and the beginning of the twentieth centuries, were editors of original texts, translators, and commentators on the works of Jewish thinkers of that period; in their writings they also described the historical and cultural milieu in which these works arose, and the influence these works had on the following centuries.

16 M. Heidegger in *Kant und das Problem der Metaphysik*, Frankfurt a. M.: Klostermann, 1929, shows Strauss how it is possible to read the philosophical works of the past in a new

perspective, oriented to problematize just that tradition which these works had helped to build. In fact this book, composed in 1927–28 – as Heidegger says in the *Preface* to the first edition – arose in connection with the elaboration of the second part of *Sein und Zeit* (1927), dedicated to the question of time in Kant, Descartes, and Aristotle, and entitled "Fundamental lines of a phenomenological destruction of the history of ontology by means of the problematic of temporality" (Heidegger did not publish this part in the following years). Cf. in the *Preface* to *Spinoza's Critique of Religion*, Strauss' positive evaluation of Heidegger as a historian of philosophy: "With the questioning of traditional philosophy – Strauss writes – the traditional understanding of the tradition becomes questionable" (p. 10). Heidegger seems to Strauss a deeper thinker than Rosenzweig on this theme. Rosenzweig's reception of the authors of the past – as he remarks (ibid., pp. 9–10) – is completely traditional. On Strauss' interpretation of Heidegger and Rosenzweig see § 5.4 of this chapter.

17 H. Cohen, "Charakteristik der Ethik Maimunis" (1908), in Cohen, *Jüdische Schriften*, III, pp. 221–89. (For the meaning of this essay in Cohen's intellectual evolution, cf. this book, Chapter 2, § 2.4; see also R. Goetschel, "Le paradigme maimonidien chez H. Cohen," in *The Thought of Moses Maimonides*, ed. by I. Robinson, L. Kaplan, J. Bauer, Lewinston-Queenstone, 1990, pp. 383–401.) Strauss himself quotes this piece by Cohen as his source of inspiration in the studies on medieval Jewish and Islamic philosophy published in the thirties (on these studies see below this paragraph). (Strauss had considered Spinoza's criticism of Maimonides in his book on Spinoza. But in this analysis of the Spinoza–Maimonides relation, in line with tradition, he had judged Maimonides to be the founder of rational theology: Maimonides was the author who had given a philosophical interpretation of the Biblical concept of God as existing, unique, creator, provident and omnipotent; in the *Guide of the Perplexed* he had given an onto-theology inspired by the Bible. After 1930 – as said – research on the possibility of a way out from the crisis of modernity drove Strauss towards a new evaluation of Maimonides: this was grounded on the concept of a relation between the law as a principle of social life and philosophical reflection.)

18 L. Strauss, *Philosophie und Gesetz. Beiträge zum Verständnis Maimunis und seiner Verläufer*, Berlin: Schocken, 1935. Eng. trans.: *Philosophy and Law. Essays Toward the Understanding of Maimonides and His Predecessors*, Philadelphia, PA: Jewish Publication Society, 1987.

19 The title of this essay by Strauss, included in *Philosophie und Gesetz*, is "Die philosophische Begründung des Gesetzes. Maimunis Lehre von der Prophetie und ihre Quellen." (Written in 1931, this essay was published in *Le Monde Oriental* in 1933.)

20 Ibid., p. 89.

21 The title of the second essay is "Die gesetzliche Begründung der Philosophie. (Das Gebot des Philosophierens und die Freiheit des Philosophierens)." The examination of Maimonides' thought is placed between that of Ibn Rushd (Averroes) and that of Levi ben Gershom.

22 J. Guttmann, *Die Philosophie des Judentums*, München: E. Reinhardt, 1933. Guttmann, influenced by Neo-Kantianism, places religion as a field of culture produced by the human spirit besides knowledge, ethics and art. Strauss asks if it is possible to truly understand medieval Jewish philosophy by means of this perspective. The title of the essay on Guttmann, mentioned in the text, alludes to the question of the relation between ancient models and modernity: this question, already raised in the Middle Ages, is especially present during the Enlightenment, for example in Leibniz, Lessing, Mendelssohn, and Kant. Julius Guttmann (1880–1950), who had studied and taught in the Rabbinic Seminar in Breslau, had been active between 1919 and 1934 at the "Hochschule für die Wissenschaft des Judentums." Then he was professor at the Hebrew University in Jerusalem. In 1947 he held a course on religion – published by N. Rotenstreich in Eng. trans. in 1976 in Jerusalem with the title *On the Philosophy of Religion* – where together with Cohen's influence as a philosopher of culture, Husserl's influence is evident. The book *Die Philosophie des*

Judentums, which was used as a guide for his courses, had an enlarged Hebrew edition in 1952. Thus, he did not think it was necessary to change his view on philosophy of religion and Jewish thought after Strauss' criticism (the English translation of the Hebrew version, however, entitled *Philosophies of Judaism. The History of Jewish Philosophy from Biblical Times to F. Rosenzweig*, trans. by D. W. Silvermann, Philadelphia, PA: Jewish Publication Society, 1964, seems to step back from introducing the various thinkers in a systematic context).

23 Strauss, *Philosophie und Gesetz*, p. 25.

24 L. Strauss, *Natural Right and History*, Chicago, IL: University of Chicago Press, 1953. After 1938 Strauss taught moral and political philosophy: between 1938 and 1949, at the "New School for Social Research," New York; between 1949 and 1968, at the University of Chicago.

25 In *Natural Right and History*, Strauss goes back from Kelsen and Weber to the Neo-Kantians and historicists of the nineteenth century, and from these to the Enlighteners, in his description of the path of western political philosophy. His method of exposition in this book coincides with the method applied by K. Löwith in *Meaning in History* (1949) (the German ed., entitled *Weltgeschichte und Heilsgeschichte*, is in the *Sämtliche Schriften*, II): the historicism of the twentieth century, the first subject in this work, is considered to be the result of an intellectual line which begins with the Bible. Strauss and Löwith are alike – with regard to their common thesis of nihilism as the last stage of western culture – and unlike – in the indications for an escape from nihilism. Strauss restores metaphysics, although giving it a new form, no longer onto-theological but ethical and political; Löwith, rather, is inspired by biology and cosmology. On the Strauss-Löwith relation, cf. O. Franceschelli, *Karl Löwith. Le sfide della modernità tra Dio e nulla*, Roma: Donzelli, 1997, pp. 34 ff., 76 ff., who considers their correspondence on modernity from 1934 onward (L. Strauss, "Correspondence Concerning Modernity. Exchange of Letters with K. Löwith," in *Independent Journal of Philosophy – Revue Indépendante de Philosophie*, 1983, 4).

26 L. Strauss, *Thoughts on Machiavelli*, Glencoe, IL: The Free Press, 1958.

27 Ibid., p. 9.

28 Ibid., pp. 13–14.

29 L. Strauss, "Political Philosophy and History" (1949), in Strauss, *What is Political Philosophy? And Other Studies*, New York: The Free Press, 1959; 2nd ed., 1976, pp. 56–77. (This essay, repr. in *The History of Ideas. An Introduction to Method*, ed. by Preston King, London, 1983, pp. 213–32, is followed by a contribution by J. G. Gunnell, severely critical of Strauss, entitled "The Myth of Tradition," 1978, ibid., pp. 233–55.) The other essay is: "Social Science and Humanism" (1956), in *The Rebirth of Classical Political Rationalism. An Introduction to the Thought of L. Strauss, Essays and Lectures by L. Strauss*, ed. by Th. L. Pangle, Chicago, IL: University of Chicago Press, 1989, pp. 3–12.

30 L. Strauss, "Social Science and Humanism," p. 6.

31 Strauss, "An Introduction to Heideggerian Existentialism," in *The Rebirth of Classical Political Rationalism*, pp. 27–46.

32 Strauss, *Preface to Spinoza's Critique of Religion*, pp. 9 ff.

33 Strauss was a severe critic of Cassirer's *Philosophie der symbolischen Formen* (1923–28) which he considered inspired by aestheticism. But he appreciated Cassirer's return to the ethico-political interests of his master H. Cohen in his book *The Myth of the State* (1945): Strauss particularly appreciated Cassirer's evaluation of Plato's *Republic* as a defense of natural right, ethics and education. Cf. Strauss's review of *The Myth of the State* in *Social Research*, 1947, 14, pp. 125–8; repr. in Strauss, *What is Political Philosophy*.

34 Strauss, *Preface to Spinoza's Critique of Religion*, pp. 7 ff.

35 Ibid., pp. 10 ff.

36 See, in particular, the essays collected by Strauss in *Persecution and the Art of Writing*, Glencoe, IL: The Free Press, 1952, which refer, besides Maimonides, to Al Farabi and Yehuda Ha-Levi; and "On the Plan of the 'Guide of Perplexed'," in *H. A. Wolfson Jubilee*

Volume, ed. by S. Liebermann *et al.*, Jerusalem: American Academy for Jewish Research, 1965, pp. 775–91. Cf. also Maimonides, *Guide of the Perplexed*, trans. with introduction and notes by S. Pines. Introductory essay by L. Strauss, Chicago, IL: University of Chicago Press, 1963. Most of Strauss' writings on Maimonides – from those of the thirties, dedicated to specific themes in Maimonides' thought, to the last ones where the main topics are the social and political milieu of Maimonides and the formal elements of his writing – have been published in French trans.: cf. L. Strauss, *Maimonide*, textes rassemblés et traduits par R. Brague, Paris: PUF, 1988. See also R. Brague, "L. Strauss et Maimonide," in *Maimonides and Philosophy*, ed. by S. Pines and Y. Yovel, Dordrecht Nijhoff, 1986, pp. 246–68.

37 Cf. on the evaluation of Spinoza as a medieval thinker, whose aim is therefore in a sense the conservation of the social and political life of the religious tradition which he as philosopher criticizes, Strauss' text "How to Study Spinoza's Theologico-Political Treatise" (1948), in *Persecution and the Art of Writing*. In French trans. there is a collection of most of Strauss' texts on Spinoza: cf. L. Strauss, *Le Testament de Spinoza*, textes réunis, traduits et annotés par G. Almaleh, A. Baraquin, M. Depadt-Ejchenbaum, Paris: Cerf, 1991.

38 See particularly, with regard to Strauss as an interpreter of the political philosophy of the ancients, his essays and lectures collected in *What is Political Philosophy?*; *The City and Man*, Chicago, IL: University of Chicago Press, 1964; *Liberalism Ancient and Modern*, New York: Basic Books, 1968; *The Argument and the Action of Plato's Law*, Chicago, IL: University of Chicago Press, 1975; *Studies in Platonic Political Philosophy*, Introduction by Th. Pangle, Chicago, IL: University of Chicago Press, 1983; *The Rebirth of Classical Political Rationalism*; *Plato's Symposium*, Chicago, IL: University of Chicago Press, 2001; the works *On Tyranny: An Interpretation of Xenophon's Hiero*, New York: The Free Press, 1948; *Xenophon's Socrates*, Ithaca, NY: Cornell University Press, 1972; and the *Introduction* to Plato in *History of Political Philosophy*, ed. by L. Strauss and J. Cropsey, Chicago, IL: University of Chicago Press, 1963 (1973, 2nd. ed.; repr. 1981). In the context of Strauss' reflection on using an ancient approach to politics – as a means to escape from the crisis of modernity – there are Strauss' discussions on one side with A. Kojève on the problem of "tyranny," on the other with E. Voegelin on "faith and knowledge." The documents of the dialogue between Strauss and Kojève, developed in the fifties, after the publication of Strauss' *On Tyranny*, together with the correspondence between them, between 1932 and 1965, have been published by Gallimard, Paris 1997. The exchange of letters between Strauss and Voegelin, with some writings of both authors, and commentaries on their debate, has appeared in *Faith and Political Philosophy. The Correspondence between Leo Strauss and Eric Voegelin (1934–1964)*, ed. by P. Emberley and B. Cooper, University Park, PA: Pennsylvania State University Press, 1993. On Strauss' interpretation of the ancient world, see also A. Momigliano, "Ermeneutica e pensiero politico classico in L. Strauss" (1969), in Strauss, *Pagine ebraiche*, ed. by S. Berti, Torino: Einaudi, 1987.

39 L. Strauss, *Preface to Spinoza's Critique of Religion*, p. 6: "Finite, relative problems can be solved; infinite, absolute problems cannot be solved. In other words, human beings will never create a society which is free of contradictions. From every point of view it looks as if the Jewish people were the chosen people in the sense, at least, that the Jewish problem is the most manifest symbol of the human problem as a social or political problem."

40 L. Strauss, *Jerusalem and Athens. Some Preliminary Reflections*, New York: The City College, 1967.

41 H. Cohen, "Das soziale Ideal bei Platon und den Propheten," in Cohen, *Jüdische Schriften*, I, pp. 306–30. On this essay cf. Chapter 2, § 2.5, and Chapter 4, § 4.4.

42 L. Strauss, "Philosophy as Rigorous Science and Political Philosophy," *Interpretation. A Journal of Political Philosophy*, 2, 1971, pp. 1–9.

43 E. Husserl, "Philosophie als strenge Wissenschaft," *Logos*, 1910–11, 1, pp. 289–341. This essay, which amounts to a program for phenomenology, is quoted by Strauss himself in "Philosophy as Rigorous Science."

44 Strauss quotes the *Krisis der europäischen Wissenschaften* (1935–36), as the text where Husserl defends the idea that the philosopher should consider the non-rational strata of consciousness, although he continues to see in science and philosophy the highest spheres produced by the human spirit. For the influence of this Husserlian text on Buber, see Chapter 4 of this book.

45 L. Strauss, *Introductory Essay* to H. Cohen, *Religion of Reason out of the Sources of Judaism*, trans. and *Introduction* by S. Kaplan, New York: F. Ungar, 1972, pp. XXIII–XXXVIII.

46 L. Strauss, "Why We Remain Jews: Can Jewish Faith and History still Speak to Us?" (1962), in *L. Strauss. Political Philosopher and Jewish Thinker*, ed. by K. L. Deutsch and W. Nicgorski, Lanham, MD and London: Rawman and Littlefield, 1994, pp. 43–79.

6 EMMANUEL LÉVINAS (1906–95)

1 Lévinas himself in "Signature (nouvelle version)," in Lévinas, *Difficile liberté. Essais sur le Judaisme* (1963), Paris: Albin Michel, 1976, 3rd ed., pp. 405–12 (Eng. trans. by S. Hand, Baltimore, MD: Johns Hopkins University Press, 1990) writes about his life and intellectual education: born in 1906 in Kovno, Lithuania (where Jewish communities had an anti-mystical and anti-pietistic tradition), he was already familiar with Hebrew, the Bible, and Russian literature, especially Puškin and Tolstoy, in the years of his childhood and adolescence. He lived in Ukraine during the Russian revolution. Between 1923 and 1928 he studied at the University of Strasbourg, where Geroult, Charles Blondel, Carteron, Halbwachs, and Pradines taught. In 1928–29 in Freibourg he met those who at that time were the most important representatives of the phenomenological direction in philosophy. (He was already introduced to the phenomenological method by Jean Hering in France.) In the thirties in Paris he was in contact with Jean Wahl, Gabriel Marcel, and Léon Brunschvicg. Between 1940 and 1945, as a member of the French army, he was a prisoner in Germany. After the second world war, in Paris, he was the director of the "Ecole Normale Israélite Orientale" whose aim was the education of French speaking teachers for Jewish schools in Mediterranean countries affiliated with the "Alliance Israélite Universelle." From 1947 onwards he lectured at the "Collège philosophique" grounded and animated by Jean Wahl. A bibliography of Lévinas' writings is in R. Burggraeve, *E. Lévinas. Une bibliographie primaire et secondaire 1929–1985* (1986), *Avec complément 1985–1989*, Leuven: Bibliothek van de Faculteit der Godgeleerdheid van de KU, 1990.

2 E. Lévinas, "Sur les 'Ideen' de M. E. Husserl,"*Revue philosophique de la France et de l'Etranger*, 1929, repr. in Lévinas, *Les imprévus de l'histoire*, Montpellier: Fata Morgana, 1994; "Fribourg, Husserl et la phénomenologie," *Revue d'Allemagne et des pays de langue allemande*, 1931, repr. in *Les imprévue de l'histoire*, pp. 94–106. In this collection of essays there is also an interview by R. Pol Droit with Lévinas, first published in "Le Monde," June 2, 1992, where he remembers his stay in Freibourg and, particularly, his participation in the discussion between Cassirer and Heidegger on Kant, the problem of man, and philosophy in Davos 1929. At that time he had shared Heidegger's ideas.

3 E. Lévinas, *La théorie de l'intuition dans la phénomenologie de Husserl*, Paris: Alcan, 1930.

4 Husserl's most important texts known until the date of the publication of Lévinas' book on Husserl, quoted by Lévinas' himself (pp. 8–9), are: *Logische Untersuchungen*, Halle, 1900–01, 2 volumes (2nd enlarged ed., volume I 1913, volume II 1920); "Philosophie als strenge Wissenschaft," in *Logos*, 1910–11; *Ideen zu einer reinen Phänomenologie und phänomenologische Philosophie*, Halle, 1913; "Husserls Vorlesungen zur Phänomenologie des innern Zeitbewusstseins," ed. by M. Heidegger, in *Jahrbuch für Philosophie und phänomenologische Forschung*, 1928.

5 Lévinas, *La théorie de l'intuition dans la phénomenologie de Husserl*, p. 15.

6 Ibid., p. 50.

7 Ibid.

8 Ibid., p. 51.

9 Ibid., p. 60.
10 Ibid., p. 62.
11 Ibid.
12 Ibid., p. 189.
13 Ibid., p. 200.
14 Ibid.
15 Ibid., p. 203.
16 E. Lévinas, "M. Heidegger et l'ontologie," *Revue philosophique*, 1932; partially repr. in Lévinas, *En découvrant l'existence avec Husserl et Heidegger*, Paris: Vrin, 1949 (2nd ed. 1967; 3rd ed. 1974, pp. 53–76, from which I shall quote).
17 Ibid., p. 57.
18 Ibid., p. 59.
19 Ibid., p. 72.
20 In the preface to the first edition of the collection of writings on Husserl and Heidegger *En découvrant l'existence*, Lévinas himself recalls that these texts of his must be seen in the context of the interest of French philosophy in authors still almost unknown at the moment of their publication. In *La théorie de l'intuition dans la phénomenologie de Husserl*, Lévinas mentions B. Groethuysen (who had written about phenomenology in *La philosophie allemande depuis Nietzsche*, Paris, 1927) and G. Gurwitsch (author of the book *Les tendences actuelles de la philosophie allemande*, Paris, 1930), in addition to J. Hering, as interpreters of Husserl and the phenomenological movement. Lévinas, together with G. Pfeiffer, translated an important contribution of Husserl into French: *Méditations cartésiennes. Introduction à la phénomenologie*, Paris, 1931. J.-P. Sartre was later inspired by Lévinas' first essays on phenomenology or expositions of phenomenological analyses (for example, as we shall see, on the phenomenon of nausea, described by Sartre in the novel entitled *La nausée*, published in 1939): on Lévinas' relation with Sartre, cf. Lévinas' writings 1947, 1948, and 1980, on Sartre's philosophy, repr. in Lévinas, *Les imprévus de l'histoire*.
21 E. Lévinas, *Quelques réflexions sur la philosophie de l'hitlérisme* (1934), suivi d'un essai de M. Abensour, Paris, 1997. In this edition there is also Lévinas' *Post Scriptum*, first published together with the Eng. trans. of the article in *Critical Inquiry*, 17, 1990, 1, pp. 63–71: here the author remembers the conviction moving him to a severe evaluation at that time – the idea that National Socialism was not an anomaly, and that against it western thought had not yet elaborated theoretical instruments strong enough to gain a victory.
22 Ibid., p. 24.
23 E. Lévinas, *De l'évasion* (1935), introduit et annoté par J. Rolland, Montpellier: Fata Morgana, 1982.
24 Ibid., p. 92.
25 Ibid., p. 93.
26 Ibid.
27 Ibid., p. 98.
28 Ibid., p. 127.
29 Ibid.
30 E. Lévinas, "L'oeuvre d'E. Husserl," in *Revue philosophique*, 1940, repr. in *En découvrant l'existence*, pp. 7–52.
31 Ibid., p. 25.
32 E. Lévinas, "L'ontologie dans le temporel," lecture in 1940, first published in Spanish in the Argentinian revue *Sur*, 1948, 167, repr. in *En découvrant l'existence*, pp. 77–89.
33 Ibid., p. 89. (In his evaluation of Heidegger's philosophy as connected to a historical age and a particular concept of human being, Lévinas precedes M. Buber who in *Das Problem des Menschen*, characterizes the *Dasein* described in *Sein und Zeit* as *homunculus*, as a fictitious being and very far from a man living in normal conditions: cf. Chapter 4, § 4.4 of this book.)
34 E. Lévinas, *De l'existence à l'existant*, Paris: Fontaine, 1947, 2nd ed. 1978; 3rd ed. 1981.

35 E. Lévinas, "Le Temps et l'Autre," in *Le Choix-Le Monde-L'Existence*, Grenoble-Paris, 1948, pp. 125–96, 2nd ed., 1979; 3rd ed., 1983.

36 The link "Plato and the Prophets," already examined by H. Cohen (cf. Chapter 2, § 2.5 in this book), is also discussed by M. Buber in his inaugural lecture to his first course in "Social philosophy" at the Hebrew University in Jerusalem in 1938 (cf. Chapter 4, § 4.4), and by L. Strauss in his lecture of 1967, entitled "Jerusalem and Athens" (cf. Chapter 5, § 5.5).

37 E. Lévinas, "De la description à l'existence" (1949), unpublished text, inserted in the 1st ed., 1949, of the book *En découvrant l'existence*, pp. 91–107.

38 After 1949 Lévinas wrote other contributions on Husserl and Heidegger: deserving of special mention, about both thinkers but especially Heidegger, are the essays, "L'ontologie est-elle fondamentale?," in *Revue de Métaphysique et de Morale*, 1, 1951, pp. 88–98 (repr. in Lévinas, *Entre nous. Essais sur le penser-à-l'autre*, Paris: B. Grasset, 1991, pp. 13–24); "La ruine de la representation," in *E. Husserl 1859–1959*, La Haye: Nijhoff, 1959, pp. 73–85 (repr. in *En découvrant l'existence*, pp. 125–36). Other texts on phenomenology, published during the sixties, are included in this volume. About Lévinas' relation with Husserl and Heidegger, cf. A. Th. Peperzak, *Beyond. The Philosophy of E. Lévinas*, Evanston, IL, 1997.

39 E. Lévinas, *Totalité et Infini. Essai sur l'Extériorité*, La Haye: Nijhoff, 1961; repr. Paris: Kluwer Academic, 1996, from which I shall quote (Eng. trans. by A. Lingis, Pittsburg, PA: Duquesne University Press, 1969). In this book F. Rosenzweig and M. Buber are recalled (the first p. 14, the second p. 64) as sources of inspiration and suggestions, although Lévinas continues to adopt phenomenological analysis. Lévinas writes on Rosenzweig in " 'Entre deux mondes'. La voie de F. Rosenzweig" (1959), repr. in *Difficile liberté*, pp. 253 ff.; "F. Rosenzweig. Une pensée juive moderne" (1965), repr. in *Hors Sujet*, Montpellier: Fata Morgana, 1987, pp. 71 ff.; Preface to S. Mosès, *Système et Révélation. La philosophie de F. Rosenzweig*. He writes on Buber in "M. Buber und die Erkenntnistheorie," in *M. Buber*, pp. 119–34 (French version in Lévinas, *Noms propres*, Montpellier: Fata Morgana, 1982, pp. 29–50), an essay which Buber himself mentions in the *Antwort* in the same volume. In 1963 there is a correspondence between Buber and Lévinas, reproduced in *Noms propres*. Three other texts of Lévinas on Buber are reprinted in *Hors Sujet*, "La pensée de M. Buber et le judaisme contemporain" (1968); "Martin Buber, Gabriel Marcel et la philosophie" (1978); "A propos de Buber" (1982). After the publication of *Totalité et Infini*, Lévinas taught in the University of Poitiers; then, from 1967 at the University of Paris-Nanterre; finally from 1973 at the "Sorbonne."

40 Lévinas, *Totalité et Infini*, p. 118.

41 Ibid., p. 141.

42 Ibid.

43 Ibid., pp. 301–2.

44 Ibid., p. 220.

45 Ibid., p. 221.

46 Ibid., p. 226.

47 Ibid., p. 230.

48 Ibid., p. 242.

49 Ibid., p. 274.

50 Ibid., p. 8.

51 Ibid., p. 23.

52 Ibid., p. 100.

53 In the French intellectual milieu Jacques Derrida is the most important critic and interlocutor of Lévinas. He wrote on Lévinas' texts published until the sixties in "Violence and métaphysique. Essai sur la pensée d'E. Lévinas," in *Revue de Métaphysique et de Morale*, 1964, 3–4; repr. in Derrida, *L'écriture et la différence*, Paris, 1967, pp. 117 ff. In the following years there were two other moments in the dialogue of Derrida with Lévinas: "En ce moment même dans cet ouvrage me voici," in *Textes pour Lévinas*, Paris 1980, pp. 21–60 (repr. in

Derrida, *Psyche. Inventions de l'autre*, Paris, 1987, pp. 159–202); *Adieu à E. Lévinas*, Paris, 1997. Lévinas discusses Derrida's philosophical position in *Noms propres*.

54 On the influence and discussion of Lévinas' philosophy, from the end of the sixties until the last period of his activity, in Germany, Holland, Belgium, Italy, United States, State of Israel, Latin America, cf. M.-A. Lescourret, *E. Lévinas*, Manchecourt (France): Flammarion, 1996, ch. 5: "Les paradoxes de la renommée."

55 The major part of Lévinas' contributions on Jewish subjects is collected in *Difficile liberté*, and in the books where he comments on pages from the Talmud, which I shall quote below. On Lévinas as a Jewish thinker, cf. particularly "L'Herne," 1991, 60, ed. by C. Chalier; C. Chalier, "The Philosophy of E. Lévinas and the Hebrew Tradition," in *Ethics as First Philosophy. The Significance of E. Lévinas for Philosophy, Literature, and Religion*, ed. by A. Th. Peperzak, New York and London: Routledge, 1995, pp. 3–12; *Pardès. Revue européenne d'études et de culture juives*, 1996, N. 26, issue entitled "E. Lévinas. Philosophie et Judaisme."

56 In *Difficile liberté*, for Lévinas' evaluations on Christianity, the Catholic Church, Christian thinkers, or Jewish thinkers in dialogue with the New Testament or Christian tradition, cf. "Le lieu et l'utopie" (1950); "Personnes ou figures. A propos d' 'Emmäus' de P. Claudel" (1950); "Une voix sur Israel" (1951), "Simone Weil contre la Bible" (1952); " 'Jésus raconté par le Juif errant' d'E. Fleg" (1953); "Pour un humanisme hébraique" (1956); "Amitié judéo-chrétienne" (1961); "Anti-humanisme et éducation" (1974).

57 E. Lévinas, "Ethique et esprit" (1952), in *Difficile liberté*, pp. 13–23.

58 Ibid., p. 15.

59 E. Lévinas, "Une religion d'adultes" (1957), ibid., pp. 24–42.

60 E. Lévinas, "Textes messianiques," ibid., pp. 89 ff.

61 Ibid., p. 101.

62 E. Lévinas, "Le lieu et l'utopie" (1950); "Judaisme" (in *Encyclopaedia universalis*); "Pièces d'identité" (1963), ibid.

63 E. Lévinas, "Les cordes et les bois (sur la lecture juive de la Bible)" (1972), in *Hors Sujet*.

64 E. Lévinas, *Quatre lectures talmudiques*, Paris: Editions de Minuit, 1968; *Du Sacré au Saint. Cinq nouvelles lectures talmudiques*, Paris: Editions de Minuit, 1977; *L'au-delà du verset. Lectures et discours talmudiques*, Paris: Editions de Minuit, 1982; *A l'heure des nations*, Paris: Editions de Minuit, 1988. After Lévinas' death the collection *Nouvelles lectures talmudiques* too was published in Paris, 1996.

65 E. Lévinas, *Quatre lectures talmudiques*, p. 12.

66 Ibid., pp. 23 ff.

67 D. Pinto ("Il terzo polo? Verso un'identità ebraica europea," in *Rassegna Mensile di Israel*, 2002, N. 1, issue on Judaism in Europe between 1990 and 2000, pp. 1–36) defends the kind of Judaism of which Lévinas is an important representative together with other French speaking Jewish intellectuals of the same generation.

68 E. Lévinas, *Autrement qu'être ou au-delà de l'essence*, La Haye: Nijhoff, 1974, repr. Paris: Kluwer Academic, 1996, from which I shall quote (Eng. trans. by A. Lingis, The Hague: Nijhoff, 1981). The articles collected in *Humanisme de l'autre homme*, Montpellier: Fata Morgana, 1972, written between 1964 and 1972, prepare the way for *Autrement qu'être* because they clarify the themes of sense, "an-archism," humanism, non-egoistic subject.

69 Lévinas, *Autrement qu'être*, p. 23.

70 Ibid., p. 26.

71 Ibid., p. 27.

72 Ibid., p. 32.

73 Ibid., p. 53.

74 Ibid., p. 75.

75 Ibid., p. 84.

76 Ibid., p. 124.

77 In *De Dieu qui vient à l'idée*, Paris: Vrin, 1982 (2nd ed., 1986), which collects essays written in the seventies and eighties, Lévinas refers to structuralism, Marxism, E. Bloch, F. Kafka and French philosophers influenced by Nietzsche or Heidegger; in *Entre nous. Essais sur le penser- à-l'autre*, a collection of writings published between the seventies and nineties, Lévinas' interest in history, law and politics is particularly evident. For the problem of history and historiography in Lévinas' work, cf. *E. Lévinas et l'histoire*, ed. by N. Frogneux and F. Mies, Presses Universitaires de Nanterre, 1998. Among the last witnesses of Lévinas, cf. *Dieu, la mort et le temps*, reproduction of his course 1975–76 at the "Sorbonne," ed. by J. Rolland, Paris: Grasset et Fasquelle, 1993.

7 A FINAL REMARK: HUMAN RIGHTS, THE TRUTH OF WITNESSING, A PHILOSOPHER'S DUTY

1 Kant, *Bemerkungen zu den Beobachtungen über das Gefühl des Schönen und Erhabenen* (1764–65), *Gesammelte Schriften*, Berlin: Akademie-Ausgabe, 1942, volume 20, p. 44.

2 Cf. E. Cassirer, "Die kritische Philosophie Kants," in Cassirer, *Das Erkenntnisproblem in der Philosophie und Wissenschaft der neueren Zeit* (1907), 2nd ed., Berlin: B. Cassirer, 1911, II, pp. 583–762; A. Guerra, *Introduzione a Kant*, Roma-Bari: Laterza, 1980, pp. 28–31.

3 Kant, *Kritik der praktischen Vernunft, Ges. Schriften*, V, "Analytic of pure practical reason," chapter 3.

4 Kant, *Grundlegung zur Metaphysik der Sitten, Ges. Schriften*, IV, § 3; *Kritik der praktischen Vernunft*, V, part 2: doctrine of the postulates of pure practical reason; *Die Religion innerhalb der Grenzen der blossen Vernunft*, VI, chapter 3: the ethical civil community.

5 Kant, *Ueber das Misslingen aller philosophischen Versuche in der Theodizee, Ges. Schriften*, volume 8, pp. 253–71.

6 Cf. H. Cohen, *Religion der Vernunft aus den Quellen des Judentums*, Chapter 8 (on the "spirit of sanctity"), pp. 123 ff.; F. Rosenzweig, *Der Stern der Erlösung*, pp. 11, 194 ff.; M. Buber, *Das Problem des Menschen*, in *Werke*, I, pp. 307–407; L. Strauss, *Persecution and the Art of Writing*, pp. 32–3 (where Strauss considers Kant as a representative of those philosophers who assume the law, as it is in a certain society, to be a necessary basis for philosophical thinking); E. Lévinas, *Autrement qu'être ou au-delà de l'essence*, Chapter 4.

BIBLIOGRAPHICAL NOTE

In this note I recall only some works which present a history of Jewish philosophy – in relation to a history of philosophy – of which Jewish thought of the twentieth century is part; the writings of the authors that this book examines (H. Cohen, F. Rosenzweig, M. Buber, L. Strauss, E. Lévinas); the English translations of their most important writings; and some introductions in English to each of these philosophers. The reader will find other bibliographical references to these authors in these translations and introductions.

For the history of Jewish philosophy within – or in a critical attitude to – the context of general philosophy, cf. E. Seidel, *"Jüdische Philosophie" in nicht jüdischer und jüdischer Philosophiegeschichtsschreibung*, Frankfurt a. M.: Lang, 1984; *Revue de Métaphysique et de Morale*, 90, 1985, N. 3, special issue on *Les philosophies juives*; Z. Levy, *Between Yafeth and Shem. On the Relationship between Jewish and General Philosophy*, New York: Lang, 1987; the collection of essays on the problems, currents and most important representatives of the history of Jewish thought, entitled *La storia della filosofia ebraica – The History of Jewish Philosophy*, ed. by I. Kajon, Padova: Cedam, 1993; the chapters on authors and Jewish philosophical milieus, from the Bible to thought on the Holocaust and the actual problems of Judaism in the State of Israel and the Diaspora, in *History of Jewish Philosophy*, ed. by D. H. Frank and O. Leaman, London, New York: Routledge, 1987. In C. Sirat, *La philosophie juive au moyen âge selon les textes manuscrits et imprimés*, Paris: Editions CNRS, 1983 there is a detailed description of Jewish thought from the first encounter of Hellenism and Judaism, through Philo of Alexandria, up to Italian Humanism and the Renaissance. Cf. also G. Veltri, "'Jüdische Philosophie'. Eine Philosophisch-Bibliographische Skizze," in *Wissenschaft vom Judentum. Annäherungen nach dem Holocaust*, ed. by M. Brenner and S. Rohrbacher, Göttingen: Vandenhoeck-Ruprecht, 1999, pp. 134–63.

The "H. Cohen Archiv," directed by H. Holzhey, at the University of Zürich, is at the moment editing all the works of Cohen: *Werke*, Hildesheim, New York: Olms, 1987. So far the following works have been published in this edition: *Kants Theorie der Erfahrung* (1871, 1st ed.; 1885, 2nd ed.; 1918, 3rd ed.), and *Kants Begründung der Ethik nebst ihren Anwendungen auf Recht, Religion und Geschichte* (1910, 2nd ed.), which form vols I and II; the "philosophical system" (*System der Philosophie*, 1. Teil, *Logik der reinen Erkenntnis*, 1914, 2nd ed.; 2. Teil, *Ethik des reinen Willens*, 1907, 2nd ed.; 3. Teil, *Aesthetik des reinen Gefühls*, 1912), vols VI, VII, VIII–IX; the *Kommentar zu I. Kants Kritik der reinen Vernunft* (1917, 2nd ed.), vol. IV; the writings *Das Prinzip der Infinitesimal-Methode und seine Geschichte* (1883) – *Einleitung mit kritischem Nachtrag zur "Geschichte des Materialismus" von F. A. Lange* (1914, 3rd ed.), vol. V; and the text, in a problematic link with the "philosophical system," *Der Begriff der Religion im System der Philosophie* (1915), vol. X. In this edition of the complete works Cohen's minor writings will appear in chronological order (vols XII–XVII): until now vol. XVI, *Kleinere Schriften V. 1913–1915* and vol. XVII, *Kleinere Schriften VI. 1916–1918*, have been published. Two *Supplementa* have also been published in this edition: vol. I, which reproduces Cohen's reflections and notes out of Natorp's *Nachlass*, and vol. II, which is dedicated to Cohen's library, both ed. by H. Wiedebach. Cohen's other writings, which are not yet available in this edition, are: *Kants Begründung der Aesthetik*, Berlin: Dümmler, 1889; *Religion der Vernunft aus den Quellen des Judentums* (1919), 1929, 2nd ed., repr. Köln: Melzer, 1959; most of the essays published in *Jüdische Schriften*, 3 vols, ed. by B. Strauss, Introduction by F. Rosenzweig, Berlin: Schwetschke & Sohn, 1924; and in *Schriften zur Philosophie und Zeitgeschichte*, 2 vols, ed. by A. Görland and E. Cassirer, Berlin: Akademie Verlag, 1928. Cohen's correspondence is important for knowing about his personality and activities: cf. Cohen, *Briefe*, ed. by Bertha and Bruno Strauss, Berlin: Schocken, 1939; and H. Holzhey, *Cohen und Natorp*, Basel-Stuttgart: Schwabe, 1986, II: *Der Marburger Neukantianismus in Quellen*. In vol. I of this work there is also a bibliography of Cohen's published writings.

Some of Cohen's religious writings were published in English translation: *Reason and Hope. Selections from the Jewish Writings of H. Cohen*, trans. and ed. by E. Jospe, New York: Norton, 1971; *Religion of Reason out of the Sources of Judaism*, trans. by S. Kaplan, Introductory Essay by L. Strauss, New York: F. Ungar, 1972; *Ethics of Maimonides*, trans. with commentary by A. Sh. Bruckstein, Foreword by R. Gibbs, Madison, WI: University of Wisconsin Press, 2004. Cf. for an analysis of Cohen's works, A. Poma, *The Critical Philosophy of H. Cohen*, trans. by J. Denton, Albany, NY: Suny Press, 1997 (Italian ed., 1988); for a reflection on the link between philosophical system and religion in Cohen's thought, *Man and God in H. Cohen's Philosophy*, ed. by G. Gigliotti, I. Kajon, and A. Poma, Padua: Cedam, 2003; for an interpretation of religious experience in Cohen's work, M. Zank, *The Idea of Atonement in the Philosophy of H. Cohen*, Providence (RI): Brown Judaic Studies, 2000.

Most of F. Rosenzweig's writings have been collected in *Der Mensch und sein Werk. Gesammelte Schriften*, Haag-Dordrecht: Nijhoff, 1976–84, 3 vols: vol. I, *Briefe und Tagebücher*, 1. (1900–18); 2. (1918–29), ed. by R. Rosenzweig and E. Rosenzweig-Scheinmann with the cooperation of B. Casper; vol. II, *Der Stern der Erlösung*, Introduction of R. Mayer; vol. III, *Zweistromland. Kleinere Schriften zu Glauben und Denken*, ed. by R. and H. Mayer; vol. IV, *Sprachdenken*, part 1: *Jehuda Halevi. Fünfundneunzig Hymnen und Gedichte, Deutsch und Hebräisch*, ed. by R. Rosenzweig; part 2: *Arbeitspapiere zur Verdeutschung der Schrift*, ed. by R. Bat-Adam. Not in this collection are Rosenzweig's books *Hegel und der Staat*, 2 vols, München-Berlin: Oldenbourg, 1920 (repr. Aalen: Scientia, 1962); and *Das Büchlein von gesunden und kranken Menschenverstand*, first ed. by N. N. Glatzer, Düsseldorf: Melzer, 1962. Cf. also the Rosenzweig-Eugen Rosenstock-Margrit Rosenstock correspondence in Rosenzweig, *Die "Gritli"-Briefe*, ed. by I. Rühle and R. Mayer, Tübingen: Mohr, 2002. A bibliography of Rosenzweig's writings is in *F. Rosenzweig. A Primary and Secondary Bibliography*, ed. by L. Anckaert and B. Casper, Leuven: Bibliothek van de Faculteit van de Godgeleerdheid van de KU, 1990 (1995, 2nd ed.).

In English translation Rosenzweig's following writings are available: *The Star of Redemption*, trans. from the 2nd ed. by W. H. Hallo, New York: Holt, Rinehart and Winston, 1971; *The New Thinking*, ed. by B. Galli and A. Udoff, Syracuse, NY: Syracuse University Press, 1999; *On Jewish Learning*, ed. by N. N. Glatzer, New York: Schocken, 1965; B. Galli, *F. Rosenzweig and Yehuda Halevy. Translating, Translations and Translators*, Montreal: McGill-Queen's University Press, 1995; *Ninety-two Poems and Hymns of Jehuda Ha-levi*, trans. by T. Kovach, E. Jospe, G. G. Schmidt, ed. by R. A. Cohen, Albany, NY: State University of New York Press, 2000; *Philosophical and Theological Writings*, trans. and ed. by P. W. Franks and M. L. Morgan, Indianapolis, IN: Cambridge Hackett Publishing Co., 2000; *Cultural Writings*, trans. and ed. by B. E. Galli, Foreword by L. Banitzky, Syracuse, NY: Syracuse University Press, 2000; *God,*

Man, and the World: Lectures and Essays, trans. and ed. by B. E. Galli, Foreword by M. Oppenheim, Syracuse, NY: Syracuse University Press, 1998; *Understanding the Sick and the Healthy: A View of the World, Man and God*, with a new introduction by H. Putnam, Cambridge, MA: Harvard University Press, 1999. Cf. also Rosenzweig's writings on the Bible in M. Buber-F. Rosenzweig, *Scripture and Translation*, trans. by L. Rosenwald with E. Fox, Bloomimgton, IN: Indiana University Press, 1994; and Rosenzweig's correspondence with Rosenstock in *Judaism despite Christianity. The Letters on Christianity and Judaism between E. Rosenstock-Huessy and F. Rosenzweig*, Tuscaloosa, AL: University of Alabama Press, 1969. Cf. as introductions to Rosenzweig's life and work, *F. Rosenzweig. His Life and Thought*, presented by N. N. Glatzer, New York: Schocken, 1953, 1961 2nd ed.; *The Philosophy of F. Rosenzweig*, ed. by P. Mendes Flohr, Hannover-London: University Press of New England, 1988; S. Mosès, *System and Revelation. The Philosophy of F. Rosenzweig*, Detroit, MI: Wayne State University Press, 1992.

M. Buber himself collected those writings which he considered most meaningful, on philosophy, the Bible and on Hasidism, in an edition of three volumes: *Werke*, München-Heidelberg: Kösel-Schneider, 1962–64, I, *Schriften zur Philosophie*; II, *Schriften zur Bibel*; III, *Schriften zur Chassidismus*. To the texts published in this edition one must add, as collections of essays edited by Buber himself, *Hinweise. Gesammelte Essays*, Zürich: Manesse Verlag, 1953; and *Der Jude und sein Judentum. Gesammelte Aufsätze und Reden*, Köln: Melzer, 1963. Recently P. Mendes-Flohr and P. Schäfer have begun to edit Buber's complete work at the "Gütersloher Verlagshaus," Gütersloh, Germany: the first volume of this edition has so far been published, entitled *Frühe kulturkritische und philosophische Schriften (1891–1924)*, ed. by M. Treml, 2001. Buber's correspondence is very important for seeing his intellectual evolution as well as the events of European and non-European Judaism: it has the title M. Buber, *Briefwechsel aus sieben Jahrzehnten*, 3 vols, ed. by G. Schaeder, Heidelberg: Schneider, 1972–75. Cf. moreover, *M. Buber. A Bibliography of His Writings 1897–1978*, ed. by M. Cohn and R. Buber, Jerusalem: Magnes Press, 1980.

On English translations of his works and English reception cf. *M. Buber and His Critics: An Annotated Bibliography of Writings in English through 1978*, ed. by W. Moonan, New York: Garland, 1981. Among the English translations of Buber's writings I note: *The First Buber: Youthful Zionist Writings of M. Buber*, trans. and ed. by G. G. Schmidt, Syracuse, NY: Syracuse University Press, 1999; *On Judaism*, ed. by N. N. Glatzer, New York: Schocken, 1967; *The Legend of the Baal-Shem*, trans. by M. Friedman, New York: Schocken, 1955; *Ecstatic Confessions*, ed. by P. Mendes Flohr, S. Francisco: Harper & Row, 1985; *I and Thou*, New York: Scribner, 1970; *On the Bible: Eighteen Studies*, ed. by N. N. Glatzer, New York: Schocken, 1968; *Kingship of God*, trans. by R. Scheimann, London, 1967, 3rd ed.; *The Prophetic Faith*, trans. by C. Witton-Davies, New York: McMillan, 1949; *Moses: The Revelation and the Covenant*, New York, 1958; *For the Sake of Heaven*, trans. by L. Lewisohn, New York: Atheneum, 1949; *Tales of Hasidim*, trans. by O. Marx, New York, 1947; *Between Man and Man*, trans. by R. G. Smith, Introduction by M. Friedman, New York: McMillan, 1965; *Eclipse of God. Studies in the Relation between Religion and Philosophy*, New York: Harper, 1952; *Two Types of Faith*, trans. by N. P. Goldhawk, London, New York: Routledge, 1951. Cf. also: *The Jew. Essays from M. Buber's Journal "Der Jude" 1916–1928*, ed. by A. A. Cohen, Tuscaloosa, AL: University of Alabama Press, 1980; *A Land of Two Peoples: M. Buber on Jews and Arabs*, ed. by P. Mendes-Flohr, New York: Oxford University Press, 1983; *The Letters of M. Buber*, ed. by N. N. Glatzer and P. Mendes-Flohr, New York: Schocken, 1991; and M. Buber-F. Rosenzweig, *Scripture and Translation*, trans. by L. Rosenwald with E. Fox, Bloomington, IN: Indiana University Press, 1994. A detailed introduction to Buber's thought has been given by M. Friedman in *M. Buber's Life and Work, I: The Early Years 1878–1923; II: The Middle Years 1923–1945; III: The Later Years 1945–1965*,

New York: E. P. Dutton, 1981–83. Cf. also, among the critical literature, *The Philosophy of M. Buber*, ed. by P. A. Schilpp and M. Friedman, La Salle, IL: Open Court, 1967 (some auto-biographical writings of Buber are also published in this volume); P. Mendes-Flohr, *From Mysticism to Dialogue: M. Buber's Transformation of German Social Thought*, Detroit, MI: Wayne State University Press, 1989.

There are two projects for publishing L. Strauss' work: the first is the edition of the *Gesammelte Schriften* by H. Meier at Metzler, Stuttgart-Weimar (in this edition, in 1996, 1997 and 2001, the first three volumes have been published with the title: I, *The Religionskritik Spinozas und zugehörige Schriften*; II, *Philosophie und Gesetz. Frühe Schriften*; III, *Hobbes' politische Wissenschaft und zugehörige Schriften*); the second project is the edition of all the writings on Judaism from 1921 onwards by K. Hart Green at the State University of New York Press, Albany, under the title *The Jewish Writings of L. Strauss* (the fifth volume of this edition has been published: L. Strauss, *Jewish Philosophy and the Crisis of Modernity. Essays and Lectures in Modern Jewish Thought*, 1997, which collects writings published after 1945). Among Strauss' writings which have not appeared in these editions until now, cf. *On Tyranny. An Interpretation of Xenophon's "Hiero,"* New York, 1948, repr. New York: The Free Press, 1991; *Natural Right and History*, Chicago, IL: University of Chicago Press, 1953; and *Thoughts on Machiavelli*, Glencoe, IL: The Free Press, 1958. Cf. also the essays, belonging to different periods of Strauss' reflection, collected in: *Persecution and the Art of Writing*, Glencoe, IL: The Free Press, 1952; *What is Political Philosophy? And Other Studies*, New York: The Free Press, 1959; *The City and Man*, Chicago, IL: University of Chicago Press, 1964; *Liberalism Ancient and Modern*, New York, London: Basic Books, 1968; *Studies in Platonic Political Philosophy*, Introduction by Th.L. Pangle, Chicago, IL: Chicago University Press, 1983; *The Rebirth of Classical Political Rationalism. An Introduction to the Thought of L. Strauss. Essays and Lectures by L. Strauss*, ed. by Th. L. Pangle, Chicago, IL: Chicago University Press, 1989. There is a bibliography of Strauss' writings in *Studies in Platonic Political Philosophy*, pp. 249–58.

Among the English translations of Strauss' essays and books in German, cf.: *The Early Writings, 1921–1932*, trans. and ed. by M. Zank, Albany, NY: State University of New York Press, 2002; *Spinoza's Critique of Religion*, New York: Schocken, 1965; *The Political Philosophy of Hobbes. Its Basis and Its Genesis*, trans. by E. M. Sinclair, Foreword by E. Baker, Oxford, 1936, repr. Chicago, IL: Chicago University Press, 1952 and 1984; *Philosophy and Law*, trans. by F. Baumann, Philadelphia, PA: Jewish Publication Society, 1987. As introductions to Strauss' thought, cf. K. Hart Green, *Jew and Philosopher. The Return to Maimonides in the Jewish Thought of L. Strauss*, Albany, NY: State University of New York Press, 1993; and *L. Strauss. Political Philosopher and Jewish Thinker*, ed. by K. L. Deutsch and W. Nicgorski, Lanham, MD: Rawman, 1994. Also remarkable is the book which collects the letters between Voegelin and Strauss and the commentaries on them by different authors: *Faith and Political Philosophy. The Correspondence between L. Strauss and E. Voegelin (1934–1964)*, ed. by P. Emberley and B. Cooper, University Park, PA: Pennsylvania State University Press, 1993.

Although he establishes a relationship between philosophy and Judaism, it is necessary to make a distinction between the philosophical writings and the writings on Judaism of E. Lévinas, as the author himself points out. The following works belong to the first group: *La théorie de l'intuition dans la phénoménologie de Husserl*, Paris: Alcan, 1930; *En découvrant l'existence avec Husserl et Heidegger* (1949), Paris: Vrin, 1974, 3rd ed.; *Quelques réflexions sur la philosophie de l'hitlérisme* (1934), ed. by M. Abensour, Paris, 1997; *De l'évasion* (1935), ed. by J. Rolland, Montpellier: Fata Morgana, 1982; *De l'existence à l'existant* (1947), Paris: Fontaine, 1947, 1981, 3rd ed.; *Le Temps et l'Autre* (1948), Montpellier: Fata Morgana, 1979, 2nd ed.; *Totalité et Infini. Essai sur l'Extériorité* (1961), Paris: Kluwer Academic, 1996; *Humanisme de l'autre homme*,

Montpellier: Fata Morgana, 1972; *Autrement qu'être ou au-delà de l'essence* (1974), Paris: Kluwer Academic, 1996; *De Dieu qui vient à l'idée* (1982), Paris: Vrin, 1986, 2nd ed.; *Entre nous. Essais sur le penser-à-l'autre*, Paris: Grasset, 1991; *Les imprévus de l'histoire*, Montpellier: Fata Morgana, 1994. These works belong to the second group: *Difficile liberté* (1963), Paris: Albin Michel, 1976, 3rd ed.; *Quatre lectures talmudiques*, Paris: Editions de Minuit, 1968; *Du Sacré au Saint. Cinq nouvelles lectures talmudiques*, Paris: Editions de Minuit, 1977; *L'au-delà du verset. Lectures et discours talmudiques*, Paris: Editions de Minuit, 1996. A bibliography of and about Lévinas is in R. Burggraeve, *E. Lévinas: une bibliographie primaire et secondaire 1929–1985*, Leuven: Bibliothek van de Faculteit der Godgeleerdheid van de KU, 1986, *Avec complément 1985–1989*, 1990. Some of Lévinas' writings were published in English: *The Theory of Intuition in Husserl's Phenomenology*, trans. by A. Orianne, Evanston, IL: Northwestern University Press, 1973; *On Escape*, trans. by B. Bergo, Stanford, CA: Stanford University Press, 2003; *Existence and Existents*, trans. by A. Lingis, The Hague: Nijhoff, 1978; *Totality and Infinity. An Essay on Exteriority*, trans. by A. Lingis, Pittsburg, PA: Duquesne University Press, 1969; *Humanisme of the Other*, trans. by N. Poller, Introduction by R. Cohen, Urbana, Chicago, IL: University of Illinois Press, 2003; *Otherwise than Being or Beyond Essence*, trans. by A. Lingis, The Hague: Nijhoff, 1981; *Of God Who Comes to Mind*, trans. by B. Bergo, Stanford, CA: Stanford University Press, 1998; *Collected Philosophical Papers*, trans. by A. Lingis, Dordrecht: Nijhoff, 1987; *Difficult Freedom. Essays on Judaism*, trans. by S. Hand, Baltimore, MD: Johns Hopkins University Press, 1990; *Nine Talmudic Readings*, ed. by A. Aronowicz, Bloomington, IN: Indiana University Press, 1990; *New Talmudic Readings*, ed. by R. Cohen, Pittsburgh, PA: Duquesne University Press, 1998. Cf. as introductions to Lévinas, E. Wyschogrod, *E. Lévinas: The Problem of Ethical Metaphysics*, The Hague: Nijhoff, 1974; *The Provocation of Lévinas: Rethinking the Other*, ed. by R. Bernasconi and D. Wood, London, New York: Routledge 1988; *Ethics as First Philosophy: The Significance of E. Lévinas for Philosophy, Literature and Religion*, ed. by A. Peperzak, London, New York: Routledge, 1995.

INDEX